All About Bowls

THE HISTORY, CONSTRUCTION & MAINTENANCE OF BOWLING GREENS

Jeff Perris

STRI
St Ives Estate, Bingley,
West Yorkshire, BD16 1AU England
Tel: 01274 565131 Fax: 01274 561891
Email: info@stri.co.uk Website: www.stri.co.uk

First Published 1988 by:

THE SPORTS TURF RESEARCH INSTITUTE, BINGLEY, WEST YORKSHIRE, BD16 1AU, ENGLAND.
FIRST EDITION : ISBN: 0-9503647-7-0

SECOND FULLY REVISED EDITION COPYRIGHT © SPORTS TURF RESEARCH INSTITUTE 1992.
ISBN: 1-873431-01-5

THIRD FULLY REVISED EDITION COPYRIGHT © SPORTS TURF RESEARCH INSTITUTE 2008.
ISBN: 1 873431 06 6 and 9781873431061

NOTE 1: The fact that photographs of particular items of equipment or machinery appear in this text should not be taken to imply that the STRI endorses one firm's products over another. When purchasing equipment for a club it is always wise to obtain details of all rival products and to make a choice based on full on-site demonstrations and on the exact requirements of the particular club, bearing in mind the supply of spare parts, local servicing facilities, etc.

NOTE 2: The application rates given in the following text for pesticides should be regarded as being for guidance only, although every effort has been made to ensure that quoted rates are appropriate. It should be understood that pesticide users are under an obligation to comply with legal requirements governing the usage of such materials and that the instructions included with each product are mandatory, including instructions regarding application rates. Users should be familiar with the Food and Environmental Protection Act (1985), FEPA, Part III: Control of Pesticides Regulations (1986). This Code of Practice is for all professional users of plant protection products in England and Wales.

Acknowledgements

The last edition of a bowling green book published by STRI was in 1992, written by my former colleague Roger Evans. That book has been out of print for several years and many with an interest in bowling greens have expressed a wish for an updated version.

Over the past few years I have managed to find time, amongst my busy consultancy activities, to eventually conclude on what I hope will be a worthwhile updated book on the history, construction and maintenance of bowling greens. The task of partly re-writing and updating the past STRI bowling green books has been made easier by the fact that the previous books were so well written by Roger Evans and I have had a great deal of help from former and present colleagues.

We live in an ever-changing world, no better illustrated by the turf and recreational industry where new materials, machines and regulations are constantly appearing. It is for this reason that I have provided limited information in certain areas, but hopefully have guided the reader in the direction of acquiring really up to date information through various websites or regularly up dated publications. Even during the preparation of this book many chemicals used in turf culture have been withdrawn or are being withdrawn!

I am particularly grateful to Tony Allcock (Chief Executive of Bowls England) for contributing to the Foreword. In addition, thanks to BMS Europe Ltd., Dennis Mowers, Par 4 Irrigation Ltd., Sisis Equipment (Macclesfield) Ltd., Sportsmark Group Ltd., Techneat Engineering Ltd. and Tillers Turf Co. Ltd. for providing certain photographs.

Finally, my thanks to Ann Bentley who has produced this book on her desktop publishing system, the third Bowling Green book she has completed.

Enjoy your bowling and bowling green.

Jeff Perris
STRI, March 2008

Foreword

The most important asset of a Bowling Club is its green and its value is proportionate to its quality. It has been stated that a game of bowls is dependent on the three "l's" namely line, length, and luck. If the sport is to be respected as a game of skill then we must endeavour to minimise the element of luck. The one sure way is to ensure that the playing surface is true and properly prepared, and that is the purpose of this publication.

Bowls England is aware of the changing social climate and the "in-house" greenkeeper is becoming a rarity and the use of contractors is becoming common. However, it is still the responsibility of the club to ensure that the contractor is performing to standard and at least one club member should be aware of the basics of greens maintenance and this book provides a 'bible' to which both the amateur and the professional can refer.

The EBA and now Bowls England have been running their Greens Maintenance and Advisory Service since 1984 and have received support from the STRI. Therefore it is with great pleasure that we support this reissue. We recommend this publication to all clubs as an authoritative reference book that will enable the clubs to maintain their greens to a standard that will make playing on them an enjoyment to bowlers of all standards.

Tony Allcock MBE, Chief Executive, Bowls England

Contents

1 The History of the Game

ORIGINS

One of the few things which can be said with complete certainty about the origins of the game of bowls is that it is a very ancient game indeed. The often-repeated legend that the game was invented by a certain bloodthirsty medieval king who was wont to pass an idle hour by rolling the severed heads of recently executed prisoners at a convenient target can fortunately be dismissed as purely apocryphal—the game is much more ancient than that.

It is in fact reasonable to assume that some version of the game was played in the dawn of prehistory—tossing or rolling rounded and conveniently-sized pebbles at some kind of marker is after all a fairly obvious way by which the members of some primitive and long-forgotten tribe may have amused themselves. Among the earliest known artefacts relating to the game are a set of nine stones, a larger stone ball and a marble archway (this latter fulfilling a somewhat similar function as a croquet hoop) found in the tomb of an Egyptian child who died about 5,200 B.C. The Polynesian game of Ula Maika, also involving stone markers and balls, is probably almost as old.

In the Europe of 2,000 years ago, prototype forms of the Italian game of Boccie, the Basque Quilles and the French Boule have been detected. Such games largely involved tossing a ball through the air towards the target rather than rolling it along a more-or-less level surface. Bowling a ball along the ground is, however, a feature of the old German game of Kegel, played as early as the 3rd or 4th century A.D. In this case the game took on a markedly religious aspect as the target clubs or skittles were regarded as representing the Heathen and the Christian bowler, in knocking him down, was hence cleansed of sin. The game thus gained full church approval and was, in fact, played along monastic cloisters. The French game of Gettre de Pere is another related sport and involved placing a ball or missile close to a small set object, probably fixed in the ground. This version probably reached England during the course of the Norman Conquest.

In this context, it is interesting to note how the ancestral game developed along divergent lines in France and England. As far as France is concerned, bowls developed into the jeu provençal (the game of Provence) where balls were tossed or rolled down a 25 metre pitch at a tiny jack (cochonnet). At the end of the 19th century the Provencal game evolved into the modern boule or pétanque, played on a shorter 15 metre rink. Now immensely popular throughout France, no visitor to that country could be unfamiliar with the sight of the boule games played casually in every village square at lunch times and early evenings. To the British visitor it seems odd that the game is played on almost

An early illustration of bowling at a conical marker. From a 14th century M.S.

A Victorian artist's impression of the famous game on Plymouth Hoe in 1588

Bowls in the Netherlands, circa 1650. Note the fixed peg aiming point and the rather primitive bowling surface. (A painting by David Teniers the Younger, Torrie Collection, Edinburgh University.)

English village bowlers – about 1850

any surface, usually grassless, but surface levels are relatively unimportant in the case of a game where the unbiased steel bowls are unusually tossed through the air at the jack, although occasionally a rolling technique is also employed. Boule can claim to be the national game of the French, with over 15,000 clubs and very keen competition in the national championships. Incidentally, a bowls variant survives in Brittany which is more akin to the British game. The Bretons play on a prepared rink of rolled sand 25-30 metres long using spherical 4 inch diameter lignum vitae bowls, biased by means of a lead plug inserted into one side. The rink has boarded sides and the rules allow bouncing the bowl off the boards to reach an otherwise obscured jack. In Brazil, a somewhat similar variant is played using unbiased ceramic bowls, for all the world like giant snooker balls. A curved line is obtained by exploiting the trough-shaped clay rink, its edges being contoured up to meet the side boards.

By 1300, German bowlers were aiming at anything between 3 and 17 target pins. In the period 1400-1600 the game had spread into Austria, Switzerland and what is now modern Poland. By this time, playing surfaces were cinders or clay, the latter being sun-baked to concrete-like hardness. Covered, all-weather rinks or courts were also gradually coming into use where the playing surface was commonly of wooden planking.

To the modern British reader, the above account of the game's development may appear a little confusing as it will be obvious that many of the games referred to are not 'Bowls' in the modern English sense of the word, but related games which in this country would be called skittles or perhaps ten-pin bowling. Duckpins, candle-pins, five-pins and nine-pins are other variants of this type of ball-game. On a worldwide scale, this form of game (particularly ten-pin bowling) remains dominant through the whole of the American continent, Scandinavia, Japan and Australia. Even billiards, snooker and pool, also internationally popular, can to some extent be regarded as a related table-top version of the same family of games. Bar-billiards, for example, even retains a form of the archetypal skittle or pin.

From the Middle Ages onwards, however, British players gradually evolved their own characteristic version of the basic game which we would now commonly refer to as 'Bowls', or, more precisely and correctly, as Lawn Bowls or Bowling on the Green. Under British influence over the last few centuries this game also has spread out on a worldwide scale and today rivals the skittle-type game in popularity on the international scene. The English variety of Lawn Bowling today predominates in the British Isles and in many of the old British Colonies—New Zealand and South Africa in particular. Canada, Australia and the USA also hold many devotees of the lawn-based game.

BRITISH LAWN BOWLING

Although the French may have brought their own version of Bowls across the Channel during the Norman Conquest as mentioned above, it seems more than probable that Saxons and Celts had been amusing themselves with similar games for centuries prior to the Norman invasion. Greco-Roman pottery and tapestries clearly show balls or rounded stones being bowled along the ground rather than tossed, and show that the target was a peg fixed in the ground rather than a set of skittles which had to be knocked over. The Greek and Roman game is therefore clearly related and may be directly ancestral to English lawn bowls in that the object is to bowl one's ball along the ground so that it contacts or lies close to a small marker which served the same purpose as the modern jack. The jack and the skittle are of course analogous but do not fulfil quite the same function. The Romans may therefore have brought this form of game to the British Isles after the 55 B.C. invasion, although historical proof of this seems unavailable. Suffice it to say that, by the Middle Ages, lawn bowls had become the preferred activity in England while skittles in its many guises predominated on the Continent of Europe. Thirteenth and 14th century manuscripts survive which show the game being played along modern lines. One contemporary illustration shows two players with one ball each bowling at a small conical target rather than a spherical jack.

English bowlers soon ran into trouble with the Authorities. Statutes prohibiting the game were issued in the reign of Richard II (1377-1399). At the time, the chief worry stemmed from the fact that the effective defence of the realm relied heavily on a citizen militia of expert archers and those in power made repeated attempts to encourage archery amongst the peasantry, regarding all other games and sports as undesirable distractions which interfered with the commoners' required pursuit of expertise with the longbow. Shakespeare is, however, historically correct in portraying Queen Isabella and one of her Ladies in Waiting discussing whether to pass the time with a game of bowls (in Richard II Act 3, Scene 4, written about 1595), as the ban was at that time only applied to the lower classes of society. The prohibition was renewed in the reigns of Henry IV (1399-1413) and Edward IV (1461-1483) but again only as far as commoners were concerned. In 1511 Henry VIII issued a statute which stated:–

"The game of bowles is an evil because the alleys are in operation in conjunction with saloons or dissolute places and bowling ceased to be a sport, and rather a form of vicious gambling."

This edict was not legally rescinded until 1845 but was only haphazardly enforced and the game hence continued to flourish. Official disapproval seems, however, to have tended to drive the game underground to a certain extent and it gained a rather unsavoury reputation at times due to its association with taverns and gambling. The wealthy, however, continued to play the game respectably with friends and family on secluded private estates. Henry VIII remained a keen player despite his prohibitions, although innkeepers during his reign were fined two pounds per day for allowing bowling and betting on their premises, and bowlers could be, and were, imprisoned. A further statute promulgated by Henry VIII (in 1541) prohibited *"artificers, labourers, apprentices, servants and the like from playing bowls except in their masters' house and presence at Christmas"*—a rather short bowling season.

The famous game played between Sir Francis Drake and Sir John Hawkins in 1588, when even the imminent arrival of the Spanish Armada was not considered sufficient reason for abandoning a game, serves very well to illustrate that legal bans were only patchily applied. In the reign of James I (1603-1625) the King was actually advocating the sport— in his Book of Sports published in 1618 he recommended the game to his son. Again, in

1630 the Earl of Derby was granted a plot of land in Chester on which a bowling alley was constructed, implying official approval.

During the Commonwealth and Civil War period Puritan attitudes and the upheavals of the conflict probably placed severe restrictions on the pursuit of the game, but with the Restoration (1660) bowls became very fashionable and, with royal approbation, grew in popularity. In 1670 a set of twenty formalised Rules of the Game were drawn up which would not seem too foreign to a modern bowler. Through the 17th and 18th centuries bowls continued as a popular recreation and most towns and villages could boast a green, usually attached to the local inn.

Sufficient emphasis has not yet been given to the role played by the Scots in the development of Lawn Bowls. In Scotland, bowls first gained a hold on the populace in the 16th century and for a time assumed the status of a national sport. North of the Border, the game never gained an unsavoury reputation through association with alehouses, drunkenness and gambling, and therefore Scots bowlers escaped the kind of prohibitive legislation imposed by the English monarchs. (Kirk Elders did, however, castigate bowlers from time to time and play on the Sabbath was definitely not approved.) James VI of Scotland (and 1st of England) came down in favour of the game as we have already seen. Curling—that characteristically Scottish form of bowls on ice—can perhaps be regarded as a monument to the Scots bowler's stubborn refusal to allow his recreation to be ruined by a harsh climate! A doctor from Jedburgh, Thomas Somerville, wrote in 1741 that:–

"Bowls were then a common amusement. Every country town was provided with a bowling green for the diversion of the inhabitants in the summer evenings. All classes were represented among the players, and it was usual for players of different ranks to take part in the same game. A bowling green usually formed part of the policy or pleasure grounds of country houses. At these private bowling greens ladies also shared in the amusement, thus rendering it greatly more attractive."

In more recent times, Scotland must have the credit for two major steps forward in the evolution of the modern game. Firstly, the Scots pioneered serious attempts at improving the quality of turf bowling surfaces and hence gave birth to the modern art and science of bowling green construction and greenkeeping. Secondly, in 1849 they formulated a code of laws which forms the basis for the game of Flat Green (Association) Bowls as it is played today. Their early contributions to bowling green improvement will be covered in more detail later in this volume.

Today, Lawn Bowling is played in all parts of the British Isles and, with well in excess of a million regular participants of all age groups, qualifies as a major sport. Certainly it cannot be slightingly dismissed as "old man's marbles" as it has sometimes been in the recent past. Incidentally, it is also perhaps worth mentioning that other non-lawn games which share a common ancestry with true bowls still thrive in places. Skittle alleys can still commonly be found in parts of England—indeed many West Country lawn bowling clubs have indoor skittle alleys to provide members with amusement and recreation in the winter months when the outdoor green is closed. Ten-pin bowling enjoyed a renaissance in Britain in the 1950s and 60s when many defunct cinemas were converted to bowling alleys, a craze which developed under influence from the USA. Mention has already been made of Scottish curling on ice—another surviving bowls variant involves bowling or hurling large bowls over considerable distances across moors or wastelands, or along miles of country lane. This form of bowls is still played in Tyneside in England, and in parts of Ireland, the basic idea being to cover the distance in the least number of throws.

British bowling today is, however, dominated by Bowling on the Green, with three variations of the game of Lawn Bowls being played on two basic forms of bowling green. In terms of the geographical area covered and in terms of numbers of players, Association or Flat-green bowling dominates the scene. It is the only form of lawn bowls played in Ireland and Scotland and is also the game which was spread, largely by Scottish emmigrants, to parts of the former British Empire. Association bowls is characteristically played on a green divided into parallel rinks, each rink being between 18 and 19 feet wide. Historically, rink bowling of this kind is a relatively recent development which probably arose to allow more individual players to use a particular green at one time without interfering with each other. It also facilitates team play with four team players acting in concert. Flat rink bowls was governed by the English Bowling Association (formed in 1903) but now comes under the auspices of Bowls England. The English ruling body is pre-dated by the Scottish Bowling Association—formed in 1892. Surprisingly enough, the oldest national flat rink bowling Associations are those of the Australian states of New South Wales and Victoria formed as early as 1890. The English Women's Bowling Association joined the scene in 1931. U.S. lawn bowlers are catered for by the American Lawn Bowls Association formed in 1915.

Crown green bowls differs significantly from the flat rink discipline in that it is played all over the green in any direction and not confined to rinks. A biased jack is employed and play is single-handed and not a team game. The game is played on a "crowned green"—in effect a low hill with the centre anything from 6 to 18 ins. higher than the four corners. Today, crown-green bowls is centred on the North of England, extending west into North Wales, Isle of Man and south as far as Worcestershire. Its governing body is the British Crown Green Bowling Association which was founded in 1907.

The third major variety of lawn bowls still played in England is Federation Bowls, governed by the English Bowling Federation (1926) and the English Women's Bowling Federation (1956). As originally played in the Durham and Northumberland (and later Norfolk) areas the Federation game resembled crown green bowls in being played with a roving jack on greens of variable size. It has now, however, developed into a rink game played on flat greens in the eastern counties of England.

Mention must also be made of indoor bowls. The popularity of flat rink bowling led to a demand for indoor facilities where the game could continue during the winter off-season. As early as 1909 the Crystal Palace and Alexandra Palace in London commenced indoor bowls, on rather primitive and unsatisfactory surfaces. The popularity of the activity has spread rapidly since that time and indoor bowls is now widespread on a variety of carpet-like surfaces (originally jute but now largely synthetic). Space restrictions have led to the development of short mat bowls in Northern Ireland which requires only a 6 x 45 ft. mat. Indoor crown-green bowls is rarely possible due to the difficulties and expense of providing a suitable slightly-domed surface. The English Indoor Bowling Association appeared in 1933 and the Women's equivalent in 1951.

Studying The State of Play. Flat Rink (Association) Bowls at the EBA Amateur National Championships, Mortlake, August 1966

The crown green game on a typical municipal green in the North of England. Myrtle Park, Bingley, June 1982

Indoor flat rink bowls. The Crystal Palace indoor facility is one of the oldest in the country. Here, England and Wales play a Hilton cup match in March 1964

2 The Development of Greens and Greenkeeping (Prior to 1945)

Although the evolution of the game of lawn bowls in the British Isles over the last six centuries or so is quite well documented, the same cannot be said for the history of bowling green construction and maintenance.

In the earliest times, it is safe to assume that the game was played on any suitable patch of ground. After all, it is possible to play the basic unrefined game on virtually any reasonably level area of sufficient size—even one lacking any form of grass cover. Actual green construction work, in the sense of the actual altering of natural contours and the preparation of areas of land specifically for bowling purposes, does however date back to a surprisingly early period. Southampton old bowling green for example may have been in existence since 1299, although it is doubtful whether this ancient club is still playing on its original green. The prize for the club which has been continuously playing a single green for the longest period of time must surely go to Hereford Bowling Club—established in 1484. This late 15th century green, tucked away behind the Bowling Green Inn near the centre of Hereford, has seen the town grow up around it.

An even older green, dating from just after the Norman Conquest, is Lewes in Sussex. Situated just inside the castle gates, this green was formerly the jousting ground of a castle built by William de Warrenne.

In subsequent centuries the quality of one's bowling surface depended on one's social status. The mass of the peasantry continued to play on any convenient area of ground which was probably subject to the barest minimum of preparation and maintenance. Bowls was played on commons or village greens, presumably on sheep-grazed turf, until legal prohibitions made overt public bowling a risky activity—playing areas then tended to be more discreetly hidden behind taverns and village inns. It was probably not until the 19th century that the bulk of the population were able to play on prepared surfaces which would come anywhere near satisfying the requirements of the modern game.

For the wealthy or aristocratic bowler however, the situation was somewhat different. Bowling greens or bowling alleys became a feature of many a gentleman's well-planned garden. Incidentally, in modern usage the term "alley" tends to bring to mind a picture of a plank-surfaced indoor skittle alley. In the past, however, the word seems to have had a wider meaning and many records of the existence of "bowling alleys" often actually refer to narrow strips of turf analagous to what we would now term a true bowling green and which resembled a single isolated rink on a flat Association bowls green.

The Tudor gentleman's garden is described in detail by Dr. Andrew Borde (*Boke for to lerne a man to be wyse in building of his House* : published circa 1500) who states that the well-planned garden should include an orchard, fish pools, a dovecote, butts for archery

Bowls on a country house alley – Bramshill House, Hampshire, 17th century

18th century bowls at White Fryers, Gloucester

and a bowling green. Queen Elizabeth's privy garden at Whitehall included both tennis court and bowling green. At this period lawns and garden walks were often of herbs, particularly camomile, rather than grass turf and there is every reason to suppose that bowling greens were often laid with a similar ground cover. Low and slow-growing herbal lawns could well have helped minimise maintenance problems in the days when grass had to be laboriously mown with scythes, sickles or hand shears.

A bill relating to the construction of a bowling green at Windsor Castle actually survives in the Royal Archives. One W. Herbert was paid, by order of Charles II in 1663, as follows:

"May 11, 1663. To W. Herbert for making ye bowling green and walks £10, and for cutting Turfe for ye green £3 12s. in all £13 12s. For 8 pairs of bowls and carriage and hampers £4 5s. 6d. Sept. 26. Iron work for ye bowling green door £1 17s. 11d."

The reference to turfing as a method of laying this 17th century green is particularly interesting.

In 1683 one Randle Holme published *'The Academy of Armory'*, a book on heraldry and other subjects. Apposite to our study are his remarks on bowling surfaces:–

"Several places for Bowling: First, Bowling greens are open wide places made smooth and even, these are generally palled or walled about. Secondly, Bares are open wide places on mores or commons. Thirdly, Bowling-alleys are close places, set apart and made more for privett persons than publick uses. Fourthly, Table Bowling, this is tables of a good length in halls or dineing roomes, on which for exercist and divertisement gentlemen and their associates bowle with little round balls or bullets."

Bowling green surfaces must have been of reasonably good quality by this time as Holme also remarks, in a section entitled *"Orders agreed upon by Gentleman Bowlers"* that *"Noe high heeles enter for spoiling the green, they forfeit 6d."* Another stated rule is that *"All stamping or smoothing is barred."* The ban on high heels surely implies that surfaces, at least on enclosed greens, were uniform and true enough to warrant such a prohibition.

In the reign of Queen Anne (1702-1714), private bowling greens continued to be popular. The Duke of Devonshire's Chatsworth house in Derbyshire had a bowling green as a central feature, overlooked by the house so that play could be watched from indoors. At another Queen Anne residence, Cassiobury, the bowling green was in a wood, the approach being via an avenue of trees. In an anonymous early eighteenth century gardening book, translated from the French, entitled *'The Solitary or Carthusian Gardener'* and dated 1706, the author says there are five ways of making green plots, *"namely by Turfs, by Spanish Clover-grass, by Hay-seed, by the Seed of Sanfoin, and by that of Medick Fodder"*. He considers turf (i.e. grass) the best. He also states:–

"A Bowling Green should be incompassed with great Trees such as Elms, Horse-chestnut trees or Acacias accompanied by Yews. They are only proper in spatious Gardens and commonly are drawn in the remotest places to prevent the confining of the prospect by the tall Trees that surround it".

Included in this book is one of the earliest-known plans for a bowling green, surrounded by trees planted at regular intervals—some trimmed in topiary work.

Mention has already been made of a plot of land in Chester being granted to the Earl of Derby in 1630. It was in St. John's Parish near the River Dee and enclosed by high walls of stone. The section of the plot used as a bowling alley was 99 yd. in length and 42 yd. in breadth and survived until the 1830s when it was eventually built over. Very old crown greens still survive in Chester, Chesterfield, Shrewsbury and Penrith. It seems likely that the game of crown green bowls as we know it today evolved as a result of the inadequate construction of these early greens. Difficulties must have been frequently encountered in the skilled task of producing a level and uniform surface. After initial construction, settlement and subsidence problems probably also played a part in producing the characteristically domed North of England green, on which this variant of the game subsequently evolved.

During the period of approximately 1300-1700 therefore there was probably very little real progress made in the improvement or design of playing surfaces. Bowling greens established themselves as desirable and artificially constructed features of the rich man's garden while, initially at least, commoners continued to play on any suitable natural area of ground. Some experimentation took place with alternatives to grass for the actual ground cover plant but constructional methods probably remained very basic and maintenance was carried out by labourers, or at best gardeners, using only hand tools. Simple tools such as garden rakes, weed forks, hand rollers, shears and scythes evolved early and 14th century examples would be recognised easily by a modern greenkeeper. Rollers were in use by the 18th century, as a foreign visitor to England remarked at that time that English greens were *"so even that they bowl upon them as easily as on a great billiard table—they have thick rowling-stones to keep the green smooth"*. Grass cutting must, however, have remained something of a headache and the virtual impossibility of achieving a really accurate and uniform playing surface with shears or scythe probably held back the development of really skilled and expert bowls for a considerable period.

The 18th and 19th century, however, saw the emergence of three factors which revolutionised the quality of bowling surfaces and hence changed the nature of the game itself. The significant innovations were:–

1. The use of sea-marsh turf.
2. The more organised and scientific approach towards green construction and maintenance pioneered by Scottish bowlers and greenkeepers.
3. The invention of the mechanical lawn mower.

The first two factors were in fact intimately inter-related as the Scots seem to have been the first to have advocated and used sea-marsh turf for bowling greens.

To deal first with mechanical grass trimming, we owe the invention of the lawn mower to Edwin Budding, a free-lance engineer of Stroud in Gloucestershire who undoubtedly conceived the idea from his familiarity with a machine used in the local woollen industry for shearing the nap off bolts of cloth. His mower was patented on 25th October 1830 and the specification refers to:–

"A new combination and application of machinery for the purpose of cropping or shearing the vegetable surfaces of lawns, grass-plots and pleasure grounds, constituting a machine which may be used with advantage instead of a scythe for that purpose... grass growing in

the shade, too weak to stand against the scythe to cut, may be cut by my machine as closely as required, and the eye will never be offended by those circular scars, inequalities and bare places so commonly made by the best mowers with the scythe, and which continues visible for several days."

Budding's criticism of the scythe is particularly interesting with reference to bowls surfaces. Budding's patent was licenced to J.R. and A. Ransome of Ipswich in 1832. One satisfied customer was the foreman at Regent's Park Zoo, who commented in 1831 that the machine did the work of six to eight men with scythes and brooms and produced a far better finish. Other manufacturers gradually appeared—Alexander Shanks of Arbroath in 1841, Thomas Green of Leeds in 1856. The spread of the use of such machines was, however, slow and many bowling greens were still being cut with scythes until the First World War. Cutting a bowling green with a scythe was always a highly skilled business. A late 19th century article in the magazine '*The Field*' remarks (rather prematurely) that:–

"The introduction of lawn mowers has effectually done away with the industry of lawn mowing by hand, for it was no ordinary wielder of the scythe who was regarded as good enough to mow a first-class green. Fifty or sixty years ago a man who had established a reputation for this kind of work was always in demand, and in many cases he could command his own price."

Writing in 1912, J.A. Manson records that:–

"In Scotland greens are mostly mown with the scythe which, in the opinion of many, is the only instrument which should be used on a first class green. But the majority of groundsmen, in other respects well up to their work, cannot handle the scythe and perforce employ the lawnmower, which is a capital substitute."

Turning to the other factors listed above, the influence which Scottish bowlers had on the development of flat rink bowling greens during a period stretching very roughly from the early 18th century to the First World War cannot be over-estimated. A measure of their influence is that flat rink greens came to be known as "Scotch Greens", to distinguish them from the North of England crown green (crown bowls is not played in Scotland). To quote J.A. Manson again:–

"In Scotland bowls first took root in Glasgow, probably in the latter half of the sixteenth century; for when the Kirk Session in 1595 forbade Sunday play it is fair to suppose the game had already acquired formidable popularity. Some have claimed Edinburgh or Haddington for its birthplace, but Dr. J.G. Wallace-James informs me that the earliest mention he found in Haddington's records is dated 1662, when the frugal grant of £160 was sanctioned for 'the laying out of ane bowling green on the sands'. But Glasgow's right to pride of place is incontestable. In 1695 the Council parted with ground in Candleriggs to Mungo Cochrane solely for the construction of a green. The Willowbank club claims to be the lineal descendant of those who played here from the very first and in that case is much the oldest club in Scotland."

The first known use of sea-marsh turf, lifted from its natural seaside environment and relaid as a bowling surface, may be found in the records of the managers of the bowling green at Cowan's Hospital in Stirling. Here, one may read that on 16 January 1738: *"the patrons considering a petition given in by several of the merchants, trades and other inhabitants showing the badness of the Bowling Green, and craving the same might be laid with salt faill,*

BUDDING'S

PATENT GRASS-CUTTING MACHINE.

SOLD BY APPOINTMENT, BY

J. R. & A. RANSOME, IPSWICH.

This Machine is so easy to manage, that persons unpractised in the Art of Mowing, may cut the Grass on Lawns, Pleasure Grounds and Bowling Greens, with ease. It is easily adjusted to cut to any length, and the beauty of its operation is, that it leaves no seam, nor any of the cut grass upon the Lawn. Other advantages of this machine are, that the grass may be cut when dry, and consequently it may be used at such hours as are most convenient to the Gardener or Workman,—while the expence of Mowing is considerably lessened, as more than double the work may be done with the same manual labour that is requisite with the scythe.

The first lawn mower was Budding's machine, patented in 1830 and manufactured by Ransomes from 1832 (advert circa 1840)

they therefore appoint the masters" of the hospital "to cause William Dawson, gardener, and keeper of the said Green, to lay the same with salt faill as soon as possible, the expense thereof not exceeding the sum of £10 sterling." In March, next year, the expense of the improvements was found to be £138 4s. Scots, or £11 16s. 8d. sterling; and the patrons ordered "the bowl meal (mail, or charge) to be augmented to one shilling Scots (a penny, sterling) from each person playing." On 22 March 1740, "the patrons appoint the master to provide half-a-dozen pair of byass bowls to the Bowling Green, and to cause make a sufficient lodge for the bowls in a proper part of the garden." The bowls seem to have served for 14 years, as on 6 April 1754, "the patrons appoint the master to provide six pair of new bowls and an odd one for the use of the Hospital Bowling Green, a great many of those already there being almost useless." Again, on 5 February 1763, eight pairs of good byass bowls and two jacks were ordered to be purchased for the use of the Green. The price was £3 6s. 10d. sterling, paid to Robert Home, merchant in Edinburgh.

Improvements in the management of the Green became necessary in 1777. On 16 May that year, "the managers considering that of late great complaints have been made to them that the Hospital Green, flower garden, and back walk are not kept in the same good order and condition which they used to be in: that people are allowed without distinction not only to make a thoroughfare of the garden, but also to use the Bowling Green contrary to the original intention thereof; they therefore authorize the Hospital master to give orders to the keeper of the said Green with regard to the proper management and regulation thereof, so as that improper persons may be prevented from taking up the Green; and appoint the said keeper to obey the orders that may be given him from time to time by the Hospital master thereanent, at his peril; and authorize the Hospital master to cause build a small brick house for holding the bowls, in such convenient situation as may be pointed out by the managers." Still there was dissatisfaction, and on 5 July 1779, the magistrates framed a set of Regulations for the Keeper of the Hospital Green, etc., the following being the principal: "Not to suffer boys and others to make a common thoroughfare of the garden and terraces, but to keep the garden doors lockt, and to give attendance to let decent people, as well as strangers and town's folk, pass through them. To await regularly on the Bowling Green, to allow none but decent people to play at bowls, and no children or servant-maids, etc., to walk on the Green."

Attention must be drawn to the use of the term "salt faill" in the above extracts. "Faill" (fail or fàl) is the Gaelic word for turf or sod, salt faill hence being synonymous with the more modern term sea-marsh turf.

During the Victorian era the practice of using sea-marsh turf as a bowling surface became well established and gradually spread southwards into England and Wales. Such turf occurs naturally around our coasts, the Morecambe Bay area and the Solway Firth being particularly rich natural sources. The Forres marshes in the north of Scotland were also commercially exploited and some in South Wales. The merits and demerits of sea-marsh turf as a bowling surface is discussed later; suffice it to say at this point that, during the 18th, 19th and the first quarter of the 20th centuries, it was the best naturally-occurring material available. It could be found in commercially usable quantities and was fairly consistent in quality and could therefore form the basis of what was to become an organised turf-supply industry. Briefly, sea-marsh turf proved attractive as a bowling surface because it tended to have a uniform, natural cover of fine, wiry grasses and areas could be selected which had only a minor broad-leaved weed content. Again, the natural soil is a fine, evenly-textured silt which facilitated turf-lifting and allowed easy trimming to a very uniform thickness. After careful laying on a bowling green, the silt could be rolled down to give a fast, even and highly accurate surface which the bowler found ideal. Sea-marsh turf thus gained such an enviable reputation that even today one encounters an older generation of bowlers who still feel that it is mandatory for the best of greens. Unfortunately, it also has many serious drawbacks which are often not immediately apparent when a green is first laid and its popularity has hence rightly declined drastically in more recent years. It is, however, true to say that for a lengthy period of time it was the best material for the purpose and its use represented a major step forward in bowling green improvement.

Sea-marsh turf.
Lifting and boxing
to uniform thickness

Besides popularising the use of sea-marsh turf, Scottish bowling green builders had, prior to the First World War, evolved a distinctive method of bowling green construction which, with minor variations, remained in vogue until the Second World War (one West Sussex contractor, is still advocating the Scottish constructional system today—and still using sea-marsh turf). The most distinctive feature of the Scots method of green construction was that no soil whatsoever was placed beneath the turf. An even subsoil formation surface was first produced, of sufficient area to allow a 42 x 42 yd. playing surface (i.e. six rinks in each direction, allowing the green to accommodate a maximum of 48 players at any one time). A pipe drainage system was then introduced into the subsoil surface consisting of 2 or 3 in. diameter clayware pipes at anything from 9-21 ft. centres, running into mains placed under the surrounds ditch and thence to a suitable outfall. Drains were sometimes omitted for drier sites. Over the subsoil was then spread some 6-12 in. of hardcore variously described as clinker, ash, broken stone or even "brick-bats". Sometimes this would be divided into fine-over-coarse layers but 3 in. gauge clinker seems to have been most often favoured. Next a 1-3 in. layer of fine ash—¼ in. grade is mentioned in one text. Finally, between 1 and 3 in. of sand was spread and the sea-marsh turf laid directly on this sand bed. The turf was cut 1¼-1½ in. in thickness. This basic constructional method was

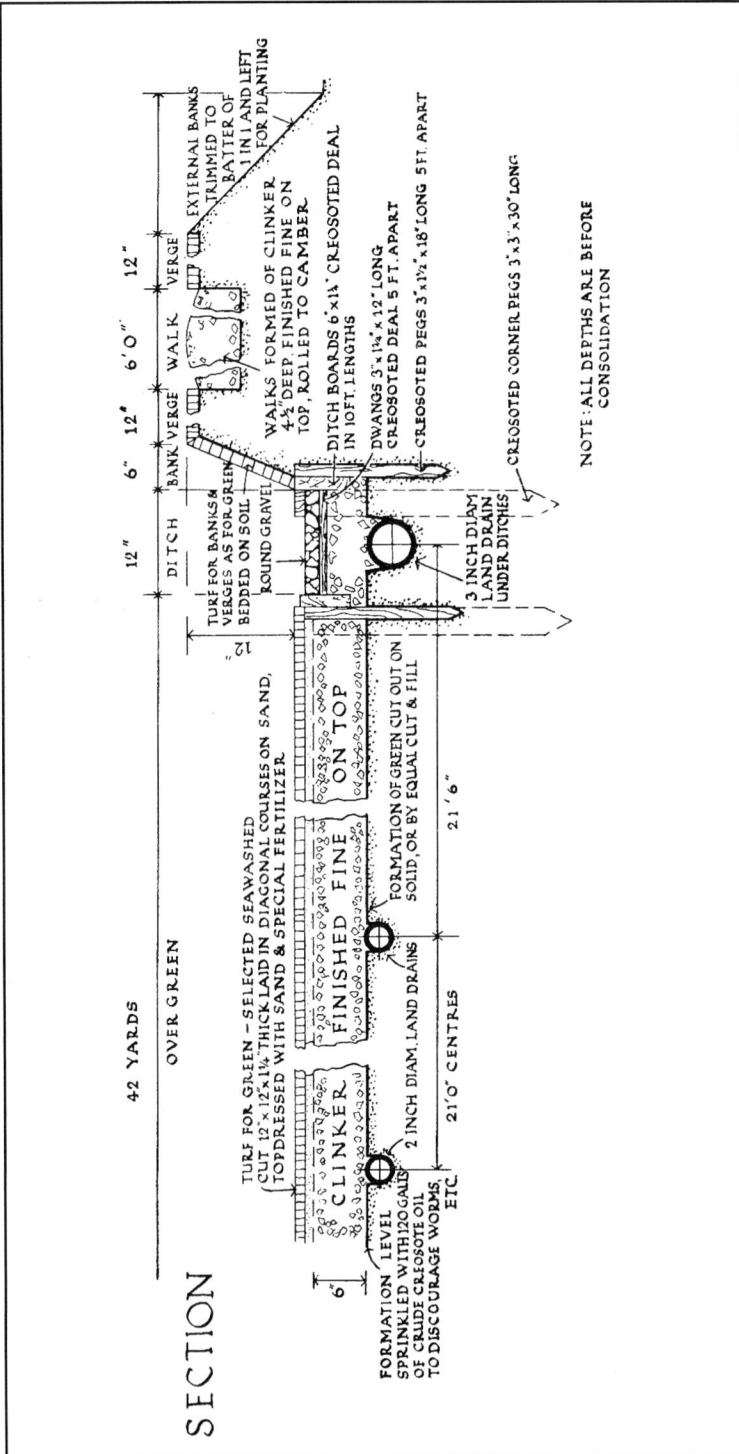

Method of green construction evolved in Scotland for sea-marsh greens advocated by the Scottish Bowling Association after its formation in 1892 and during the 1920s and 30s also became a standard English Bowling Association requirement.

This Scottish method of construction had a number of advantages. Greens so made had good underlying drainage—important in wetter areas like the West of Scotland. The stone or clinker foundation is a firm one, could be well consolidated and hence minimised subsidence after the green had been laid. The sand layer beneath the turf was easy to grade to an accurate surface level and, together with accurately cut turf, helped form an almost instant bowling surface of high quality.

The growth of Public Parks as a result of the Public Health Acts of 1875, 1890, 1906 and 1925 and a related increase in the demand for bowling greens led to a spate of green-building following the above constructional methods. Many greens were built by Welfare organisations in the Depression of the inter-war period using volunteer labour drawn from the ranks of the unemployed.

Of course, not all greens were constructed using this standard Scottish method. Sea-marsh turf was expensive, particularly if transported long distances. In 1920 the cost of building a green by the above system was about £120, of which £25 represented the cost of the turf alone—a quite considerable proportion of the total. As a result, impecunious clubs sought cheaper substitutes. Moorland or Mountain turf was sometimes used, but material of the required uniform quality was difficult to find in quantity in natural situations and underlying soils tended to vary more with stones, etc. making uniform cutting more difficult. Seeding was of course also an alternative method of green establishment but initially it was difficult to obtain seed of suitable quality. Hay loft sweepings were cheap and widely employed where money was short but developing swards tended to contain weed and coarse grasses. Some early advocates of seeded greens insisted that seed should be harvested from moorland pastures, thereby ensuring a higher proportion of the desirable fine grasses. Gradually of course seed quality improved and the commercial availability of good seed slowly led to an increase in the acceptability of the seeded green. Old-established seed firms like Sutton's of Reading did much to improve seed quality and demonstrate in the face of established prejudice that it was possible to form a perfectly satisfactory bowling green by seeding rather than turfing. Sutton's laid a bowling green at their own recreation ground in Reading in the late 1920s, partly to demonstrate the point. Their green was sown in September and was ready for play the following June. The majority of bowlers, however, continued to regard seeded and non-sea-marsh greens as an inferior substitute for the real thing, even in the face of accumulating evidence to the contrary.

For a seeded green, soil had to be used as a surface layer. One early specification details a 4 in. layer of topsoil, ameliorated if necessary with sand, over the standard fine ash/clinker base.

In the case of crown greens, construction was of course complicated by the definitive "mushroom top" contours of the finished surface. Such greens vary between 30 and 60 yd. square, with 45 x 45 yd. being most usual. Circular greens were sometimes constructed but were always relatively rare. Scottish flat green specifications were adapted for crown green construction. Drains were usually (but not always) omitted beneath the actual bowls surface as the contours shed surface water into the surrounding ditches. The rough shape of the finished surface was first formed by crowning the subsoil formation surface, subsequent layers reflecting the slightly domed effect. For the best crown greens, clinker foundations were again used, topped with fine ash and sand which were carefully spread to pre-set concentric circles of level pegs so that the centre of the finished green was between 6 and 14 in. above the corners. Sea-marsh turf could then be laid. It was normal to turf a flat green working from corner to corner, laying turf in diagonal lines with staggered joints like brickwork. For crown greens, an alternative method was sometimes advocated, starting at the centre on the crown and then laying concentric circles of turf to the level pegs previously placed in position. Some expense could be spared in the case of crown greens in that ditch and bank requirements are not nearly as rigorous as in the case of flat rink Association greens. (The same is true of flat Federation greens.) Indeed, ditches and banks were sometimes omitted altogether. Although not a requirement of the game, it was, however, realised that ditches were useful for drainage purposes. It is interesting to note that Manson (in 'The Complete Bowler' 1912) states that perimeter ditches were virtually unknown around English greens prior to 1870, either flat or crown.

Association green established by seeding at Sutton's Recreation Club at Reading. Photographed in 1931

One source gives the cost of a crown green built to modified Scottish specification in 1936 as £470 excluding labour. With crown greens also money could be saved by seeding or by omitting the clinker and ash base layers, but sea-marsh turf and clinker foundations were used whenever funds permitted.

BOWLING GREEN MAINTENANCE PRIOR TO 1930

There seems to have been little attempt made to produce a rational system of bowling green maintenance prior to the late 19th century. Traditionally the process of bowling green upkeep was probably left to individual greenkeepers working largely on a trial and error basis, aided only by hand tools and a limited range of chemicals—manures and so on which had proven their value in general agricultural and horticultural usage.

As had been mentioned previously, it was the Scottish bowling fraternity who took the first steps towards a more systematic and rational approach towards green maintenance and during the first third of the 20th century they gained an enviable reputation as the leaders in the field, their influence spreading throughout the British Isles. Developments were of course brought virtually to a standstill by the exigencies of the 1914-18 war, but with the cessation of hostilities the Scottish influence on greenkeeping matters became even more marked. It must be stressed that the Scottish approach was by no means a really scientific one—there was no experimental work as such. Strictly pragmatic thinking was the order of the day and greenkeeping techniques were evolved as a result of long practical experience.

Scottish greenkeeping methods were originally specifically developed in connection with flat rink sea-marsh greens laid with soil-less sand and clinker foundations as we have already seen. Their methods soon spread, however, with varying degrees of success, to turfed and seeded greens in general, of both flat and crown types.

One of the most vociferous and influential among Scottish greenkeepers was William Paul of Paisley, an ex-president of the Scottish Bowling Association and for 30 years secretary of the Renfrewshire Bowling Association. He is now probably best remembered as the inventor of the hollow tine fork (still known as a Paul fork in some parts of the country), but during the 1920s he produced a stream of articles and booklets which did much to popularise Scottish greenkeeping practices. A privately published booklet 'The Care and Upkeep of Bowling Greens' produced in the 1920-25 period is typical and provides a very good summary of current techniques.

Briefly, Paul's recommendations for the upkeep of a green built in the Scottish manner are as follows:–

Commencing in the spring, the green should be brushed with a stiff besom. Repeated rolling was then advised, continuing this operation right through the playing season (¼ ton rollers were widely used at the time). The importance of harrowing is also stressed, using a heavy wooden harrow with 2 in. nail-like tines, to remove moss and creeping growth. Harrowing should be continued fortnightly through the playing period. Weed should be controlled by close scything of clover and pearlwort, etc. in the spring. Commencing in March, fertiliser should be applied—Peruvian guano or sulphate of ammonia. Paul's fertiliser recommendations vary but applications of sulphate of ammonia, sulphate of iron and a sandy carrier are usual, given every three weeks through the growing season. Watering is considered vital—the Scottish soil-less construction is very free draining and two weeks' drought was thought dangerous.

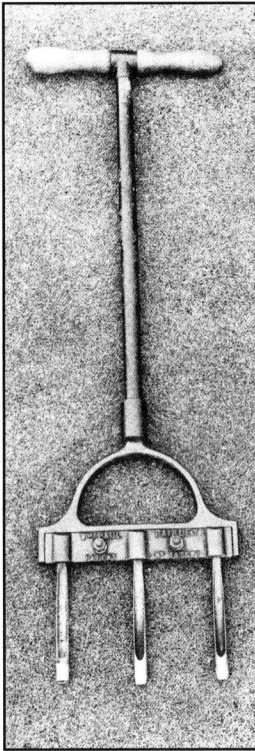

One of William Paul's original hollow tine forks first used in 1919 on the Abercorn bowling green at Paisley, Scotland

Autumn end-of-season work commenced with scarification with a fine sharp rake to remove moss. The green should then be 'graiped', i.e. hand forked using a tool with straight solid tines, this being described as having been in vogue "for generations". In cases where greens are felt to be over-compacted (or "skin-bound"), Paul's own hollow tine fork is strongly advocated. Hollow tine forking was first carried out on greens at Abercorn, Paisley, in 1919, much to the consternation of some more conservative members of the bowling fraternity who thought the operation too severe. After forking, Paul recommended autumn fertiliser (nitrogen, potash and basic slag) followed by top dressing using either 7 ton sharp sand or a 5 ton sand/2 ton compost mix. Top dressing should be worked in with a long rake or straight edge to improve levels. Autumn wormkilling could sometimes also be necessary. (The seed firm, Carters of Raynes Park, London, had introduced the first expellent wormkiller in 1902.)

In the light of modern knowledge, such a system of greenkeeping is open to a number of criticisms. There are, for example, several glaring omissions—there is no mention of the important questions of mowing frequency, mowing heights or mowing patterns. Turf diseases are entirely ignored—admittedly few effective treatments were available but trouble must have been encountered at times with damaging diseases and one might reasonably expect some comment as to possible causes and remedial action. Fusarium patch disease must for instance have occurred periodically, also dollar spot disease to which sea-marsh turf is particularly prone.

28

GENERAL DIRECTIONS

— FOR —

"PAUL'S PROCESS" OF TURF TREATMENT.

IF moss exists it shows unhealthy conditions of some kind. Bowling green turf should be of an open, sandy nature. Much of it of recent years is of clay or peat structure, which, under the roller and playing becomes compressed, making life for the grasses very difficult. They die out and moss comes in their place. Older greens also suffer in time from a "skin bound" condition although their subsoil may be of quite a healthy texture. There are others whose subsoil has become caked from various causes—the use of too fine sand perhaps being the most common.

They all want "digging up by Paul's Process." Even where the turf and conditions are good, "Paul's Process" will still further better them.

First of all cut out a small plug from the green and examine it. If it is of this putty-like clay or of peat fibres, the ejected wads of turf from the cutting implement should be taken away.

To begin with the moss must all be broken up and scratched out of existence. If you have a large bowling-green harrow, trail it several times in all directions over the turf; or a little spiked roller machine for extracting the moss is excellent. Where much moss exists it may also be necessary to carefully scarify the moss with fine rakes made by driving 2 rows of wire nails through an 18" narrow flat board. The scarifying must be thorough, crisscrossing it to carefully moulder away the moss—not to tear it out. Considerable grass will also be lost in this operation. (It is not unusual for a full cart load of moss to be taken off a badly infested green). The green must afterwards be clean swept of the loose moss.

Then perforate the turf with the "Paul's Process" Implement every 4" or 5", doing a rink at a time and taking away the wads at completion of rink. If the wads, however, are good healthy material let them lie and roughly break them up with a flat rake to await the final top dressing. After the whole green has been perforated apply the feeding. I recommend 2 or 3 cwts. bone flour, 1 cwt. good grass fertiliser and $1\frac{1}{2}$ cwts. basic slag. A change of feeding is at times beneficial.

This should be scattered on by hand. 3 cwts. dry carbonate of lime is also good for sweetening the ground and liberating potash in the soil. If the wads have been removed, 8 tons of top dressing will be necessary to fill up the holes by the spring. 6 tons good sharp sand put through a $\frac{1}{4}$" riddle and 2 tons good clean soil. The sand should be as coarse as possible. Even the finer riddlings swept into the bottom of the holes make excellent drainage. If the ejected wads are healthy, break them up roughly and apply about 5 tons good sharp open sand, spreading as evenly as possible. Leave for the rains to act on it, but an occasional rake over will help in its distribution. Before the winter sets in the little turfs of remaining grass roots should be raked off the surface. In satisfactory greens the soil could be omitted or reduced, and it need not be repeated too often in subsequent years on the others.

Many of the holes may still be partly open till the green is swept in the spring. After thorough sweeping in March the roller will complete the closing of them. About the middle of March a cwt. of good grass fertiliser (Ichthemic Guano or other) should be applied to the turf and no cutting done, of course, until it has been washed in to the soil. Throughout the playing season occasional light dressings of 8 lbs. of Ammonium Sulphate mixed with 5 times its own weight of fine sand or clean soil will keep the grass up to concert pitch.

Replacements of cutters 5/- per set of 3.

WILLIAM PAUL,   :   :   :   41 CAUSEYSIDE STREET, PAISLEY.

One of Paul's many leaflets on bowling green maintenance, circa 1925

MOSS EXTRACTOR.

(Illustrated on right.)

This machine is invaluable wherever moss infests the surface of Putting Greens, Bowling Greens, or Lawns, and its use proves it to be a great boon and labour-saver to Greenkeepers and Gardeners. It is very speedy and effective in tearing out the moss, while combing and aerating the grass. Even if there is no moss, its use is very beneficial to the grass, and it is altogether better and quicker in action than a rake. Can be employed during the whole season, and will be found very serviceable when used prior to the application of top dressings.

16 inches wide (with Box) ... ... **£5 5s. net.**

GREEN'S PATENT 'SILENS MESSOR' LAWN MOWER.

The 'Silens Messor' is a very light running machine and produces a fine even surface on the lawn. The cylinder, which is reversible, has eight cutters. *(Illustrated.)*

Complete with Grass Box. Drawing rope and handle supplied with all hand machines from 14-inch size upwards. If required for 12-inch size, **2/6** extra.

	£	s.	d.		£	s.	d.
8-inch cutter	5	15	0	16-inch cutter	11	0	0
10-inch ,,	6	15	0	18-inch ,,	12	10	0
12-inch ,,	8	0	0	20-inch ,,	13	10	0
14-inch ,,	9	10	0	24-inch ,,	16	0	0

This type of machine can be supplied with gear instead of chain drive, if required, at above prices.

Special close-cutting machines for Golf and Bowling Greens, which include one or two additional cutters in cylinder, can be supplied at an extra cost of **7/6** each additional cutter.

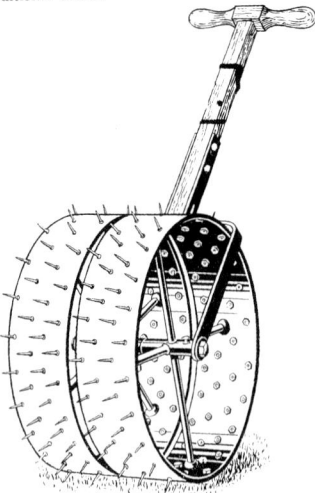

RANSOMES' 'CERTES' LAWN MOWER.

Designed to ensure perfect cutting on Golf Greens. The machine-cut gearing is totally enclosed and grease lubricated. Cutting cylinders with eight knives, and thin bottom blades for close cutting. Steel front roller running on ball bearings; screw adjustment to front roller. *(Illustrated.)*

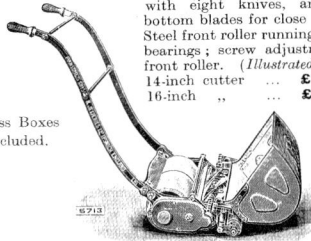

14-inch cutter	...	**£10 15s.**
16-inch ,,	...	**£11 10s.**

Grass Boxes included.

Bowling green maintenance machinery 1920-1939

30

Turfing and Edging Tools

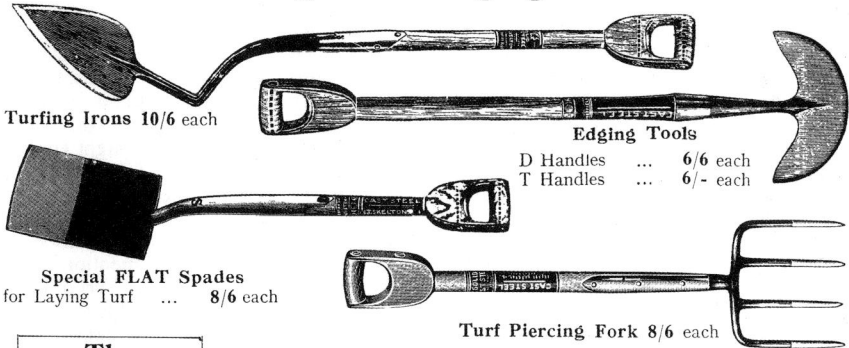

Turfing Irons 10/6 each

Edging Tools

D Handles	...	**6/6** each
T Handles	...	**6/-** each

Special FLAT Spades
for Laying Turf ... **8/6** each

Turf Piercing Fork 8/6 each

The PROVAN

Price 22/6

Hollow Prongs.

Turf Races

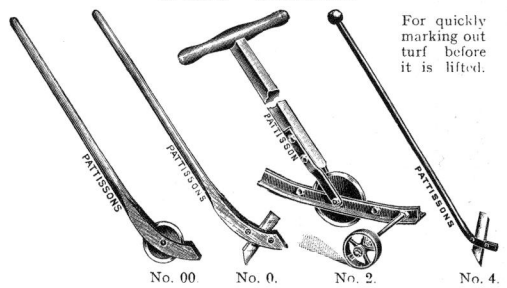

For quickly marking out turf before it is lifted.

No. 00   No. 0.   No. 2.   No. 4.

PRICES

No. 00.	**Ash Handle,** with Disc Knife	...	...	...	**12/6**	each
No. 0.	**Ash Handle**	...	...	...	**10/-**	,,
No. 2.	**Ash Handle,** with disc cutter and gauge	...		**21/-**	,,
No. 4.	**Tubular Iron Handle**	...	...	...	**11/-**	,,

Turf Gauge Boxes and Knives

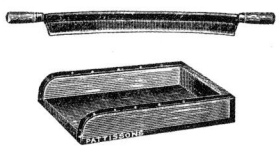

The boxes are strongly made with edges bound in half-round steel. Ensures accurate thickness of the Turves.

PRICES

No. 1.	24″ × 12″ × 1½″	...	...	**7/-**	each
No. 2.	24″ × 12″ × 2″	...	...	**7/6**	,,
No. 3.	36″ × 12″ × 1½″	...	...	**8/-**	,,
No. 4.	36″ × 12″ × 2″	...	...	**8/6**	,,
Knives, double handled	...	...	...	**10/6**	,,

SPECIAL BOWLING GREEN ROLLER.

(*Illustrated below.*)

Single steel cylinder, with cast-iron rounded ends. Fitted with roller bearings and extra long balanced handle. Size : 33 inches diameter by 33 inches wide. Weight 4 cwt. 2 qrs. 14 lb. **£14**

Special Bowling Green Roller

Carriage paid to any Station in England and Wales, Scottish Stations, and to Irish east coast ports.

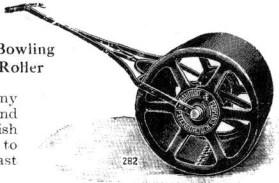

This Roller is also largely used for Hard Tennis Courts.

Hand tools for greenkeepers, circa 1930

By today's standards the amount of rolling advocated is excessive, although one must bear in mind that mowing was predominantly carried out with hand machines which do not have the rolling action of the heavier motor mowers used today—more frequent rolling as a separate operation was therefore justified, although perhaps not with rollers as heavy as the ones then in favour. Fertiliser recommendations are obviously rather arbitrary and understandably not based on any scientific understanding of plant nutritional requirements. The amount of fertiliser used over a 12 month period is excessive but this criticism must be tempered to a certain extent by the fact that Scottish greens were soil-less and free draining and therefore have a higher nutritional requirement than more conventional constructions. Weed, worm and moss control measures were barely adequate but of course were limited by the lack of suitable herbicides and other more recently developed chemical treatments.

Whatever their deficiencies however, Scottish constructional and maintenance techniques provided consistently better bowling surfaces than had been possible previously and helped increase the popularity of lawn bowls in the inter-war period. The upsurge in the number of bowling greens being constructed and the increasing attention being paid to greenkeeping had another beneficial aspect—it stimulated machinery manufacturers to produce and perfect an ever-increasing range of equipment. By the early 1930s a wide range of efficient hand-pushed mowers had been developed from the original Budding machine. Models with extra blades on the cutting cylinder giving a finer cut were introduced for bowling and golf green mowing. Machines such as the Webb Deluxe of 1929, the Ransomes Hand Certes and the Green's Patent Silens Messor were capable of producing an excellent finish and were widely used. Power-driven lawn mowers were very slow to displace the hand machines and many greenkeepers resisted the advent of powered mowers on the grounds that they produced an inferior standard of bowling surface. The first powered lawn mowers were unwieldy and heavy steam-driven machines which were briefly used for general sports ground cutting in the 1893-1910 period. They proved far too large and weighty for bowling green usage. Petrol-driven machines appeared on the scene with a 1902 Ransomes machine but early models were again large, weighing about 1 ton and hence unsuitable for bowling green cutting. By the Second World War, motor mowers suitable for bowling green purposes had been developed but the reactionary attitude of many greenkeepers and bowlers delayed their general acceptance until well after the 1939-45 conflict.

By the 1930s fertiliser distributors, rake scarifiers and spikers were all being produced for the bowling green market. Spinner-type distributors, Sarel spiked rollers, drag brushes and hand-powered rotary scarifiers were all available in catalogues issued in the early 1930s. A notable pioneer was William Hargreaves who invented a mechanical spiker and founded W. Hargreaves & Co. Ltd. in 1932 (now Sisis Equipment Ltd.). Pattissons of Stanmore, Middlesex were also active and originated as far back as 1896.

Chemicals for turf maintenance 1920-1935

33

THE SCIENTIST AND THE GREENKEEPER

The scientific study of turf for lawns and sporting facilities commenced in Connecticut in the USA in 1885 when J.B. Olcott initiated detailed studies aimed at finding the best strains of grass for fine turf. Rhode Island State College of Agriculture was another pioneer, setting up experiments in 1890. Many state agricultural colleges in the U.S.A. followed suit and in 1920 the U.S. Golf Association established its "Green Section" comprising both research and advisory services.

In the British Isles, turf research began in 1929 when the British Golf Unions' Joint Advisory Council set up the Board of Greenkeeping Research. A research station and experiment ground was set up at the St. Ives Estate in Bingley, West Yorkshire and work commenced under the leadership of the Board's first Director, R.B. Dawson. The Board was reconstituted in September 1951 as the Sports Turf Research Institute, extending its work to formally cover all turf for sport and amenity purposes, but it should not be imaged that the Research Station's sphere of interest was confined to golf course management, even in its earliest years. The bowling fraternity showed a keen interest in research from the start and in February 1930 the London and Southern Counties Bowling Association made a grant of £60 to the Research Station "to allow tests to be carried out during the next 12 months, with a view to explaining in an unbiased fashion better methods of treatment for Cumberland Turf Greens". In response, a miniature bowling green was laid down at the Bingley experiment ground, turfing being completed in April 1930. The Scottish pattern of construction was followed with about 10 in. clinker (finer towards the top) underlying 2 in. of sharp Bedford sand on which Silloth sea-marsh turf was laid. Experimental work commenced at once, two important objects being to find out why sea-marsh turf was prone to broad-leaved weed and coarse grass invasion when moved away from its natural coastal environment, and to investigate and possibly prevent the encroachment of annual meadow-grass (*Poa annua*) into the turf. Questions of turf acidity and alkalinity were also investigated and the new green was divided into ten plots, each of which was subjected to a different fertiliser regime. A convenient outbreak of fusarium patch disease allowed some fungicide trials to be completed—Bordeaux/Malachite green fungicide was subsequently recommended to many bowling clubs as a result of this investigation work. By 1932, an effective leatherjacket expellant had also been developed (based on a now banned chemical, orthodichlorobenzene) and for a time the Research Station sold the material in commercial quantities as St. Ives Leatherjacket Exterminator. In 1934 the Director was able to report on the suitability of New Zealand browntop bentgrass for seeded greens, the importance of mechanical work (particularly aeration) in bowling green maintenance, and on the suitability of mowrah meal and lead arsenate for wormkilling purposes. An improved strain of slender creeping red fescue (cv. Dawson) was also developed.

Significant progress in the scientific management of bowling greens was therefore made at Bingley prior to the Second World War, although this aspect of the Research Station's activities was severely limited by lack of funds during this period. The 1939-45 war of course severely curtailed all aspects of turf research but the St. Ives station continued to tick over on a wartime footing until the Armistice.

Construction work on the miniature experimental bowling green at the Bingley Research Station, April 1930

3 Bowling Green Evolution: 1945 to the Present Day

POST WAR DEVELOPMENTS IN GREEN CONSTRUCTION

In the years following the Second World War, weaknesses in the traditional Scottish method of green construction gradually led to a preponderance of new greens being built using alternative techniques. However, conservative bowlers and contractors kept the Scottish system viable for a long time. Maintenance techniques also evolved a long way during this period, partly as a result of the abandonment of sea-marsh turf and Scottish construction, but of course also as a result of the appearance of vastly improved equipment and new chemical treatments, etc.

The main changes which have taken place in bowling green construction are a move away from sea-marsh turf in favour of seeding or alternative types of turf, and the provision of a layer of soil (or sand/soil mix) immediately beneath the sward.

A certain proportion of new greens had in fact always been constructed using soil, even during the heyday of the Scottish system. In the inter-war period the Scottish construction with sea-marsh turf was regarded as the De Luxe system, soil construction being reserved for seeded greens or greens turfed with sea-marsh turf substitutes. Soil greens were cheaper to build and traditionally regarded as very much inferior, particularly during the inter-war years. In the face of much prejudice however, it was gradually appreciated that in the long-term such "inferior" greens showed a number of significant advantages. The presence of good quality soil beneath the surface made long-term maintenance much easier—greens with this feature were less drought prone and grass growth and vigour were superior. By not using sea-marsh turf the insuperable problem of maintaining maritime grasses under inland conditions was eliminated and troublesome silt layers were no longer present. The decline of sea-marsh turf was accelerated by the over-exploitation of the marshes. After the 1939-45 war it became increasingly difficult to find turf of top quality and the use of inferior sea-marsh turf containing much broad-leaved weed or the weedgrass *Puccinellia*, plus spiralling costs, all contributed to its waning popularity. The pioneer selections of improved strains of turfgrass (like Dawson and New Zealand browntop) available in the 1930s and the beginnings of seed certification made seeded greens a more viable alternative. The very slow but significant appearance of a turf-growing industry producing high quality material specifically for fine sward establishment also made sea-marsh turf a less attractive proposition than it had formerly been.

Initially, where soil was used in green construction only shallow layers 63-75 mmin depth were used. Where cost considerations permitted, the soil was spread over a traditional Scottish foundation of clinker blinded with fine ash. Relatively shallow soil layers were favoured to maintain good water penetration into the underlying clinker and hence produce a fast-drying bowling surface.

By the time that the Research Station at Bingley (now The Sports Turf Research Institute) became actively involved in the supervision of bowling green construction projects in the 1950s, thinking on soil depths was changing and deeper layers were being advocated. (As a matter of interest, the first bowling green construction project that the Institute was involved in was a flat green for Rowntrees, the confectionery manufacturers, at York. This was as early as 1949.) As the Institute's then Director, J.R. Escritt, wrote in 1975 (in conjunction with R.B. Gooch of the NPFA in Sports Ground Construction Specifications, 1975 Edition):–

"The depth of 'topsoil' specified is related to the current commercial practice which produces satisfactory bowling greens. There is increasing evidence that a greater depth of specially pre-pared 'topsoil', say 150 mm (6 in.) or as much as 250 mm (10 in.) would be more satisfactory both for drainage and for moisture retention in dry weather. Obviously, if an increased depth of soil were to be used this would mean increased excavation and deeper drains."

This trend has continued to the present day, now with a minimum of 200 mm usually being used.

Bowling green drainage has evolved to some degree since the Second World War. In the case of flat rink greens, a grid system of parallel lateral drains running diagonally beneath the surface has emerged as standard practice, as opposed to the variety of drain-age patterns which have been advocated in the past. For crown greens, drains beneath the actual playing surface are often still considered unnecessary as surface contours shed water effectively into surrounding ditches. For flat and crown greens, perimeter ditch drains should always be included. The traditional clayware pipe drains (75 mm diameter for flat green laterals and 100 mm for ditch drains) have now been superseded by plastic pipes of equivalent sizes (60-80 mm for laterals and 100-110 mm for perimeter ditches).

For the foundation layers, the unavailability of clinker and ash of good quality has led to the use of gravel or broken stone as substitutes, blinded by a suitable grade of coarse sand. Synthetic material such as Lytag is occasionally used for backfilling drain trenches, although not for the foundation layer itself as the even-sized and rounded particles of such materials do not give sufficient stability and lead to difficulties with consolidation.

In recent years the use of standard laboratory techniques has removed the guesswork from determining an ideal sand/soil mix for the "topsoil" layer. (Rarely the admixture of a small proportion of granulated peat may also sometimes be deemed necessary if the organic matter content of the mix is found to be inadequate.) Such soil analysis work was originally carried out in the late 1950s and early 60s by the United States Golf Association but since the early 1970s has been used by the Sports Turf Research Institute to determine ideal drainage rates for soils for all sporting purposes, bowling greens included. In recent years there has been a steady tendency to increase the proportion of sand in the mix and a minimum saturated hydraulic conductivity of 150 mm per hour in the laboratory is now insisted upon. Sand of even particle size within strictly defined limits gives best results. Free-draining greens so constructed must have adequate watering systems.

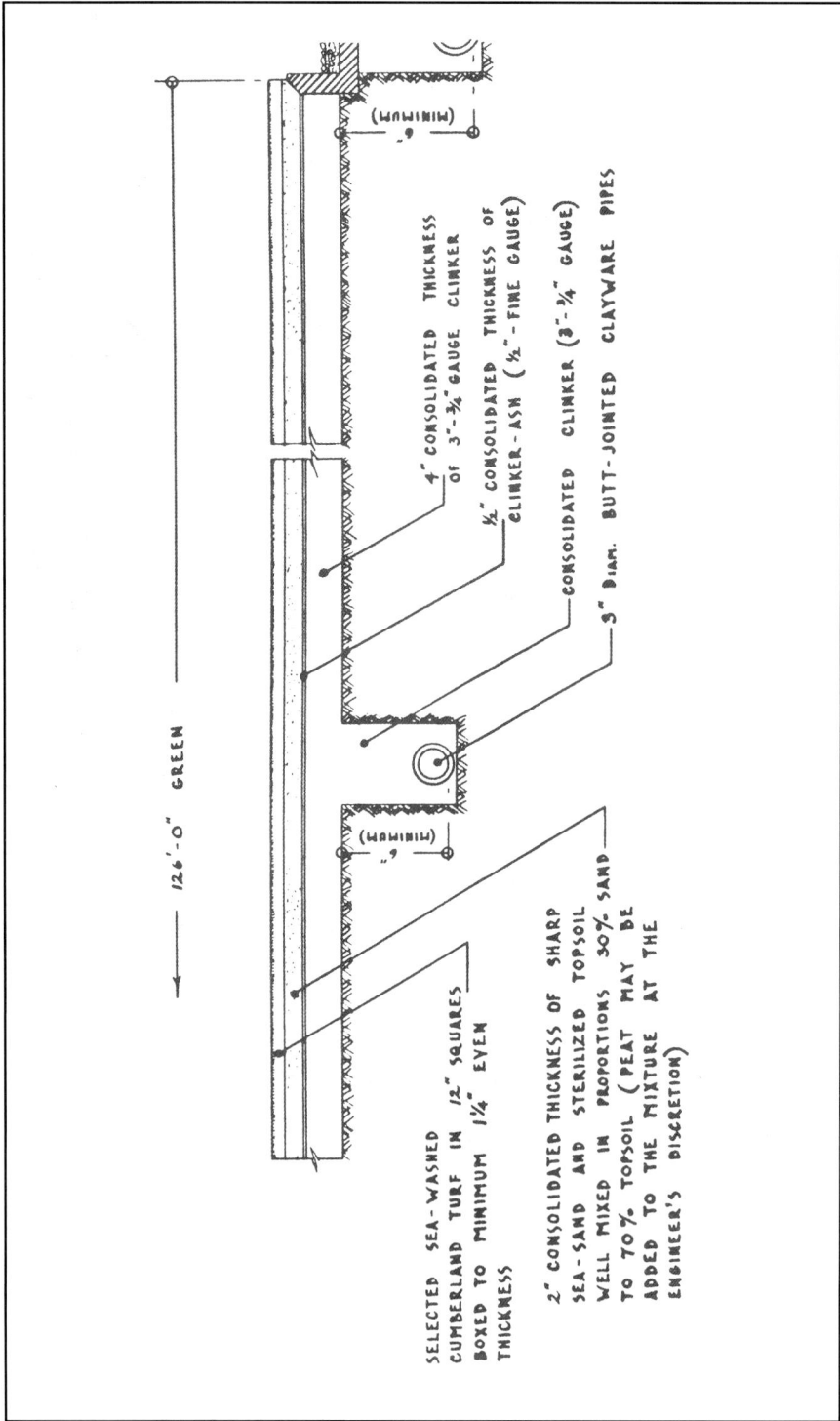

126'-0" GREEN

6" (MINIMUM)

6" (MINIMUM)

4" CONSOLIDATED THICKNESS OF 3"-¾" GAUGE CLINKER

½" CONSOLIDATED THICKNESS OF CLINKER-ASH (½"-FINE GAUGE)

CONSOLIDATED CLINKER (3"-¾" GAUGE)

3" DIAM. BUTT-JOINTED CLAYWARE PIPES

SELECTED SEA-WASHED CUMBERLAND TURF IN 12" SQUARES BOXED TO MINIMUM 1¼" EVEN THICKNESS

2" CONSOLIDATED THICKNESS OF SHARP SEA-SAND AND STERILIZED TOPSOIL WELL MIXED IN PROPORTIONS 30% SAND TO 70% TOPSOIL (PEAT MAY BE ADDED TO THE MIXTURE AT THE ENGINEER'S DISCRETION)

Typical bowling green construction of the 1950s. Note the shallow 2 in. layer of soil/sand mix and the continued use of sea-marsh turf

The first bowling green construction project in which the STRI was involved. Rowntrees bowling green at York, built in 1949

OUTER PITCH BOARD 100mm ABOVE GREEN SURFACE.

13mm THICK TURF.

127mm THICK SOIL MIX.

50mm THICK COARSE SAND.

45mm THICK 10mm GRADE AGGREGATE.

SUBSOIL FORMATION SURFACE.

25mm THICK TURF EDGE

INNER PITCH EDGE.

PITCH 300mm WIDE

100mm

90mm THICK PEA GRAVEL OR SAND

100mm EARTHWARE FIELD DRAIN.

10mm GRADE AGGREGATE

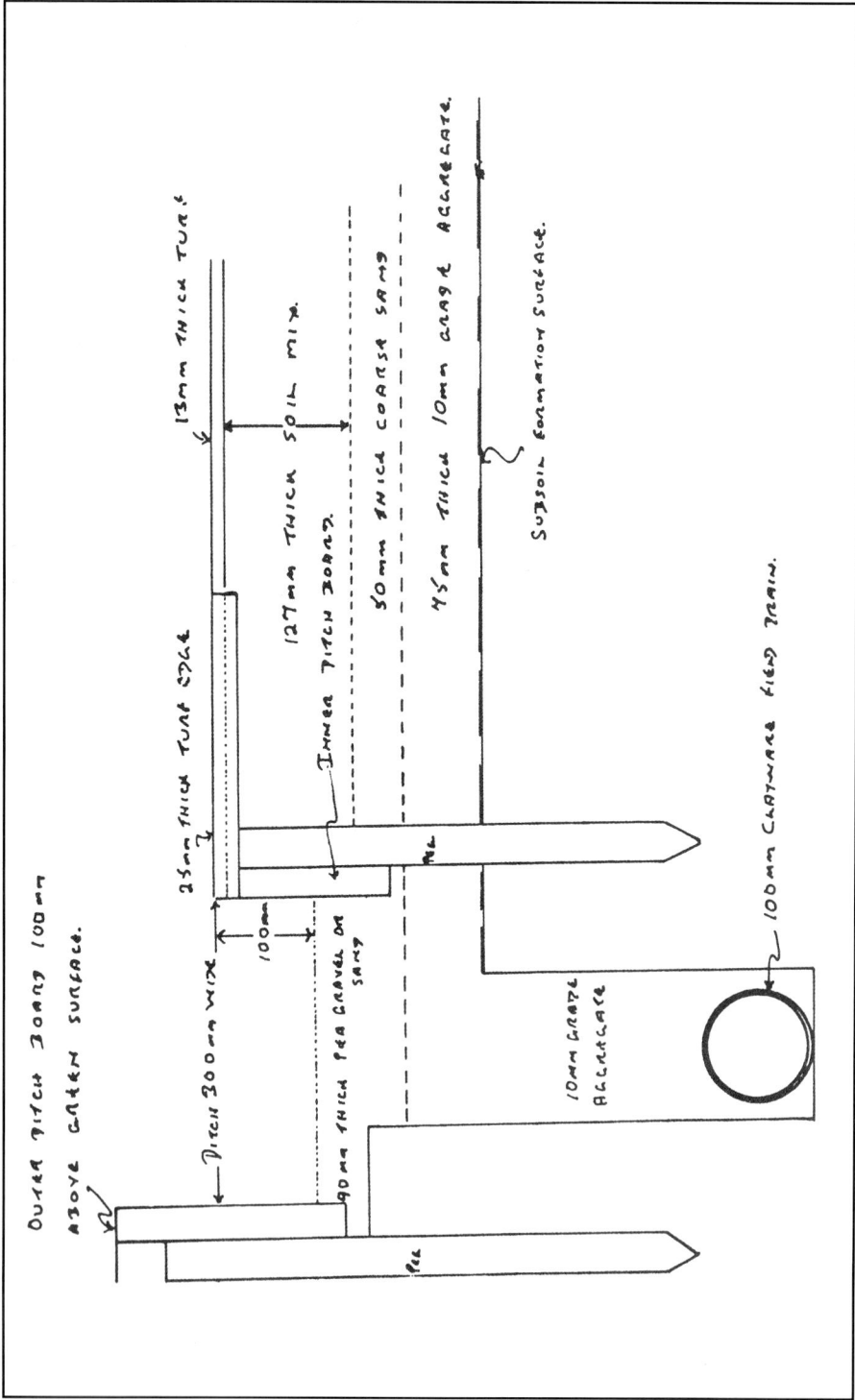

Typical bowling green construction in the 1970s. Note the deeper 127 mm (5 in.) soil mix layer

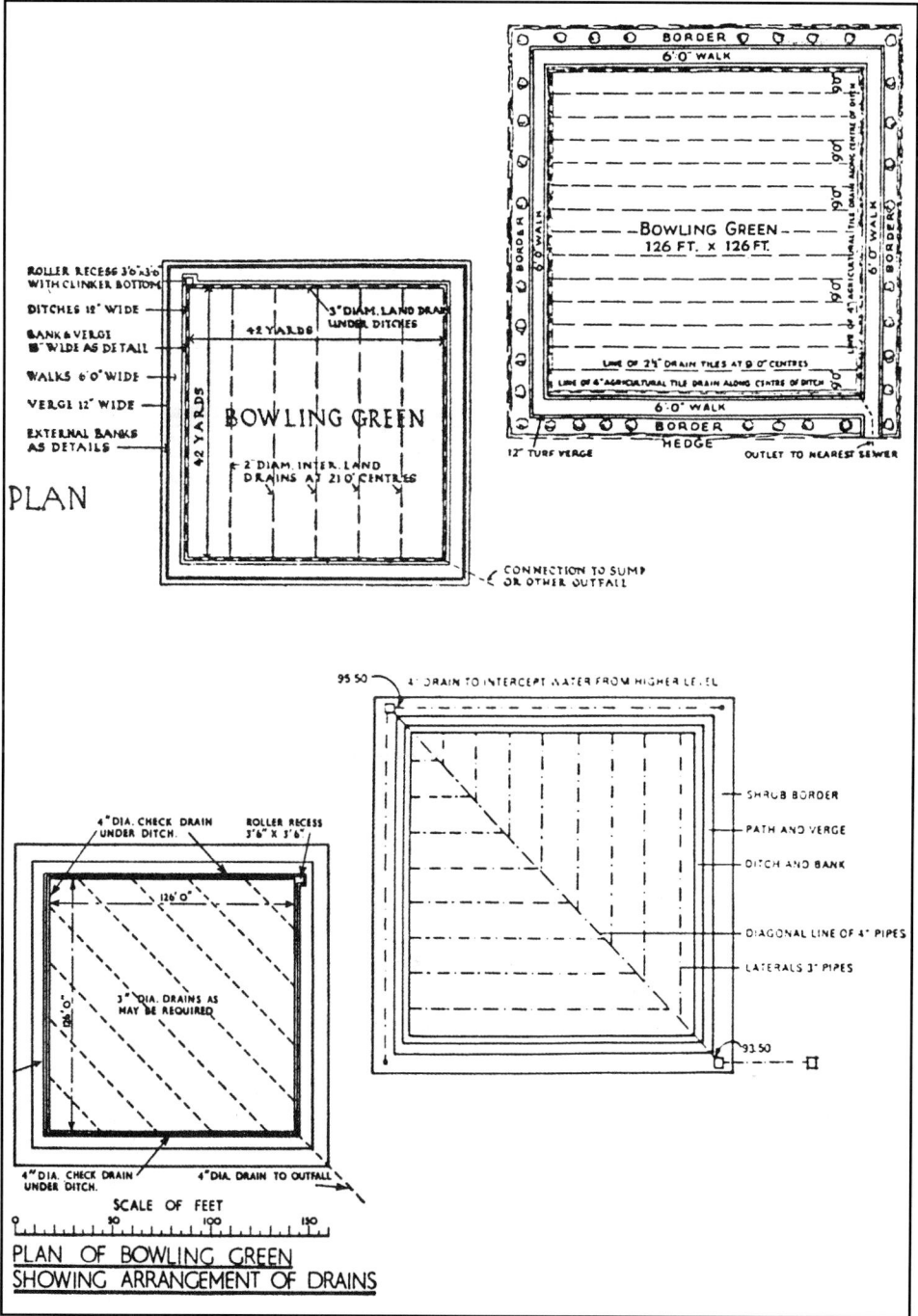

PLAN

ROLLER RECESS 3'6"x3'0"
WITH CLINKER BOTTOM

DITCHES 12" WIDE

BANK & VERGE
18" WIDE AS DETAIL

WALKS 6'0" WIDE

VERGE 12" WIDE

EXTERNAL BANKS
AS DETAILS

BOWLING GREEN

42 YARDS

42 YARDS

3" DIAM. LAND DRAIN
UNDER DITCHES

2" DIAM. INTER. LAND
DRAINS AT 21'0" CENTRES

CONNECTION TO SUMP
OR OTHER OUTFALL

BORDER
6'0" WALK

6'0" WALK

BORDER

6'0" WALK

BORDER

BOWLING GREEN
126 FT. x 126 FT.

6'0" WALK

LINE OF 2½" DRAIN TILES AT 9'0" CENTRES

LINE OF 4" AGRICULTURAL TILE DRAIN ALONG CENTRE OF DITCH

6'0" WALK
BORDER
HEDGE

12" TURF VERGE

OUTLET TO NEAREST SEWER

95.50

4" DRAIN TO INTERCEPT WATER FROM HIGHER LEVEL

SHRUB BORDER

PATH AND VERGE

DITCH AND BANK

DIAGONAL LINE OF 4" PIPES

LATERALS 3" PIPES

93.50

4" DIA. CHECK DRAIN
UNDER DITCH.

ROLLER RECESS
3'6" X 3'6"

126'0"

126'0"

3" DIA. DRAINS AS
MAY BE REQUIRED

4" DIA. CHECK DRAIN
UNDER DITCH.

4" DIA. DRAIN TO OUTFALL

SCALE OF FEET
0   50   100   150

PLAN OF BOWLING GREEN
SHOWING ARRANGEMENT OF DRAINS

Bowling green (flat rink) drain layouts. A variety of patterns have been advocated in the past. Here, four systems from 1931, 1937, 1950 and 1968

41

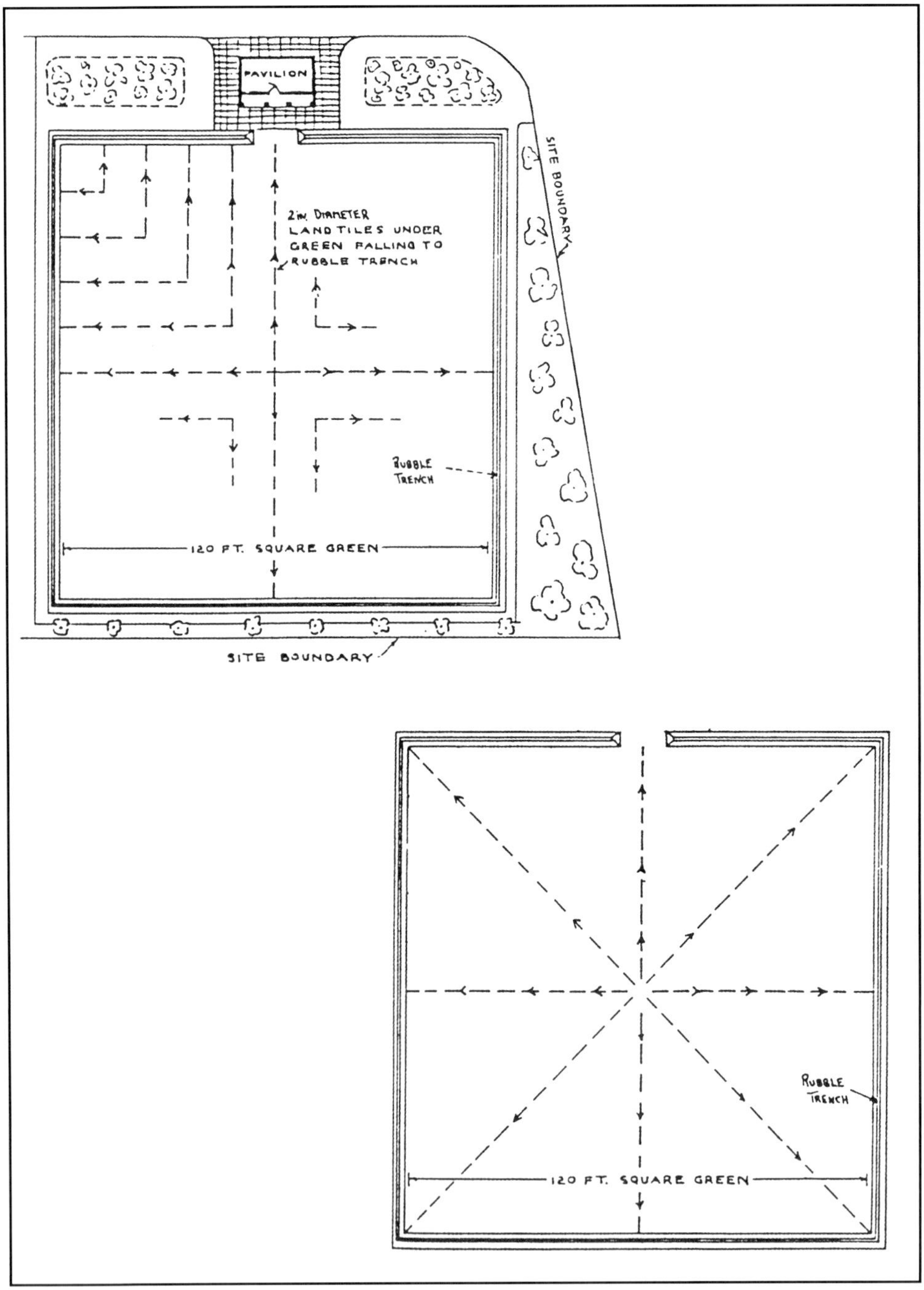
PAVILION
SITE BOUNDARY
2in. DIAMETER LANDTILES UNDER GREEN FALLING TO RUBBLE TRENCH
RUBBLE TRENCH
120 FT. SQUARE GREEN
SITE BOUNDARY
RUBBLE TRENCH
120 FT. SQUARE GREEN

The majority of crown greens do not have pipe drains below the playing surface, merely perimeter ditch drains. Drainage systems were however sometimes laid beneath the body of a crown green as indicated in these two plans from the 1930s. The possible presence of such systems should therefore be borne in mind when dealing with an old-established crown green

SAND
SIEVE TEST RESULTS

SAMPLE RE: **DATE:**

ORIGIN OF SAMPLE: **REF. NO.**

CATEGORY	DIAMETER mm	%
Stones	>8	0
Coarse Gravel	8-4	0
Fine Gravel	4-2	0
V. Coarse Sand	2-1	2
Coarse Sand	1.0-0.5	38
Medium Sand	0.50-0.25	55
Fine Sand	0.250-0.125	5
V. Fine Sand	0.125-0.050	0
Silt + Clay	<0.050	0
Lime Content (as $CaCO_3$)		<0.5

A typical laboratory sheet showing a sand with an ideal particle size distribution for inclusion in a soil-sand mix for present day bowling green construction

CATEGORY	DIAMETER mm	%	SOIL TEXTURE:
			SANDY LOAM

SOIL SAMPLE RE:

BRIEF DESCRIPTION:

DATE:

SOIL REF. NO.

CATEGORY	DIAMETER mm	%	SOIL TEXTURE:
			SANDY LOAM
Stones	>8	–	
Coarse Gravel	8-4	–	
Fine Gravel	4-2	–	

Particle size distribution of mineral matter smaller than 2 mm

CATEGORY	DIAMETER mm	%	
V. Coarse Sand	2-1	1	**COMMENTS:**
Coarse Sand	1.0-0.5	32	MIX OF ONE PART SOIL TO TWO-THREE PARKS SAND AS PER SAMPLE
Medium Sand	0.50-0.25	44	
Fine Sand	0.250-0.125	9	
V. Fine Sand	0.125-0.050	6	
Silt	0.50-0.002	5	
Clay	<0.002	3	
Loss on Ignition (% of oven-dry fine-earth)		3-5%	
Calcium carbonate (% of air-dry fine-earth)		<0.5	
Water dispersibility of the clay (%)		–	

Laboratory analysis of ideal sand-soil mix for present day bowling green construction

For seeded greens, a seeds mixture made up of browntop bentgrass and Chewings fescue is normally recommended. The seeds mix gives a 50/50 sward of the two species but because bentgrass seed is a quarter the weight of the fescue seed, four times as much fescue must be included, i.e.

- 80% by weight Chewings fescue (*Festuca rubra* spp. *commutata*)
- 20% by weight browntop bent (*Agrostis capillaris*)

Sometimes the 80% Chewings fescue is split, with 40% slender creeping fescue included.

BSPB/STRI produce an annual booklet, *Turfgrass Seed,* covering current grass varieties and their performance.

Turfing remains an alternative method of bowling green establishment which, although more costly than seeding, produces a playable surface after a shorter time. If a green is seeded in early autumn, as is usual, then about 12-18 months must elapse before play can take place. A surface turfed in autumn can usually be played on the following summer given a good standard of construction work and adequate initial maintenance. If turf is chosen as an establishment method, then it is essential to use purpose-grown turf from one of the few specialist firms who produce top quality turf in this country. Turf grown from suitable grass cultivars (as would be used for a seeded green) is mandatory and should be free of that ubiquitous weedgrass, annual meadow-grass. It is also an advantage to employ turf grown on a substrate which resembles as closely as possible the soil/sand mix used in the construction of a particular green.

Considerable progress has been made since the War in the construction of bowling green perimeter ditches. Traditionally for flat greens, preservative-treated wood boards and stakes have been used but modern difficulties in obtaining suitably seasoned high-quality timber have encouraged the use of alternative ditch formation methods. Precast concrete kerb units were the first alternative to wood, the outer taller kerb being faced with a softwood striking board to avoid damage to the bowls. (Artificial turf is an attractive alternative to a wood striking board, glued to the kerb face.) Subsequently, purpose-made precast concrete and glassfibre reinforced cement ditch units have been produced to EBA-approved patterns, complete with mitred corner units. Some of the these units could well be used for crown green construction, although crown green ditch requirements are far less rigorous than for the flat rink game and such refinements might therefore be considered unnecessarily expensive for the average crown green.

ARTIFICIAL OUTDOOR GREENS

Natural grass bowling greens are the subject of the present text, but some mention of artificial outdoor greens is an obvious requirement as there are a number of such installations up and down the country, both flat rink and crown artificial greens having been constructed.

Installation costs are comparable to those for natural grass greens. Day-to-day maintenance costs are on average less, although artificial surfaces are not maintenance-free as they require cleaning, moss or algae control, etc. However, this saving must be offset against the fact that carpets do not last forever and have to be replaced after a few years at relatively high cost. The playing surfaces of artificial greens may also change progressively with time, the surface becoming faster and faster as the carpet pile wears down.

The advantages claimed by manufacturers of artificial greens can be listed as follows:–

- True, flat playing surface for flat rink bowls.
- Completely porous system and therefore minimal drainage difficulties.
- High usage level.
- Potential evening and winter usage.
- No specialist maintenance procedures.
- Multi-directional pile carpet.
- Continual usage of same lanes.
- Easily repairable vandalised areas.

The counter-argument might be that winter or poor weather usage is not a real advantage for flat rink bowlers as they would prefer to play on one of the many indoor facilities under such inclement weather conditions. Also, that a well-maintained grass green should be largely self-repairing and that wear can be significantly reduced by correct rink-changing policies. A purist might also argue that British lawn bowling should by definition be played on a lawn, i.e. a natural grass surface.

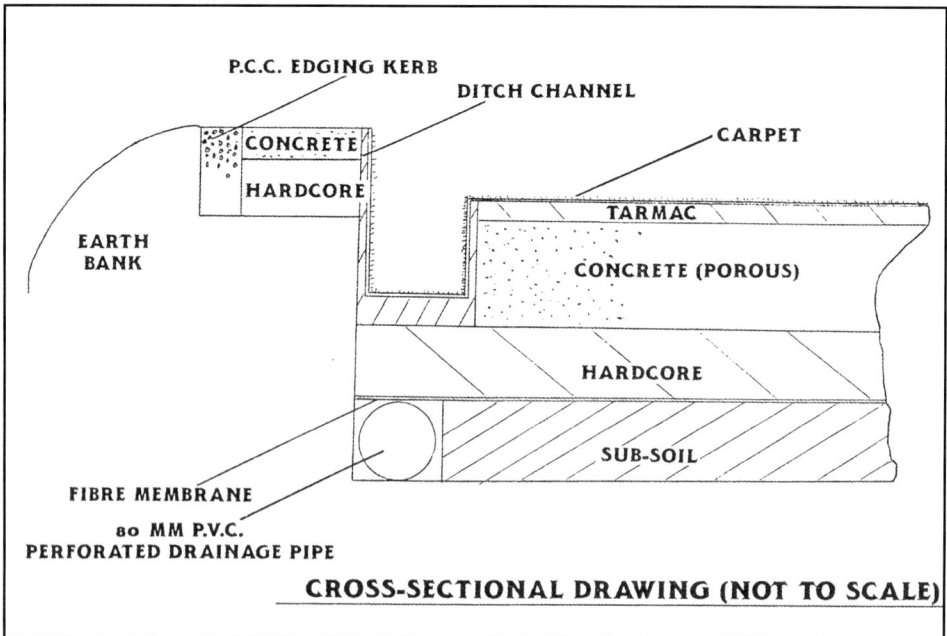

Typical artificial outdoor green construction

POST WAR DEVELOPMENTS IN GREEN MAINTENANCE

Progress in bowling green maintenance techniques since 1945 has been a result of the commercial introduction of a wide variety of effective chemicals for various greenkeeping purposes, the development of vastly more efficient mechanical equipment and a better scientific understanding of the management of turf.

The development of selective herbicides in the late 1940s, and the pioneer studies in the application of these materials to turf which were carried out at Bingley, represented a major breakthrough in greenkeeping. Lawnsands and other early weedkilling materials have now been almost entirely surplanted by 2,4-D and other growth-regulating chemicals. The traditional lawnsand (a mixture of sulphate of ammonia and sulphate of iron) is still used to some extent for mosskilling purposes. Mercurised turf sands and mercurised mosskillers proved effective and popular for a period until the health hazards of mercury use became apparent and the use of mercury banned by a more environmentally responsible society. It is indeed environmental considerations, together with a broader approach to chemical use through European Union legistslation, that are determining the available of so many turf products these days. For this reason alone, it is difficult to specifically guide on pesticide use within the context of this book as almost certainly some chemical would be withdrawn between the writing of this text and its publication!

Progress in the identification and scientific description of a number of damaging turf diseases has been paralleled by the introduction of a wide range of fungicides. The pre-war use of such materials as Bordeaux mixture, sulphate of iron, copper sulphate and mercuric chloride gave way initially to the use of both organic and inorganic mercury products, together with cadmium-based materials. Increased safety consciousness in recent years again led to legislation against the use of such chemicals on amenity turf but alternatives have fortunately appeared. A good range of effective fungicides are currently available. What will be interesting in the next few years is to see whether climate change fetches fresh disease problems to these shores, and whether we will have appropriate, approved fungicides available.

Turning to next to pest control... the chemicals originally developed for worm eradication were all expellants—in other words they brought worms to the surface without necessarily killing them and large numbers of worms hence had to be swept up and disposed of. Such chemicals were short-term in their action and treatment at quite frequent intervals was therefore necessary. Materials like potassium permanganate, derris dust and mowrah meal were employed for this purpose but were replaced by products which actually kill worms below the surface. After the War, lead arsenate and to a lesser extent calcium arsenate were used which gave very long-term control, but the very toxic (i.e. to humans) nature of arsenical compounds led to their prohibition. An organo-phosphorus compound called chlordane then appeared and was used regularly through the late 1970s and 80s achieving very good worm control for five years or more. Again for environmental and human toxicity reasons, chlordane was withdrawn in the early 1990s. There remain (at the moment) a small range of permitted wormkillers for use on turf areas, although their effects are relatively short lived. The current approach to worm control is to acidify surface soil conditions and reduce organic matter content.

The main insect pest of turf in the UK, the leatherjacket, caused headaches for years until the development at Bingley of the "St. Ives Leatherjacket Exterminator", an expellant material based on orthodichlorobenzene—a substance since banned as carcinogenic. DDT enjoyed a relatively brief period as a popular insecticide but public concern regarding health factors led to it gradually falling from favour. At the moment chlorpyrifos is used to control leatherjackets but in view of the ongoing reviews of approved pesticide use, one should always refer to the *UK Pesticides Guide* to check the situation.

Fertiliser usage on bowling greens since the war has involved fewer basic changes than is the case with pesticides and fungicides, but significant changes in thinking have taken place. It was appreciated early that the fine turfgrasses, browntop bent and Chewings fescue, are favoured by acidic soil conditions and this encouraged the use of materials like sulphate of ammonia and sulphate of iron which have an acidifying effect, so helping to reduce worm activity, broad-leaved weeds and some coarser grasses. (Sea-marsh turf has a naturally alkaline soil and the use of acidic fertilisers on greens built with this material contributed to the gradual deterioration of the sea-marsh sward.) Sulphate of ammonia was used for a long period as an acidic inorganic nitrogen source, supplemented by the use of longer-lasting, slower-acting organic nitrogen sources such as dried blood or hoof and horn meal. Sulphate of iron remains popular for its acidifying effect, the pleasing dark green grass colour which it produces, and its useful moss and disease controlling properties. For several decades after 1945 it was considered necessary to fertilise bowling greens with nitrogenous materials every five to six weeks through the playing season, so maintaining good growth and counteracting wear. In addition, spring use of fertilisers containing phosphate and potash (usually in the form of powdered superphosphate, bone meal and sulphate of potash) as well as nitrogen was advocated, with perhaps additional potash in the early autumn. Most greenkeepers made up such dressings to individual requirements out of basic ingredients. Pioneering early work at Bingley quickly established that the late or excessive use of nitrogen in the autumn was undesirable, mainly because it was a major factor in the encouragement of damaging fusarium patch disease and because rank growth late in the year is unnecessarily wasteful, particularly for a summer game surface.

By modern standards the kind of fertiliser regime described above is excessive. It is now appreciated more fully that the heavy use of nitrogen may not only encourage fusarium patch disease but also favours undesirable annual meadow-grass at the expense of browntop bent and particularly fescue—the better grasses occur naturally under conditions of relative soil poverty and survive best where fertiliser is not overdone. The results of a most revealing and interesting survey of bowling green soils published by the Sports Turf Research Institute in 1985 (see Appendix A), involved an assessment of soil samples from 225 bowling greens nationwide and showed extremely high phosphate and potash levels for the majority of greens surveyed. Phosphate in particular is a major factor in encouraging the weed, annual meadow-grass. The excessive use of fertiliser is also undesirable from the bowler's point of view—over-fed greens tend to be lush, slow and heavy, and better, faster surfaces result from a reduction in feeding. Unfortunately, it is probably true to say that many greenkeepers, as a point of pride, try to maintain greens of attractive appearance and nitrogenous fertiliser does help provide a good-looking turf. Playing quality should, however, never be sacrificed for the sake of sward appearance—a bowling green is not an ornamental lawn!

During the early 1980s there was a steady decline in the use of fertiliser dressings made up of basic ingredients—greenkeepers then using ready-made fertilisers available from commercial manufacturers. A wide range of proprietary fertilisers are now available which give excellent results in practice. Mini-granular preparations are often easier to distribute evenly using modern fertiliser spreaders than more traditional powdered mixtures bulked with sand or compost carriers. Many commercial fertilisers contain slow-release nitrogen formulations which tend to give slower, but more sustained and hence more uniform, growth through the playing season. The development of a good range of liquid fertilisers has also resulted in more widespread use of this form of fertiliser.

More spectacular than the gradual improvement in the chemical weapons in the greenkeeper's armoury has been the evolution of new mechanical equipment. By 1960 most British bowling greens were being cut using petrol-driven motor mowers (electric mowers were tried but never proved successful). Older and more reactionary greenkeepers still swore by the old hand machines but powered machines were faster and hence made better use of increasingly costly labour resources, allowing greens to be cut more quickly and perhaps more often. Refinements in the design of powered mowers ultimately ensured that the finish which they produced was in no way inferior to that produced by the hand-pushed models. An extremely useful development was the provision on some professional mowers of a small rake or comb which fits between the front roller and the cutting cylinder, a very useful mowing aid to remove flat growth and debris from the bottom of the sward. In recent years the development of groomer facilities on many of the better mowers (a revolving reel of fine blades between the front roller and the cutting cylinder) provides similar benefits.

The universal use of motor mowers has resulted in a marked decline in the need for rolling as a separate operation. Motor mowers are heavy enough to have a significant rolling action and have made frequent rolling unnecessary. Increasing appreciation of the damaging effects of heavy rolling, producing poor surface drainage, excessive soil compaction, poor grass growth and moss invasion, has fortunately led to a decline in the use of the more weighty rollers. It is after all possible to produce uniformly fast and true bowling surfaces without resorting to road-rollers, vibrating rollers or other similar juggernauts.

Spiking equipment developed between the two wars as we have already seen, with pedestrian-pushed machines appearing first as alternatives to the humble hand fork. Experiments commenced in 1934 by William Hargreaves were particularly significant in the subsequent development of such machines. After the Second World War spikers remained basically similar to pre-war versions until the advent of motorisation in the 1950s. The Pattisson S.P. spiker of 1953 proved a popular machine, as did the 1963 Sisis Auto Turfman and 1964 Auto-Outfield spiker. Some machines of this type could be fitted with alternative tine patterns—flat knife, round solid or hollow coring. Earlier machines were basically of drum-type with the tines pushed into the ground by the rolling action of a horizontally-revolving drum. A later development was the cam-action or punch-type machine with tines actually driven into the ground by powered cams, giving better penetration into compacted ground, particularly with hollow tines. The Ryan Greensaire, an American design, typifies this class of machine and, although relatively expensive, this type of machine is preferred when it comes to aerating fine turf.

To counteract the very deep-seated compaction found on some greens as a result of faulty construction or repeated heavy rolling over a long period, machines which penetrate more deeply than the l50 mm or so, which is about the maximum achievable with smaller spikers, have been developed. These depend on mole-plough shares or vibrating subsoiler-type shares for their effect or, in the case of the Verti-Drain, on long heavy tines power-driven into the ground with an accompanying prising action. Other machines shatter compaction by means of long tines down which high-pressure air is forced, or achieve the same result using jets of water directed down from the surface.

Rotary scarifiers represent another invaluable advance, using rapidly revolving vertical blades as a far more effective alternative to the hand or two-wheeled wire or rigid-tined rake. The Ransomes Gazelle was the first British powered machine, economically built from a modified motor mower by removing the sole-plate and welding nail-like scarifying tines onto the blades of a conventional mower cutting reel. Purpose-designed powered scarifiers followed with an American import, the Rose Verticut appearing in l956 and the Sisis Rotorake in spring l957. In recent years we have seen the appearance of even more robust deep verticutting machines from Sisis and Graden where it is possible to remove thatch from even greater depths.

As for other equipment, spinner and belt-type fertiliser distributors appeared pre-war and have not changed fundamentally since. Sprayers have, however, developed beyond the old knapsack type—the Drake and Fletcher 'Groundsman' constant-pressure machine of l959 proving particularly successful. The development of C.D.A (Controlled Droplet Application) sprayers offered another option, using low-volume pre-packaged herbicides, fungicides, etc. which require no dilution and which simplify accuracy in application rates.

In the years after the war most bowling clubs could boast adequate irrigation equipment, using rotary or oscillating sprinklers, spray-lines or perforated hose. Since l965 automatic watering using pop-up sprinklers has become a possibility, but cost factors invariably mean that this refinement is only possible for the more affluent bowling clubs.

In the face of all this engineering however, the basic hand tools have survived and still occupy a vital place in the greenkeeper's toolshed. The drag-mat, drag-brush, switch, daisy grubber and spiked Sarel roller still have a role to play, as does the Scottish greenkeeper's "graip" or solid-tine fork and William Paul's hollow-tined variant. Another necessity which has not changed over the years is of course the services of a knowledgeable and dedicated greenkeeper!

The alert reader, when perusing the above account of progress since l945, may have noticed a distinct lack of detailed references to any basic scientific research directed specifi-

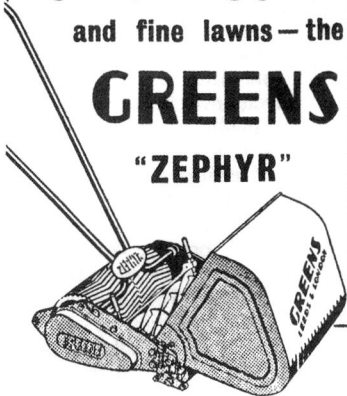

A selection of advertisements 1947-1950. Note the introduction of selective weedkillers and the continuing use of hand mowers and sea-marsh turf

cally towards the problems of bowling green upkeep. The omission is a reflection of the fact that funds for research into bowling green problems have been woefully inadequate to date. A rare exception to this state of affairs was a detailed investigation carried out by the STRI into the quality of bowling surfaces and reported on in 1986 (see Appendix B), made possible by a Sports Council grant. Fortunately, much basic scientific work into turf culture generally has been carried out and many advances are applicable to bowls surfaces. Much research primarily directed towards other sports (golf green studies in particular) has also proven invaluable when applied to bowling green work. A need for specialised bowling green research still remains, however, and it is to be hoped that this will one day be practicable.

4 Modern Bowling Green Construction

The following method of construction for flat and crown bowling greens is based on some 50 years of experience in supervisory work accumulated at the STRI and makes full use of all relevant scientific research. If you are planning the construction of a bowling green, more detailed information should be sought from STRI's Construction Department who are able to assist with design, specification production, supervision and monitoring work. There are also some useful and helpful points made in Sport England's design guidance note *Natural Turf for Sport* (which was written by STRI) and is currently available on download from **www.sportengland.org**.

ADVANCE PLANNING

An early start to planning is essential for construction work since timing has a great bearing on the final result for many of the necessary operations. Several approaches may have to be considered depending on site characteristics, for example the aggregate drainage layer could possibly be omitted for a site which has exceptional drainage characteristics—as perhaps on a gravel subsoil. Again on sites where there is very sandy topsoil, there might be less of a requirement for amelioration of the upper layer. The approach to construction ultimately adopted may also depend on available finance. A penny-pinching approach to bowling green construction should, however, be avoided if at all possible. Undertaking construction work correctly in the first place saves money in the long-term.

An eight to ten week contract period should be offered in documentation, culminating in sowing or turfing and allowing for some initial maintenance work to be completed by the contractor. Timing is important, it is usual to sow in late summer or early autumn or to aim for autumn turfing. Spring/summer seeding or turfing need not, however, be entirely ruled out if an adequate water supply is available so that drought damage can be prevented during early establishment. It is necessary to obtain planning consent from the Local Authority before work is intended to commence.

Advice should therefore be sought at an early stage from the STRI on the particular aspects of each site, e.g. the general construction procedure appropriate to the type of green (flat or crown) required, design of drainage system in relation to outfall and suitability of existing topsoil (although one has to say that there are very few sites where it is possible to reuse the topsoil, even ameliorated, as the final rootzone).

At the outset, a survey drawing is required showing existing levels, site features, including underground or overhead services (if any) and drain outlets, e.g. ditches or public surface water drains. If the latter are to be used, permission will have to be obtained from the Water Authority and/or the Environment Agency. Usually these days surveys are carried out with sophisticated equipment that records survey data in digital format which can then be downloaded quickly and easily into a CAD (computer-aided design) system. The following drawings of an existing green show the intensity of surveying requirements and the resultant contour map and 3 dimensional plan that is possible.

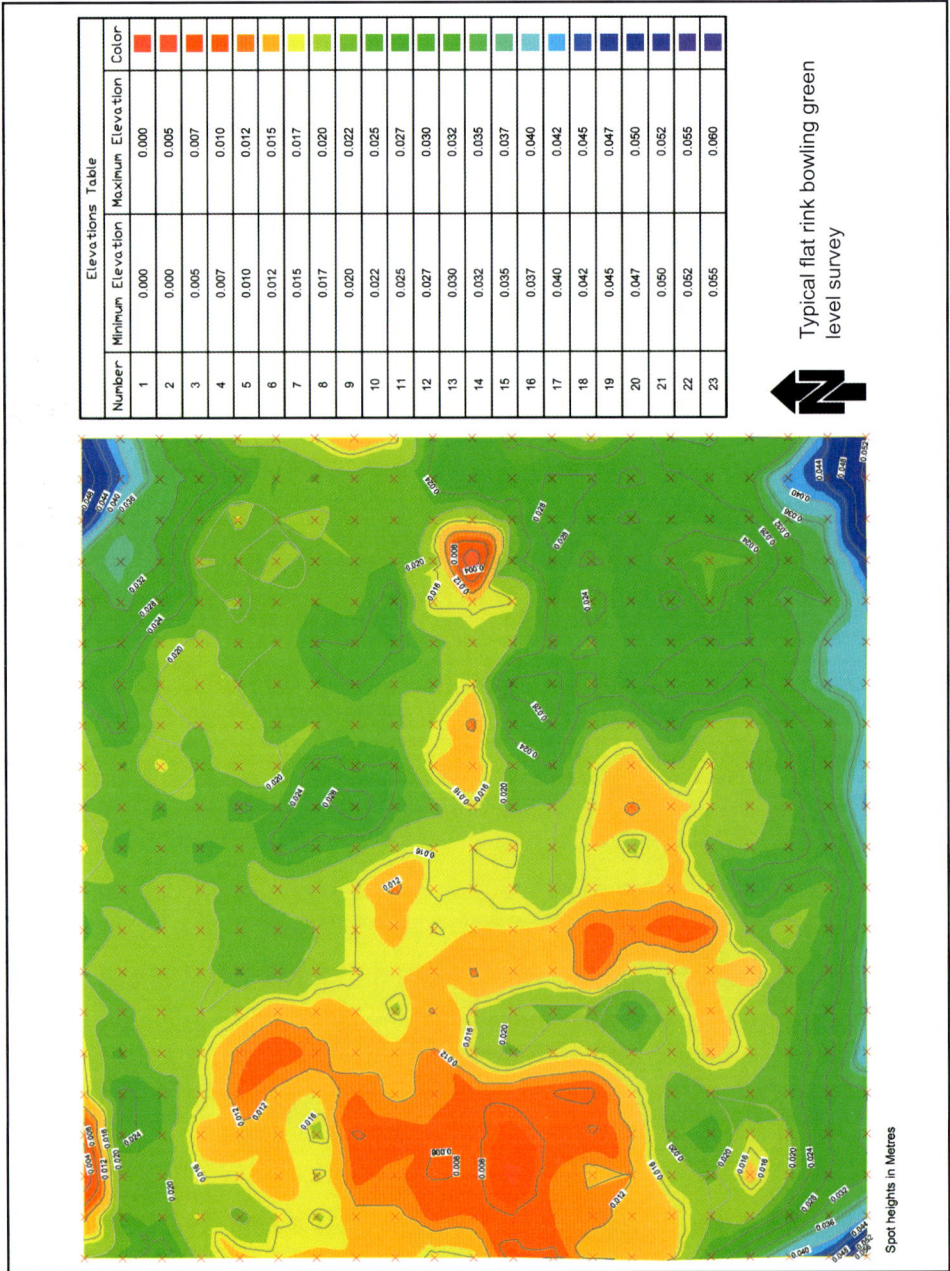

Typical flat rink bowling green level survey

Elevations Table			
Number	Minimum Elevation	Maximum Elevation	Color
1	0.000	0.000	
2	0.000	0.005	
3	0.005	0.007	
4	0.007	0.010	
5	0.010	0.012	
6	0.012	0.015	
7	0.015	0.017	
8	0.017	0.020	
9	0.020	0.022	
10	0.022	0.025	
11	0.025	0.027	
12	0.027	0.030	
13	0.030	0.032	
14	0.032	0.035	
15	0.035	0.037	
16	0.037	0.040	
17	0.040	0.042	
18	0.042	0.045	
19	0.045	0.047	
20	0.047	0.050	
21	0.050	0.052	
22	0.052	0.055	
23	0.055	0.060	

Spot heights in Metres

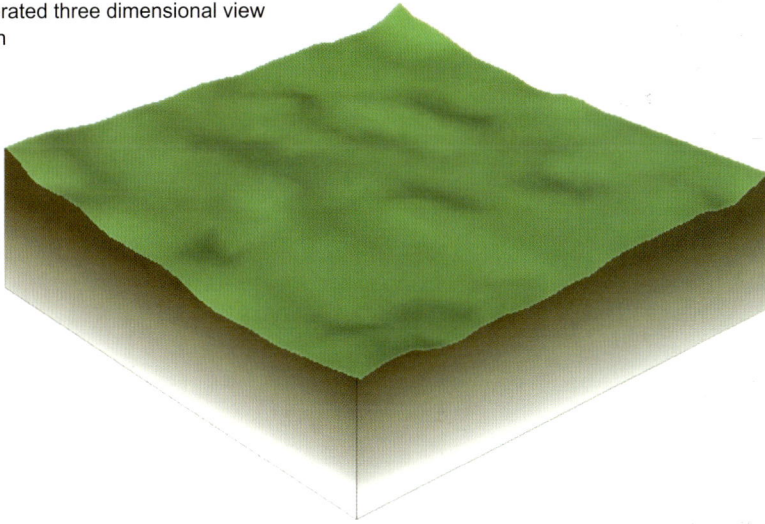

Exaggerated three dimensional view of green

The existing levels are used to establish finished levels related to the surrounds. The pipe drainage system can also be planned at this stage. While it is preferred that bowling greens are constructed on unfilled land, a certain amount of cut and fill or importation of suitable fill to give required finished levels is sometimes inevitable. The levels provided on the survey drawing in conjunction with calculated finished levels are used to determine quantities relating to excavation, materials required and all other operations specified for the construction of the green and any ancillary works which may be required.

GRADING

Following site clearance as required, grading to provide the required subsoil formation surface is carried out with specialised equipment operated by skilled personnel. The work should be undertaken when the ground conditions are dry.

Firstly, topsoil is removed from the bowling green area and surround, taking care not to disturb any subsoil material. Any surplus topsoil should be disposed of as directed by the engineer or architect. The exposed subsoil is then accurately graded to the required levels of the green, ditches, banks, verges and paths, allowing for the appropriate build-up of the drainage layer, rootzone mix over the green, and topsoil over the surrounds. If any material has to be imported to produce the subsoil formation level (preferably avoided if possible), it is crucial that this fill material is of a non-degradable nature and is carefully introduced in layers (of no more than 15 cm thickness), firming any such layer before adding the next. This should minimise the risk of future settlement which would be disastrous, especially on a flat green.

On a flat rink green, grading is completed so that the top of the bank surrounding the green should be no less than 230 mm above the finished green surface, the bank being at an angle of not more than 35° from the perpendicular but preferably upright. The green

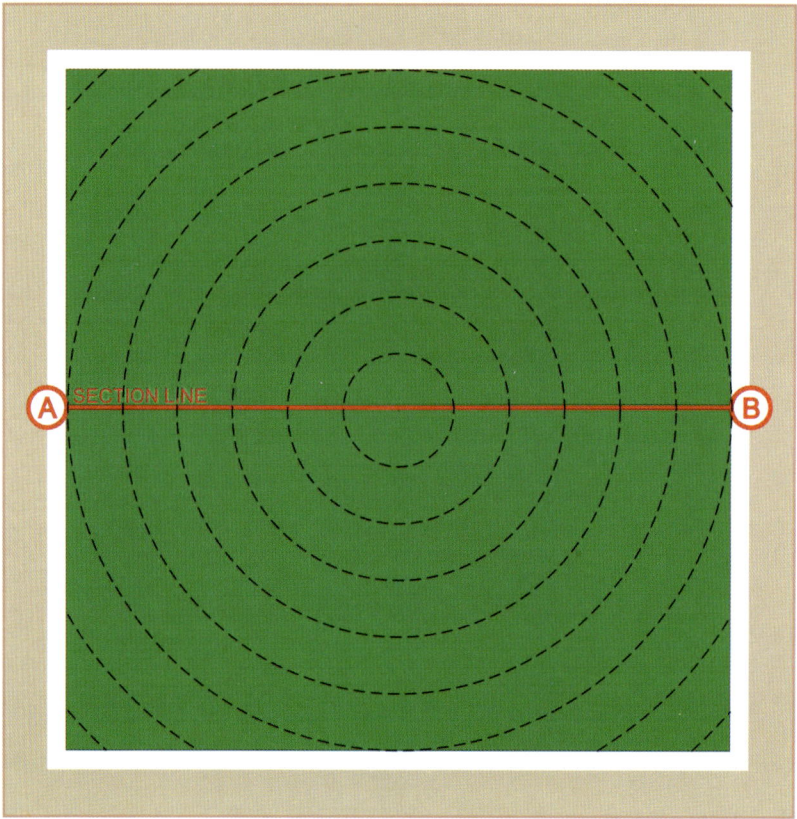

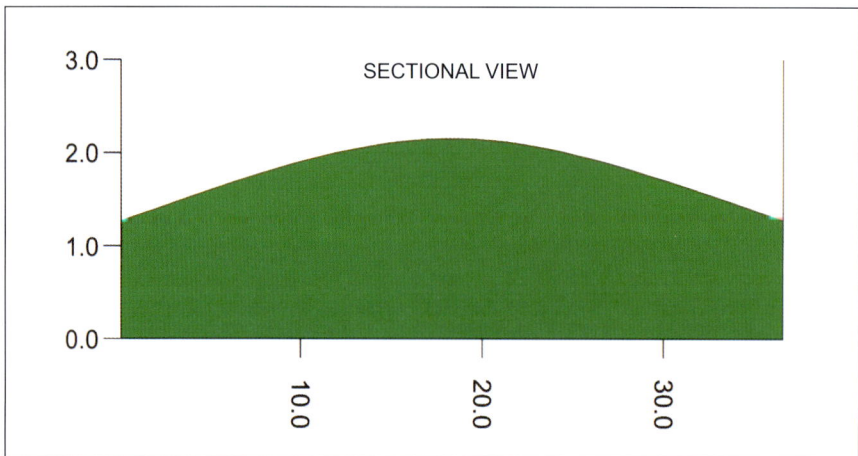

Plan view of crown bowling green including contours and sectional view

should be square in shape with a length of no less than 34 m and no more than 40 m in the direction of play.

On a crown green, adjustment to subsoil levels is completed bearing in mind that the level at the centre of the green can be 254 mm, 305 mm or 380 mm above the corner levels. 380 mm is now the British Crown Green Bowling Association's recommended height for a 36.6 x 36.6 m (40 x 40 yd.) crown green, and pro rata for greens of other sizes. Crown greens may vary in size between 27.4 x 27.4 m (30 x 30 yd.) to a maximum of 54.9 x 54.9 m (60 x 60 yd.). The top of the outer ditch board should be a minimum of 100 mm higher than the green surface on completion of a crown green.

With both flat and crown greens, pegs should be set at the correct levels and the subsoil graded to conform to them using laser levelling equipment to obtain the true and even formation surface required. In the case of a crown green, the subsoil formation surface is crowned to conform to the contours of the finished bowling surface.

WATER SUPPLY

A water supply is usually necessary. This can consist of a system which provides one or two water hydrants to operate spray-lines or moveable sprinklers. Alternatively, an automated pop-up irrigation system can be introduced. A specialist irrigation contractor should be engaged if automated irrigation is to be included in the specification.

DRAINAGE

Good drainage is essential and this is normally provided on a flat green by installing pipe drainage through the formation surface of the green and within the ditches. The drains should connect to a positive outfall and have suitable aggregate backfill.

On a crown green pipe drains are introduced in the ditches but are often omitted in the body of the green as the contouring of the formation carried through to the surface permits for speedy run-off of surface and sub-surface water.

Ditch drains for both flat and crown greens should be introduced with a fall of no less than 1:200 (0.5%) using perforated plastic drain pipes of 100-110 mm outside diameter to BS standard. Approved plastic bends are used at the corners except at the lowest corner where an appropriate plastic junction is introduced to connect the ditch drains to a non-perforated outlet drain.

Normally for a flat green 80 mm outside diameter perforated plastic drain pipes are introduced into the body of the green with appropriate falls at anything between 4-7 metre intervals, the spacing depending on individual site characteristics. Drain trenches are excavated into the subsoil formation surface. Each drain is accurately constructed to connect with the ditch drains, and forms part of a grid system of parallel drains.

Pipes are laid to true line and steady fall on a firm foundation and backfilling is then completed carefully up to subsoil formation surface using approved predominantly single sized hard aggregate, e.g. angular gravel of 6-10 mm gauge. Backfilling is then adequately firmed if necessary.

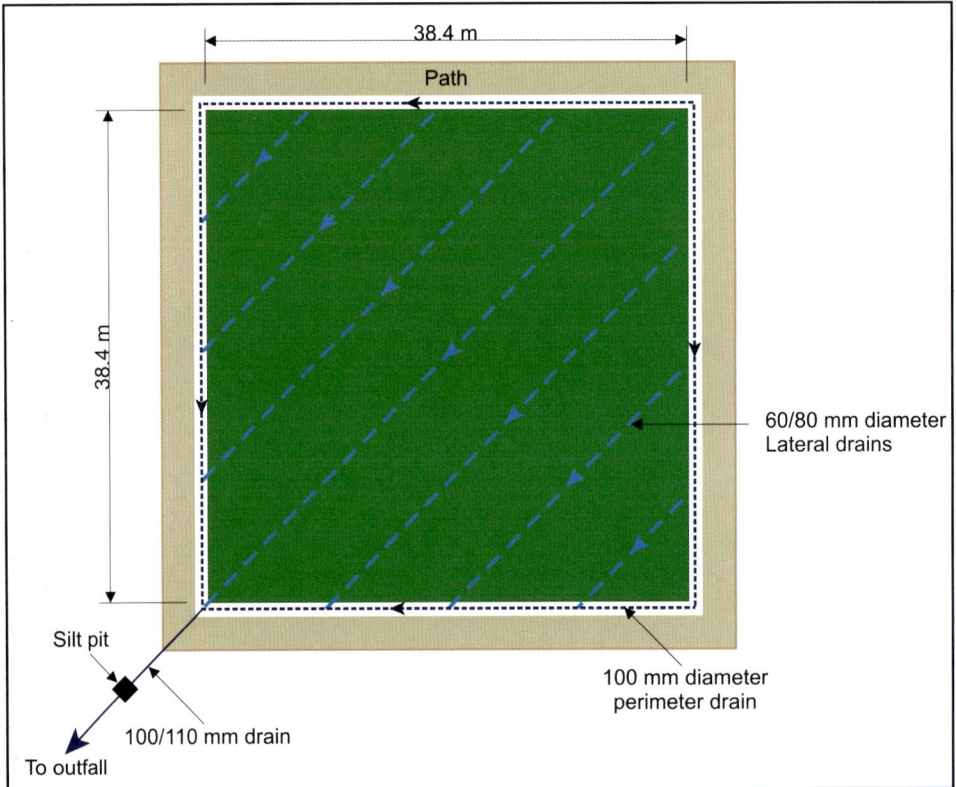

Flat green with drainage layer

Depending on the ultimate location of the drainage outlet which may, by permission, be on neighbouring land or a local authority surface water system, it might be necessary to provide a silt chamber on the line of the outlet drain.

Commonly, silt chambers are built with purpose-made reinforced precast concrete units to BS standard, each unit being set in cement mortar. The chamber is fitted with a removable cast iron cover for inspection and cleaning purposes.

APPLICATION OF HERBICIDE TO SUBSOIL FORMATION SURFACE

It may be necessary to apply an approved total residual herbicide to the whole of the green, ditch and path subsoil formation surfaces. Ensure that spraying is carried out strictly in accordance with the manufacturer's instructions and current spraying regulations following completion of a COSHH assessment.

DITCH FORMATION—FLAT GREEN

Flat rink bowling green ditches should be no less than 200 mm and no more than 380 mm wide. In the past, ditches on flat greens have been formed by a variety of methods such as:–

- Preservative treated wooden boards and stakes or precast kerb edging to form the inner and outer ditch faces with a turf bank.
- Treated wooden boards/stakes or precast kerb edging on the inner ditch face but with a vertical wall replacing the sloping turf bank.

These days, however, most new flat greens use purpose-made, high-backed precast or reinforced concrete ditch units with the outer face then covered in artificial turf.

When using traditional ditch boards, concrete kerbs, or purpose-made ditch units, the top edge of the inner side of the ditch support should finish 25 mm below the finished green level. This allows for a double thickness of turf (cut about 12 mm thick) to be laid around the edge of the green, over the top of the inner ditch support. This minimises subsequent maintenance problems with the extreme edge of the turf tending to dry out rapidly and be prone to weak growth and moss invasion. Even for seeded greens it is normal to lay turf around the perimeter as difficulty is otherwise experienced in stabilising the extreme edge until seed is established. Here also a double thickness of edging turf is to be preferred.

In the final stages of construction small rounded pebbles, or other suitable material, are spread in clean ditch beds to 50 mm depth. Its surface should be not less than 50 mm or more than 200 mm below the grass level. Other materials may be used for this purpose provided they are non-injurious to the jack or bowls—in some cases ingenuity has been demonstrated in choice of some materials, which range from discarded wine bottle corks to rubber ends for badminton shuttlecocks!

DITCH FORMATION—CROWN GREEN

For crown greens where ditch requirements are rather less rigid, traditional timber edging or precast concrete kerbs are usually employed. Kerbs are set either side of the ditch to the required height.

Flat top precast inner edging kerbs of 150 x 50 mm dimension are set in position to true line and 25 mm below the finished level of the green on concrete foundations and raised 75 mm on both sides. The outer edging kerb is set up as above but using 300 x 50 mm edgings set 125 mm above the inner kerb level and well haunched up, particularly along the ditch side. The space between the ditch kerb foundations must allow the passage of water. Drainage aggregate is then introduced to a level that will allow for 50 mm depth of approved pea gravel or rounded pebbles to finish 100 mm below the green level.

An added item for the crown green is the provision of striking boards along the outer ditch kerb. These are composed of 3.5 m x 175 mm x 30 mm tanalised seasoned softwood, reasonably free of knots, cut to profile at the ends of each board to allow close butting. Painting striking boards white can be very helpful to players bowling in poor light. Each

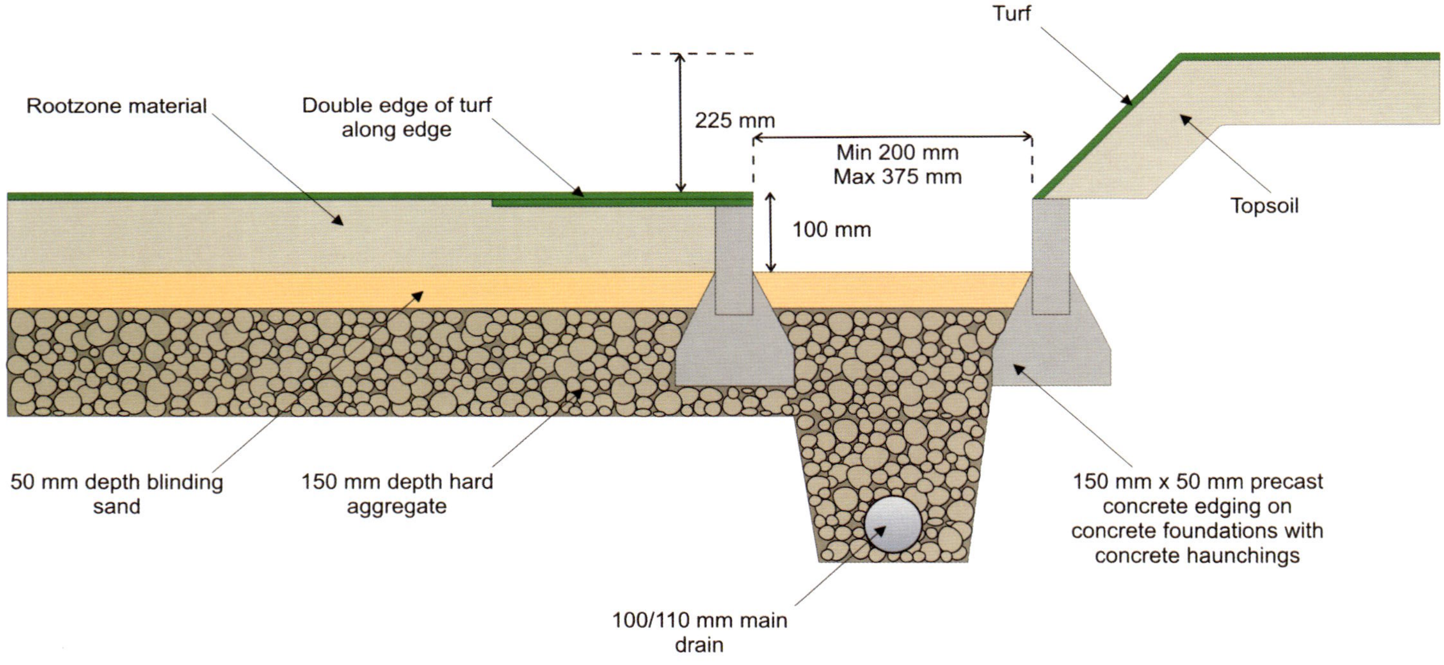

Flat bowling green with concrete kerb edging

Turf

Topsoil

150 mm x 50 mm precast concrete edging on concrete foundations with concrete haunchings

Min 200 mm
Max 375 mm

100 mm

225 mm

100/110 mm main drain

Double edge of turf along edge

150 mm depth hard aggregate

Rootzone material

50 mm depth blinding sand

High-backed ditch units ready to be installed

Artificial turf outer face with moulded rubber mat ditch base infill

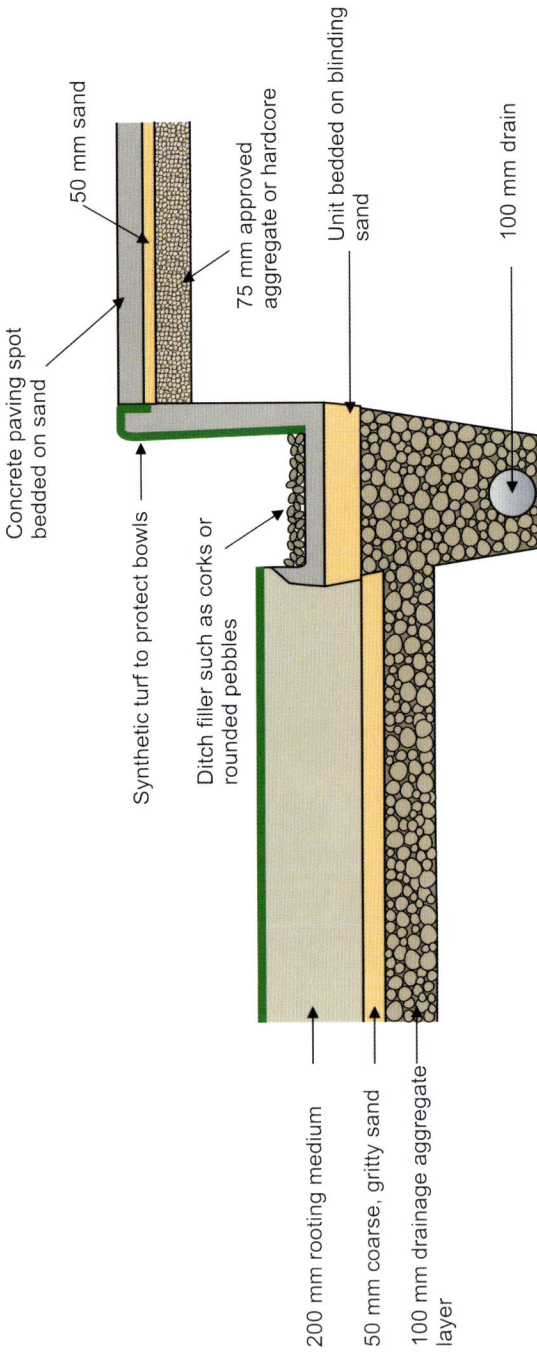

Flat bowling green with precast concrete ditch units

- 50 mm sand
- Concrete paving spot bedded on sand
- 75 mm approved aggregate or hardcore
- Unit bedded on blinding sand
- 100 mm drain
- Synthetic turf to protect bowls
- Ditch filler such as corks or rounded pebbles
- 200 mm rooting medium
- 50 mm coarse, gritty sand
- 100 mm drainage aggregate layer

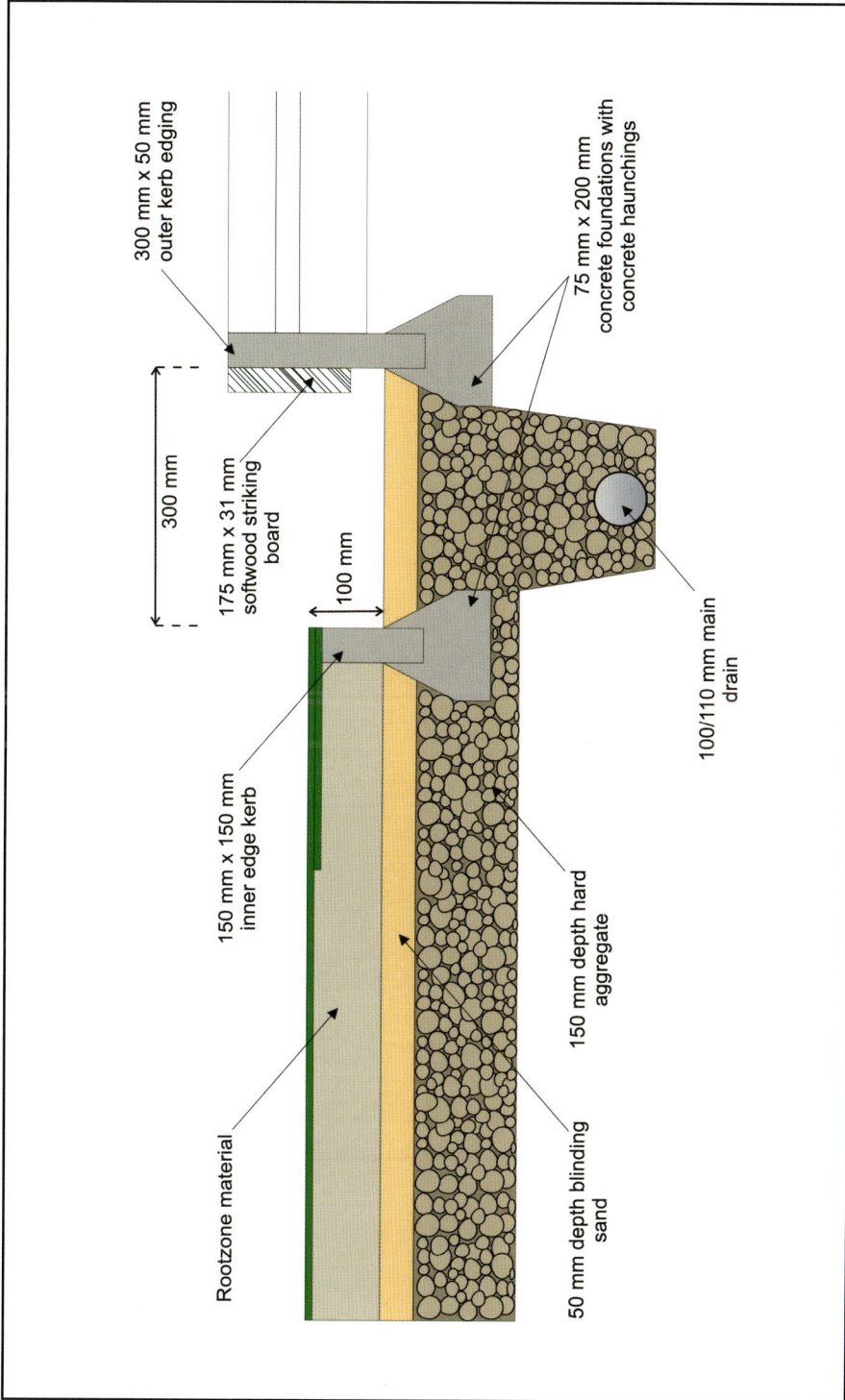

300 mm x 50 mm outer kerb edging

175 mm x 31 mm softwood striking board

300 mm

100 mm

75 mm x 200 mm concrete foundations with concrete haunchings

100/110 mm main drain

Rootzone material

150 mm x 150 mm inner edge kerb

150 mm depth hard aggregate

50 mm depth blinding sand

Crown bowling green with concrete kerb edging
(aggregate and drainage in the "body" of the green is often omitted)

board can be fitted with three galvanised mild steel brackets to fit over the tops of the kerbs forming the outer edge of the ditch. Alternatively, synthetic grass may be used.

DRAINAGE LAYER

When the ditches have been formed, spread over the green formation surface a 100-150 mm firmed depth of approved hard aggregate (6-10 mm gauge). The aggregate is carefully transported on to the green area with machinery no heavier than mechanical dumpers. The drains must be protected with, for instance, metal sheets. If necessary the drainage layer is then adequately rolled to produce an even firmness with accurate levels being maintained throughout. In some situations the 150 mm firmed depth of aggregate could be reduced to 100 mm firmed depth. In conjunction with this, an approved constructional geotextile membrane could be laid over the subsoil formation surface (but not over the backfilled drain trenches) in order to maintain the integrity of the full depth of aggregate as laid. Such a membrane prevents the mixture of subsoil and aggregate and may be very useful if there are softish areas in the subsoil.

The layer is then blinded with a 50 mm firmed depth of approved coarse sand or fine grit which will rest on the surface of the drainage aggregate without migrating downwards and causing consequent blockage and which will support the rooting medium without itself becoming contaminated.

The surface of the blinding layer on a flat green is left smooth and level, and if used on a crown green it is also left smooth but maintaining the required contours.

Drainage layer being introduced

Grading curve for the aggregate in drain trenches and drainage layer if an intermediate layer is used

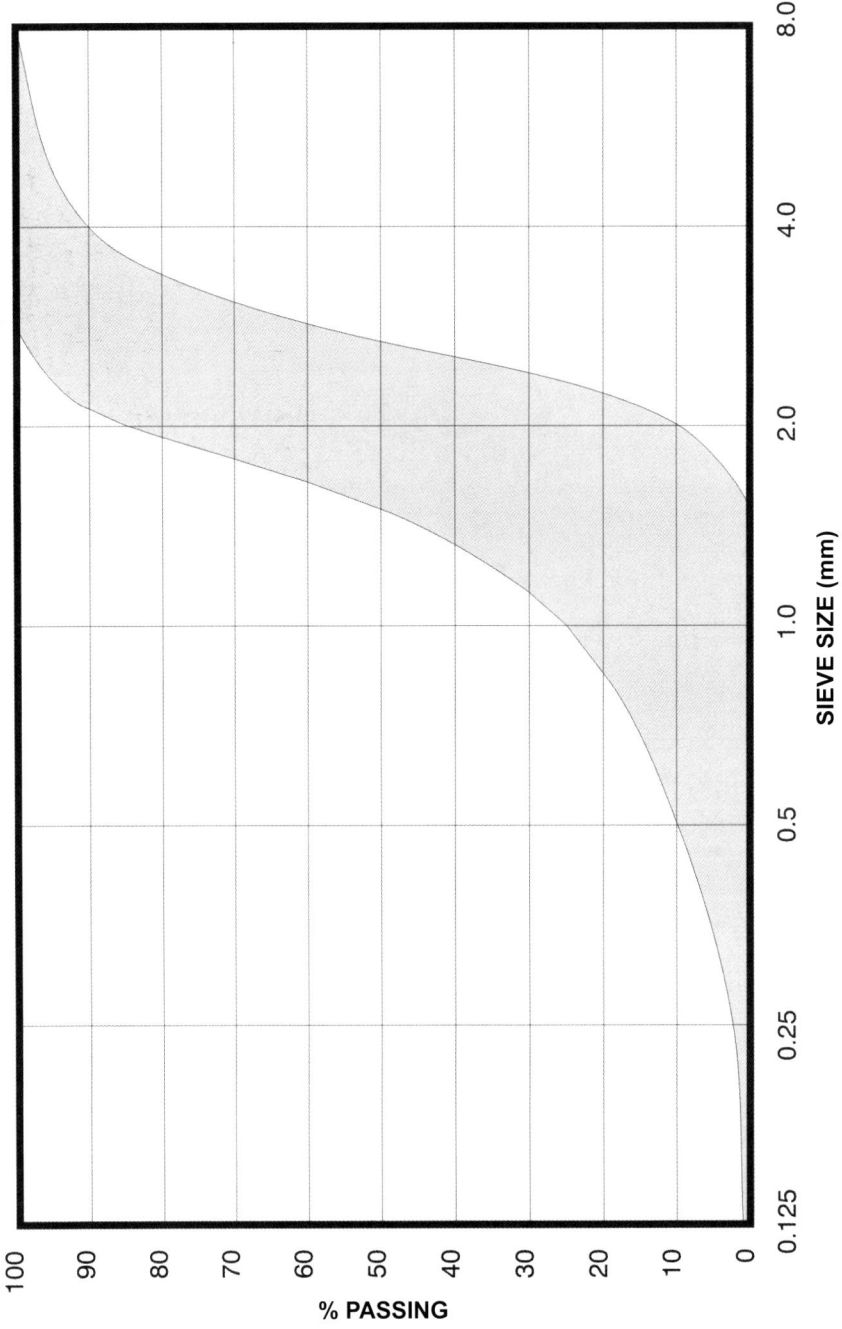

Grading curve for the intermediate layer (if required)

66

It is crucial that both the drainage aggregate and the blinding sand/grit layer meet certain physical and chemical criteria otherwise there could be problems. If the distribution of particle sizes in both the aggregate and the blinding material are wrong, there could be migration of particles from the blinding layer into the aggregate (which may eventually result in loss of levels and reduced drainage in the aggregate). Indeed, the wrong type of blinding sand could be very poorly draining in itself, which would be disastrous as the whole idea is to create a free-draining profile. Aggregate and blinding materials should ideally be lime free (if in doubt consult the Construction Department at STRI).

To complete the picture regarding drainage aggregate and blinding materials and the need for them to be appropriate and compatible, there is another way forward. This is to use one drainage material which does not need a blinding layer but whose particle size, distribution and particle shape not only drains but also supports the overlying rootzone. Sometimes 1-4 mm grit can be appropriate, but before deciding you should really take advice from a consultant agronomist.

During the later stages of grading, drainage, formation of ditches and spreading of the drainage layer, work can proceed with the preparation of the rootzone.

PREPARATION AND SPREADING OF ROOTZONE MIX

The rootzone for bowling greens, i.e. the topsoil in which the grass will establish, should be of a particularly free-draining nature and yet contain sufficient fine particles and organic material to sustain reasonably healthy growth and prevent over-susceptibility to drought and leaching of nutrients. The majority of the bulk material should therefore comprise sand, which should fall within the medium to coarse category, and should comprise approximately 75-80% of the total. Bowls has benefited significantly from much of the research done by golf in relation to developing golf greens—there are very many similarities between the rootzone requirements.

Once again it has to be stressed that it is crucial that the rootzone characteristics are correct, indeed there are very well researched and tested criteria that must be satisfied for success. Suitable rootzones for bowling greens must meet certain physical and performances criteria. The following tables show the criteria which ideally should be met.

A minimum of 200 mm firmed depth of rootzone should be introduced. Indeed, to satisfy the theory of critical tension and pore space criteria for good drainage, the depth of rootzone should probably be nearer 300 mm firmed depth. However, with bowls being a summer sport with significant moisture losses from the turf by means of evapotranspiration, experience has shown that it is possible to reduce the theoretical optimum depth.

In today's litigious world, using the wrong construction materials can be a very expensive mistake in many ways and it is always wise to seek professional advice. The sports turf industry has moved forward over recent years and many of the quarrying companies and rootzone suppliers now offer consistent products meeting strict performance and quality control criteria. As far as rootzones are concerned, it is invariably best and most convenient to use a material purchased from a specialist supplier, e.g. a member of the British Rootzone and Top Dressing Manufactures Association at **www.brtma.com**. Laboratory

Particle size distribution of rootzone mixture

Name	Particle diameter (mm)	Recommendation (by weight)
Fine gravel Very coarse sand	2.0-3.4 1.0-2.0 }	Not more than 10% of the total particles, including a maximum of 3% fine gravel (preferably none)
Coarse sand Medium sand	0.5-1.0 0.25-0.50 }	Minimum of 60% of the particles must fall in this range
Fine sand	0.15-0.25 }	Not more than 20% of the particles may fall within this range
Very fine sand Silt Clay	0.05-0.15 0.002-0.05 <0.002 }	Not more than 5% } Not more than 5% } Total particles in this range shall not Not more than 3% } exceed 10%

Physical properties of the rootzone mixture

Physical property	Recommended range
Total porosity	33-55%
Air-filled porosity (at 30 cm tension)	15-30%
Capillary porosity (at 30 cm tension	15-25%
Saturated conductivity	Minimum of 150 mm/hr

Physical and chemical properties for the rootzone

Parameter	Requirement
Total porosity	>35%
Air-filled porosity (30 cm tension)	>14%
Capillary porosity (30 cm tension	>17%
Hydraulic conductivity	>150 mm/hr
Organic matter content	0.5-3.5%
Lime content	<0.5%
pH	5.5-7.0

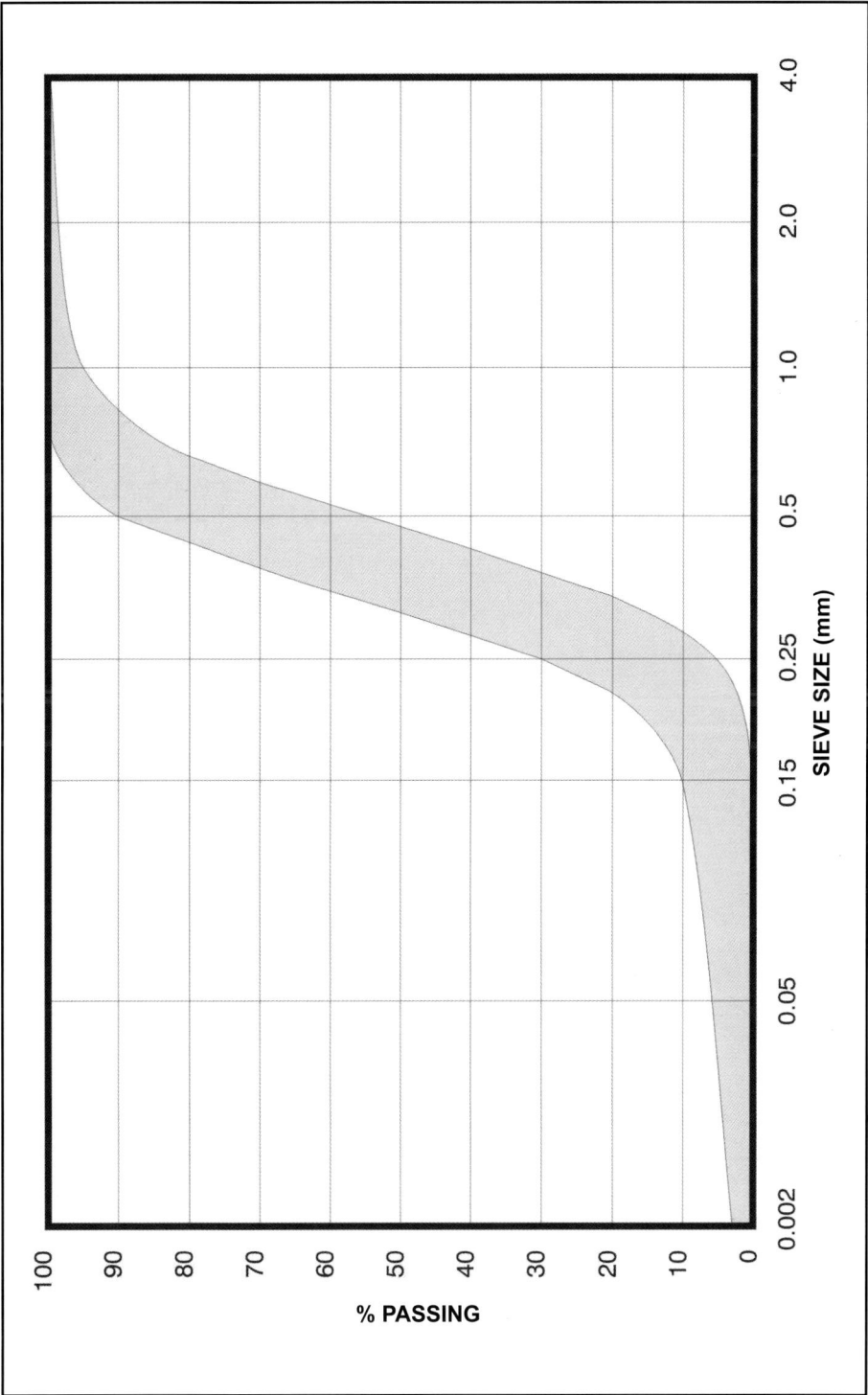

Grading curve for rootzone layer

testing is still nevertheless essential to identify suitable materials for construction as well as monitoring the incoming materials.

Only very rarely would the natural soil available on the site conform to the required performance criteria but very occasionally the available soil might be improved considerably by mixing with a suitable sand to produce a suitable mixture. Laboratory tests are necessary to identify the optimum proportion of sand and soil to mix together to obtain a formula which conforms to the design criteria.

Spreading of the special mix over the surface of the green is done by transporting with small mechanical dumpers or wheelbarrows, disturbance of the drainage layer being avoided by running the vehicles or barrows over planks or suitable protective sheets. The mix is then raked out to give the even depth required.

Extra material should be allowed for over and above the quantity required for the actual construction. This can then be used for top dressing purposes on completion of turfing or seeding and repeated as necessary during the first 12 months of maintenance to provide a true and uniform surface. This also ensures that the top dressing used matches the underlying soil mix—an essential requirement. Top dressing prepared in advance should be adequately protected from the weather.

CULTIVATIONS

Deep cultivation is not necessary after the rootzone has been spread and levelled but if required it is done with a hand-operated mechanical cultivator, care being taken to avoid disturbance of the blinding and drainage layers.

TURF/SEED BED PREPARATION

The rootzone mix is evenly firmed by alternate hand raking and heeling to provide a fine, smooth turf/seed bed. Before the heeling and raking is commenced, it may be appropriate to carefully track over the surface with a small compact tractor with balloon tyres to commence the initial firming

On a flat green the production of a level surface is imperative and this should be checked by laser level and corrected where necessary.

On a crown green it is also important to maintain correct contours and levels. This is done by accurately setting in level pegs at 3 m centres on each contour line, the top of the peg representing the finished level of the turf.

During the course of turf/seed bed preparation work any stones having one dimension of 12 mm or more are raked up and removed off site.

In the final stages of turf/seed bed preparation the required pre-turfing or pre-seeding fertiliser (determined by previous soil analysis) is evenly spread and lightly raked into the immediate surface, maintaining true levels.

ESTABLISHMENT OF GRASS COVER AND INITIAL MAINTENANCE

The method chosen, turfing or seeding, affects both timing and cost. Turfing is now the most usual method of establishing a grass cover although seeded greens are not unknown. As mentioned earlier, seeded greens usually have a turfed perimeter to ensure stability of the extreme edges.

Where turfing is to be adopted as the means of establishing the grass cover, this is best done in the autumn although it could also be done in the spring/summer if a good irrigation facility is available. The turf used should consist of clean fescue/bent free of weeds and weedgrass and have a grass cover no longer than 12 mm. It should be cut to convenient size and to a uniform thickness.

Care has to be taken with material from commercial turf suppliers. Non-indigenous soil can be imported with the turf which effectively caps-off the rootzone material when laid on the green. Turf suppliers have moved to counteract this problem with the introduction of custom-grown turf and washed turf.

Custom grown turf is produced to a specified seeds mixture and sown into a specified approved rootzone. The turf may also be grown a little longer for added maturity and a harder wearing capability.

Washed turf is passed through high-pressure water jets after harvesting to remove all soil on the turf. This material also prevents soil contamination on a new green construction but correct early care is essential with washed turf.

Turf is normally delivered to site in convenient loads as laying proceeds and it should not be kept stacked or in rolls longer than several hours. It is laid only when ground conditions are favourable commencing with a band of turf around the perimeter of the green, two turves wide. Traditionally turfing would then proceed diagonally commencing from one corner and working progressively to the opposite corner. This method does produce some wastage and nowadays is often superseded by the introduction of wider turf rolls (often 30 x 1 m) laid by a specialist machine operating parallel to the sides, this minimising the number of joins across the playing surface.

Particularly when working with smaller sized turf, workers will use boards placed on the turf already laid so that the prepared surface is not disturbed and all necessary materials are transported over boards so that the newly laid turf is not subjected to any direct traffic. Following turfing, the green surface should be rolled with a 250 kg hand roller or mower, two passes only being made (the second in a transverse direction to the first). The green is then top dressed with an approved material preferably conforming with the rootzone material at the rate of 3.0 kg/m^2, the top dressing being evenly applied and drag brushed into the surface.

With seeding, the work should be geared to sowing in late August, though sowing in spring or summer is again permissible if a reliable water supply is available.

Advance ordering of seed is required, high performing cultivars of bent and fescue being used (consult the most recent BSPB/STRI Turfgrass Seed booklet for cultivar performance). The total quantity of seed to be sown at 35 g/m^2 is divided in half, each half being sown evenly in transverse directions and then lightly raked in.

Requirements for seed bed or turf bed fertiliser depending on soil analysis			
NUTRIENT	**TEST METHOD**	**SOIL ANALYSIS RESULT**	**APPLICATION**
Nitrogen	Nitrogen needed in all cases	Not applicable	4-6 g/m² N (Note: the product should contain some slow release element)
Phosphate	Lawson (1995	0-15 mg/litre 16-30 31-50 >50	g/m² P_2O_5 12 9 6 0
Potassium	Lawson (1995)	0-35 36-60 61-90 >90	g/m² K_2O 8 6 4 0
Magnesium	MAFF (1986)	0-25 26-50 >50	g/m² MgO 2 1 0
Iron	Olson (1965)	0-0.3 0.4-2 >2	g/m² Fe 2 1 0
Manganese	MAFF (1986)	0-0.5 0.6-2 >2	g/m² Mn 0.4 0.2 0
Copper	MAFF (1986)	0-0.5 0.6-1.5 >1.5	g/m² Cu 0.2 0.1 0
Zinc	MAFF (1986)	0-0.3 0.4-1.0 >1.0	g/m² Zn 0.2 0.1 0
pH	MAFF (1986)	≥5.5 5.0-5.4 4.5-4.9	No lime should be applied 1 kg lime/tonne rootzone (250 g/m² cultivated through 150 mm) 2 kg lime/tonne rootzone (500 g/m² cultivated through 150 mm)

Traditional turf laying

Machine laying Big Roll turf

Good initial maintenance of seeded greens is required and this involves:–
- When the young grass is about 20 mm in height remove any surface stones.
- Rolling under suitable conditions, with a 250 kg hand roller or mower.
- Carrying out a first mowing when the grass is, say, 30 mm in height with no more than 10 mm of the grass foliage being removed.
- If growth remains vigorous the height of cut is gradually reduced to 12 mm before growth ceases for the year.

In the following year special attention is required to fertiliser treatment, which must be adequate but not excessive, as well as top dressing with compatible material to prevent layering in the soil profile. Several applications of top dressing will be necessary to help perfect the bowling surface.

Returning to the turfed green, good initial maintenance is again crucial, top dressing being the main item to help seal the joints between the turf and create a smooth surface. Several applications of a good quality top dressing material (matching the rootzone mix) are essential. Other items of importance such as mowing and fertiliser treatment are carried out as required.

SURROUND BANK AND VERGE

If conventional grass banks are being provided, use similar fine turf species, e.g. fescue and bent, so as to avoid contamination onto the green from coarser species. The top of the turf bank is a minimum of 225 mm above the finished level of the green with the face normally inclined 35° from the vertical. The verge is formed level between the bank and the path, the finished level being 25 mm above the kerb top adjoining the path.

A minimum 150 mm firmed depth of topsoil is spread on the prepared subsoil formation surface, the topsoil being raked to provide a satisfactory tilth. Pre-turfing fertiliser is then applied and turfing carefully completed. As laying proceeds, turf on the banks should be pegged down with wooden pegs or by other approved means until the turf is established. On completion, top dress with approved material and brush in as on the surface of the bowling green.

CONSTRUCTION OF SURROUNDING PATH (1.22-1.83 m WIDE)

The formation level of the path is properly consolidated and trimmed to the required levels and with a cross fall of 50 mm towards the bowling green.

For a macadam surfaced path a foundation of approved hard aggregate is then laid to a consolidated depth of 100 mm and blinded with approved stone chippings to 25 mm depth. (For a paved surface path the foundation is to 75 mm consolidated depth and this is blinded with 25 mm firmed depth of coarse sand.) In both cases rolling is carefully completed with a 2.5 tonne roller.

Approved 150 x 50 mm precast concrete kerbs are laid and light type gullies complete with appropriate galvanised gratings are then introduced. The gullies are connected to the 100 mm ditch drains.

The macadam surfacing is then laid in two layers to a depth of 55 mm (alternatively, only one course may be laid). For a paved path approved paving slabs are set on cement mortar pads to true line and flat with 6 mm gaps between; the gaps are grouted with cement mortar.

ANCILLARY WORKS

These are completed as required. This can involve formation of a concrete ramp, external banks for seeding or planting, catchwater drains, roller recess, seat recess, litter bin recess, borders, turf nursery (usually 50 m^2) and fencing.

5 Modern Bowling Green Maintenance: The Assessment of a Green and the Calendar of Required Work

Let us imagine for a moment that we are in the position of a newly-appointed, inexperienced greenkeeper, green ranger or chairman of green committee who is faced with the task of maintaining and, if possible, improving a particular bowling green.

The first point which should be considered is the advisability of obtaining the services of a competent consultant agronomist to assess the present condition of a green, and who could then lay down a detailed maintenance programme for future treatment. An experienced adviser can pinpoint weaknesses and suggest appropriate remedial measures which may save the club much expenditure in the long-term, so justifying in financial terms any fee that he or she might charge. Without wishing to be in any way disparaging of the very praiseworthy efforts made by amateur committee members up and down the country, one should always bear in mind that bowling green maintenance is a complex and skilled task and a high level of scientific and technical skill is required to achieve a consistently first-class playing surface. Although it is hoped that the present text will be helpful to greenkeepers and club members in the time-consuming and sometimes frustrating task of achieving the perfect bowls surface, expert advice should always be sought if at all possible. Mistakes can, after all, take a long time to correct and can occasionally be disastrous. A textbook can be an indispensable guide to a subject, but ultimately no amount of reading can compensate entirely for the absence of experience and practical skill.

It is also essential to bear in mind that it may take several years to achieve the full benefit of any maintenance programme. Unfortunately, the rapid turn over of committee members at some clubs, plus the fact that all clubs are full of self-styled expert greenkeepers all too ready to say in loud voices exactly what is needed to transform the quality of a green overnight, tends to work against consistency of maintenance. Once a sound basic maintenance programme has been decided upon, it should be adhered to for at least a three year period. It is therefore worth repeating again—CONSISTENCY AND CONTINUITY IS VITAL. Obviously there may be a need on occasions for unplanned extra work, such as the fungicidal treatment of a disease attack, but every bowling green requires a series of seasonal primary maintenance operations which must be followed each year if a good green is to be achieved and preserved.

Before planning an appropriate maintenance programme for a particular green, it is essential (for beginners, experienced greenkeepers and consultant agronomists alike) to make a detailed assessment of the condition of the green. The existing features which should be fully investigated are as follows.

PLAYING CHARACTERISTICS AND SURFACE LEVELS

Anyone who discusses the general quality of British bowling greens with expert bowlers or those who have experience of advisory work in this field will soon reach the conclusion that the two commonest problems on both crown and flat greens are excessively slow bowling surfaces and poor surface levels. In the case of flat bowling greens, both features have been scientifically investigated and a report on the survey carried out is reprinted here as Appendix B. This investigation supports the view that deficiencies in both the pace of bowling greens and uniformity of surface levels are commonplace, so when planning the future maintenance of a particular green it is worthwhile to try and assess these two aspects of its surface in some detail.

As far as the question of surface pace is concerned, club members and particularly the more expert bowlers should be consulted in order to determine whether the speed of the green is adequate or excessively slow. Opinions should be gathered regarding the playing qualities of the green at all times during the bowling season—spring, summer and early autumn. Remember, however, that bowlers frequently complain unjustifiably of the lack of pace of outdoor grass greens in the spring. This often is merely a reflection of the fact that they have spent the winter bowling on artificial, indoor surfaces, which are often fast (sometimes excessively so) and therefore take time to readjust to the natural turf green. Obviously, the pace of a particular green will vary according to weather conditions—most greens are relatively slow after heavy rain, while in some instances one finds that a green will show an increase in pace after light drizzle as compared to its performance when completely dry. Ignoring such day-to-day variations, it should be possible to gain a general impression of the performance of a green and to then slant future maintenance towards producing a necessary improvement in pace.

Alternatively, a more objective method of assessing green speed may be employed. There are two ways of doing this on a particular green. The first method simply involves bowling straight across the green, standing as near as possible to the ditch and aiming to stop the bowl just short of, or having it just topple into, the ditch on the opposite side. The time taken for the bowl to travel across the green should be determined, preferably with a stop-watch. This procedure should be repeated several times in opposite directions and at right angles and an average time obtained. In the case of flat greens, the process should be carried out on several rinks as different rinks on the same green can vary quite significantly in pace. For a crown green, repeat the process in different positions near the edge or over the middle of the green to cancel out, as far as this is possible, the effect of sloping surfaces. No test allows one crown green to be reliably compared with another. They may, however, allow objective comparison of a single green's performance under different weather conditions or at varying times of year. If the bowl takes 18 seconds to travel ditch to ditch, the green would be very fast by average club standards. A time of 14 seconds is generally considered satisfactory while a travel time of 12 seconds would make the green too slow for most players. The fact that the rate of travel of a bowl over a slow green is more rapid than on a green with good surface pace may seem confusing, but it should be realised that for a slow green a bowl must be bowled much harder and faster to reach the opposite ditch. Although a bowl decelerates more rapidly on a slow green, it leaves the bowler's hand at a much greater speed and hence crosses the green more rapidly.

The above figures were worked out for a standard 42 x 42 yd. flat green—a second or two should be added to the times quoted above if one is dealing with larger crown greens.

Since the size of a particular green influences the figure obtained by the above method, and even EBA-approved flat greens can vary quite considerably in size, a second method of determining green speed is used with a view to allowing more reliable comparisons between greens. This second procedure is advocated by the EBA, and involves placing a jack 27 m in front of the mat and timing the travel of the bowl from the time it leaves the bowler's hand to a point when it stops within about 200 mm of the jack. Again, this should be repeated on various rinks and in different directions and an average obtained. According to the EBA, 12-13 seconds indicates an acceptable surface pace, and a time of 10 seconds or less is very definitely unacceptably slow. It is doubtful whether this EBA speed test has any value in the case of crown greens where results are complicated by the effects of surface gradients. A third speed test, involving the rolling of an unbiased bowl onto the green down an inclined plane is described in Appendix A. Speed tests of these kinds cannot be regarded as totally reliable, particularly for crown greens, but they do give some objective indication of the pace of a particular green and can usefully show how its speed varies from season to season and under differing weather conditions.

At this point it is worth stressing that those bowlers who feel that deficiencies in green speed can be overcome by closer mowing or by the use of a heavier roller are usually totally in error. Although it is true that a temporarily faster surface can be obtained in the short-term by rolling or close mowing in preparation for a particular game, neither rolling nor close mowing do anything to influence the causes of long-term problems with the pace of a green. Both operations can also have deleterious side effects. Long experience indicates that the most common causes of excessive slowness are the dominance of an-nual meadow-grass in the sward and the presence of a sub-surface thatch or fibre layer. It is these faults which must be eliminated if a faster green is to be obtained and neither rolling nor close mowing has any effect apart from possibly making these problems worse in the long run. Annual meadow-grass and thatch will be more fully dealt with a little later in this chapter.

The second point which should be considered when assessing the condition and future maintenance needs of a bowling green is the question of surface levels. Here of course there is considerable divergence between the needs of flat rink and crown green bowlers. For the rink game, the ideal is a perfectly level surface, although this is something which is seldom, if ever, entirely achieved in practice. Most flat greens show some degree of surface undulation as a result of either imperfections in initial construction or level changes over years of use. Land subsidence over long periods of time is not an uncommon problem and can be particularly severe in coalmining areas. Long hot, dry spells can also shrink some underlying clay subsoils to upset surface levels. In time, the rink game itself can also result in surface irregularities. This is particularly true where players bowl continuously on popular rinks without changing strings regularly to utilise other rink positions, and always in one direction across the green. Where particular rink positions are over-used, the green gradually develops a "ridge and furrow" surface with the troughs coinciding with the centre of each rink and the ridges with the string positions. Ultimately such a surface has a marked and deleterious effect on bias and skilled and accurate bowls becomes unacceptably difficult, if not impossible. Uneven or inadequate top dressing can also contribute to surface irregularities.

There are a number of methods available for attempting to gain a picture of the surface contours of a flat green. Habitual bowlers can of course be consulted and the rink strings can also give a valuable indication—if pulled taught they rest on the high spots and bridge the relatively low areas. Heavy rain leaving standing water on a green also usefully indicates low areas as puddles lie in the hollows. Alternatively, a long straight edge can be used—a 3-4 m plank is often employed fitted with convenient D-shaped handles on its upper edge. By far the best method, however, is to have the green surveyed—a specialist surveyor is not required as most local general surveyors would be perfectly capable of carrying out the task. The results of a typical survey are shown on page 54 (contour map) and high and low areas can clearly be seen. This is of course invaluable if attempts are to be made to improve surface uniformity. Survey levels should be taken at 2 m centres. Levels taken along the top of surrounding banks should be included as these are a useful check on whether bank heights conform to EBA requirements in the case of flat greens. Levels taken along inner ditch kerbs are also useful to determine if kerb sinkage has occurred. All levels should be related to a fixed benchmark.

Modern computer-aided design and drafting systems (CAD), if fed with the level figures from a particular green, can produce three-dimensional representations of surface contours or grid gradient maps, which give a very clear visual representation of surface levels. Most surveying companies have equipment of this kind and produce print-outs which are very helpful in clarifying the irregularities which an individual green may show.

It is extremely difficult to lay down guidelines as to what degree of irregularity is acceptable in a flat green. It is not only a question of differences in height between high and low spots, but also where these irregularities occur within the body of the green and how abrupt the changes in contour are. New flat greens should be constructed within plus or minus 6 mm of the desired level but few old-established greens would meet such an exacting standard. On older greens, variations of up to plus or minus 18 mm can be regarded as capable of correction by maintenance work, i.e. by selective top dressing of low areas. Variations of more than this figure could probably only be corrected in practice by removing turf, adjusting soil contours and then returfing. In the case of a very severely uneven green, this could involve returfing the entire surface. Such work requires skilled and careful turfing and is best regarded as beyond the scope of all but very experienced greenkeepers or specialist contractors.

In the case of crown green bowls, it is even more difficult to put exact figures on what degree of departure from a true surface is acceptable or what is not. Very few crown greens conform to the theoretical requirement of a uniform mushroom-top contour—indeed many show quite considerable humps and hollows apart from the actual crown itself. Crown bowlers are generally happy with this situation, as level variations add interest to the game and give some advantage to the Home Team familiar with the runs and irregularities of their own green. Even for crown green bowls, however, some greens show level variations which are unacceptable and a green survey can be of considerable help in pinpointing the problem and allowing remedial measures to be undertaken.

SWARD COMPOSITION

If a green is to be efficiently maintained, then it is vital that those responsible have some idea of sward composition—the species of grasses present and the approximate proportion of each. Unfortunately, grass identification can be quite difficult—it is certainly not as easy to distinguish two grass species as it is to correctly name a daisy or a dandelion! Close mowing makes grass identification doubly difficult—correctly naming a grass species in its natural flowering condition is one thing, identifying it in turf cut regularly at 5 mm is quite another matter. For the amateur inexperienced in such activities, by far the easiest solution to the problem is to enlist the help of a competent greenkeeper, groundsman or other turf specialist who should, if he is worth his salt, be able to give a reasonably accurate estimate as to sward composition after ten minutes examination of the average green. If a co-operative expert is not readily to hand, however, then the following guidelines may be of value and should allow anyone of reasonable commonsense to reach some idea of the kind of sward he is dealing with.

There are about 27 species of grasses which are commonly encountered in amenity or agricultural grassland in this country, but as far as bowling greens are concerned the majority are likely to be of very little significance. There are only three grass species which are likely to be of much significance in fine bowling green turf. These are:–

Chewings fescue (*Festuca rubra* spp. *commutata*)

The most obvious characteristic of fescue is the fact that the leaves are bristle-like and appear virtually circular in cross-section to anything but an extremely close examination. Fescue produces a tough, wiry type of turf and a fast bowling surface. Theoretically, fescue should form about 50% of the sward and this is often true of newly-sown greens or greens recently established using high quality turf from a specialised turf grower. The traditional seeds mixture for the finest turf, still standard today, is designed to produce a sward containing 50% Chewings fescue and 50% browntop bent. Unfortunately, mis-management of many greens in the past has resulted in a reduction in the proportion of this valuable grass species and sadly many older greens now contain very little or none at all. Fescue can only be preserved in a sward by maintaining conditions of relative poverty—avoiding over-fertilising, over-watering, etc. Another key requirement in sustaining fescue in turf is the avoidance of particularly close mowing heights, anything less than 5 mm is likely to see a rapid decline in the fescue content of fine turf.

In may mixtures sold for bowling green use, the fescue comprises 40% Chewings fescue with 40% slender creeping red fescue. This is perfectly acceptable.

Browntop bentgrass (*Agrostis capillaris*)

Bentgrasses have rather dull green leaves which taper uniformly along their length to a fine point. It is much more common in bowling green turf than fescue and most greens contain at least some. Indeed, a proportion of the better greens contain a very high percentage of browntop bent. Bent can be better at withstanding the effects of poor maintenance than the fescues and has hence tended to survive more successfully even in very old greens. In many other situations, however, it has tended to suffer from competition from far less desirable annual meadow-grass.

Annual meadow-grass (*Poa annua*)

Annual meadow-grass occupies a very paradoxical position as far as fine turf is concerned. It is never sown deliberately and has a number of major disadvantages as a turfgrass and is hence best regarded as a weed. On the other hand, it is probably the very common grass on bowling greens in this country. Indeed, it is probably no exaggeration to say that if annual meadow-grass became extinct overnight, many British bowling greens would, on the following morning, be seen to consist largely of bare ground.

Annual meadow-grass is quite easy to identify. It is usually a light delicate green and commonly produces silver-white seed heads at any time during the growing season but particularly in late May-June. Its leaves have distinctive tips shaped like the bow of a boat and there are two distinct grooves, commonly called 'tramlines' running down each side of the mid-rib of each leaf. The tramlines are most easily seen if the leaf is bent back over a finger and are quite translucent if the leaf is held up to the light.

In the past it has been argued that annual meadow-grass fulfils a useful function on the grounds that any grass cover is better than bare ground. There is an element of truth in this but a more sensible attitude is that the disadvantages of annual meadow-grass far outweigh any possible advantages. The single botanical name and the word "annual" are misleading. Annual meadow-grass covers a wide range of plant types, ranging from true annuals, through various biennial and short-lived perennial forms (perhaps with creeping stolons that root at the nodes), to longer-lived perennials (small-leaved and forming very low dense rosettes which spread only slowly). The perennial forms are hard-wearing and tolerant of close mowing. They can produce viable seed which has a long dormancy and it is not uncommon for plant fragments to take root, both characteristics facilitating the species to establish on thin or bare areas. Growth rate is fast and plants can flourish in spite of soil compaction (and the shallow rooting which it enforces) in a way which other grass species cannot. Annual meadow-grass is not necessarily a shallow-rooting species but it is better able than other species to tolerate compacted soil.

In fine turf, annual meadow-grass may occur either as isolated patches in the sward, that look unsightly and spoil the playing surface's uniformity (in texture and height of growth),

Browntop bent

Chewings fescue

Annual meadow-grass

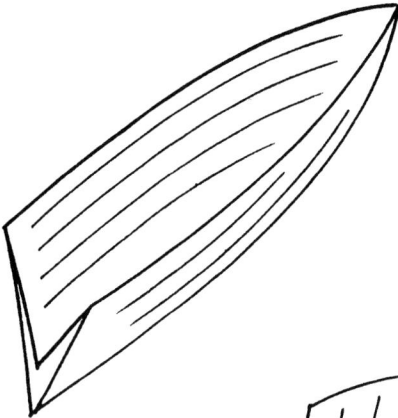

**Annual meadow-grass has
boat-shaped leaf tips and
"tramlines" down the centre
of the leaf blade**

Tramlines

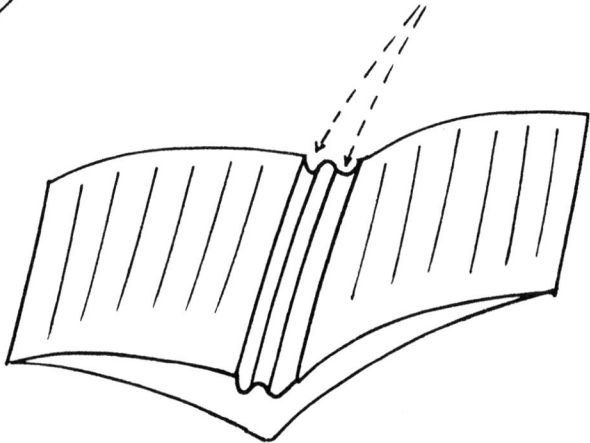

Grass identification

or as a more or less complete cover that has supplanted the sown species. Its main draw-backs are susceptibility to fusarium patch disease, anthracnose of annual meadow-grass, poor performance in drought and in winter, and the seed heads which are unsightly and may affect playing surfaces on fine turf. It is often associated with thatch problems, partly because it produces thatch quickly and partly because it is then well adapted to survive in thatchy conditions. The poor colour in drought is associated with this: if annual meadow-grass is the only grass able to survive on a thick layer of thatch, it will inevitably be the only one to show effects when deep thatch and dry weather combine to cause drought stress. Sub-surface thatch will be described in detail a little later in this chapter.

In established fine turf areas where annual meadow-grass has become dominant be-cause it is better adapted to prevailing conditions than anything else it will not be possible to eliminate the annual meadow-grass unless those conditions are changed. Even if herbi-cide treatments are developed which can be recommended for selective control of annual meadow-grass in swards of fescue and bent, the treatments would need to be backed up by appropriate management. It would also be necessary to ensure that the change-over of species could be accomplished gradually, without unsightly treatment effects and without adversely affecting the playing qualities of the surface in the short-term.

A careful programme of seed bed preparation and subsequent management may succeed in keeping annual meadow-grass out of a bowling green or at least limiting or delaying its spread. This would involve:–

- Providing a really clean seed bed, in which clean seed of good turfgrass cultivars can produce a dense, weed-excluding sward before seeds of annual meadow-grass arrive.
- Purchasing seed which is free of annual meadow-grass from a reputable turfgrass seed supplier who can vouch for its purity and viability.
- Irrigating sensibly: annual meadow-grass thrives in moist conditions.
- Using fertiliser correctly: in particular avoiding excess phosphate. Phosphate assists seedling establishment, rooting and seed production—three essential stages in take-over by annual meadow-grass.
- Maintaining a fairly low pH for inland fescue/bent turf (about 5.0-5.5).
- Providing adequate aeration to get rid of compaction and surface water.
- Undertaking careful and appropriate scarification.
- Making sure top dressings are not too heavy, i.e. that they contain a high percentage of a suitable sand, and are worked in well to avoid providing a seed bed for annual meadow-grass.
- Using sterilised top dressing whenever practicable.
- Avoiding worm casts which provide a seed bed for the weed and bring dormant seed to the surface.
- Removing clippings and hence seedheads
- Avoiding, if possible, carrying seed in from heavily infested areas on mowers, other equipment and boots.
- Avoiding continuous mowing at very low levels.

Annual meadow-grass has been covered at some length because it is one of the major problems encountered on British bowling greens. The fact that it produces soft, lush growth, particularly if heavily fertilised or watered, means that it tends to produce excessively slow bowling surfaces. Its association with sub-surface thatch layers tends to intensify this undesirable characteristic as thatch itself also makes for a slow green. It also tends to lose growth and colour rapidly in the autumn, perhaps remaining weak all winter and recovering only slowly in the spring. This tends to make an annual meadow-grass green weak at the end and again at the start of the bowling season. Late springs tend to worsen early season problems with annual meadow-grass. Its weakness in the autumn when the weather starts deteriorating is more of a problem for crown green bowlers who tend to continue play later in the year than the flat rink fraternity. The management of greens containing a high percentage of annual meadow-grass should therefore be slanted towards the reduction of this undesirable species and towards the corresponding encouragement of better bent and fescue grasses. Annual meadow-grass reduction (if not total elimination) is certainly possible for the majority of greens, although it is a gradual process and involves following a consistent policy for a period of several years.

Before leaving this brief guide to the identification of bowling green grasses, two other grass species should be mentioned, namely perennial ryegrass (*Lolium perenne*) and Yorkshire fog (*Holcus lanatus*). These are coarse grass species which occur in bowling greens as distinct and obviously undesirable patches of coarse growth rather than being intermingled evenly with other more desirable grasses over a green as a whole. Perennial ryegrass is the most desirable species as far as football fields and other coarser turf areas are concerned and is sometimes found in bowling greens as a result perhaps of careless greenkeeping, for example, overseeding worn rink ends on a flat green with the wrong seeds mixture or returfing with coarse turf. Alternatively, plants may seed naturally in a green from surrounding agricultural land. Ryegrass is a very tough species with flat leaves which are very shiny on the underside and its shoot bases are often purple in colour. Yorkshire fog on the other hand is a weed in all turf situations and is never deliberately sown, although it is a very common plant of hedgerows and waste places. It has soft grey-green leaves with distinct narrow pink stripes on shoot bases and patches usually have a very distinctly grey colour against the greener background of the rest of the bowling surface. Both species may be removed and replaced with turves containing more suitable grasses or discouraged by correct management practices, particularly raking and scarification.

Given some practice with grass identification, it should be possible to undertake a rough estimate of the proportions of the above grasses in the sward of a given bowling green. In practice the commonest situation which emerges is that a green will be basically composed of browntop bent and annual meadow-grass in varying proportions, with smaller and sometimes insignificant quantities of fescue or the coarse weedgrasses. On newly established greens there is usually a reasonable quantity of fescue with correspondingly less annual meadow-grass. If the amount of annual meadow-grass present is less than that of the bents and fescues, one may congratulate oneself in having a green with an above-average botanical composition.

The estimation of sward composition may be complicated by the fact that the green may not show an even mixture of grasses over its entire surface. In the case of flat greens for example, annual meadow-grass is often more common on rink ends, and on heavily used rink ends may frequently form 100% of the grass cover. Localised improvement of sward composition would obviously be beneficial in such a situation. Patches of annual meadow-grass colonising rink ends are often very easy to spot early or late in the year when the poor off-season colour of this species makes it appear very yellow against the greener background of the rest of the surface. A patchy distribution of annual meadow-grass on a green is a greater handicap than an even mixture of it with other grasses, as patches of different grasses tend to destroy uniformity, with bowls travelling at different speeds over patches of one grass as compared to another, as well as bobbling up and down.

OTHER SURFACE FEATURES

The remaining surface features which need to be noted when a green is being assessed for future maintenance requirements are fortunately less problematical than the question of sward composition. The presence or absence of a broad-leaved weed population should prove fairly easy to establish (the term broad-leaved is used to distinguish such weed from the weedgrasses already mentioned.) Weed identification is again something which is made easier by experience, but at least most weeds are easier to tell one from the other than the grasses. Identifying the weed species which may be present is useful as weeds vary in their susceptibility to the range of selective weedkillers available today and the product appropriate for use on a particular green should be chosen on the basis of what weeds need to be eliminated. The variety and extent of the weeds present should be noted so that appropriate control measures may be taken at an appropriate time of year. One of the commonest of bowling greens weeds, pearlwort, is easily mistaken for moss, so particular care should be taken to ensure that this species is correctly named.

Moss itself is a particular class of weed which is frequently troublesome in the bowling green situation. It is necessary to determine whether moss is a persistent problem, obvious at all times of the year and lingering from year to year, in which case it may be an indicator of some other fundamental weakness in the condition of the green. On the other hand, moss can be merely a seasonal problem, appearing in the winter or during a prolonged spell of wet weather. Such points should be decided upon so that appropriate remedial work can be planned.

The efficient greenkeeper should also be familiar with the symptoms of a range of fungal diseases of the turfgrasses, or at the very least should be able to diagnose the more serious and common ones such as fusarium, anthracnose or red thread. If disease symptoms do appear then very prompt treatment may be required if significant damage to the quality of the bowling surface is to be averted—under the right conditions disease can spread very rapidly indeed.

The industrious and almost ubiquitous earthworm is another cause of an obvious problem on bowling surfaces. Worm casts if present in sufficient numbers can reduce the quality of a playing surface very significantly, particularly during mild, moist weather when the worms tend to be most active. It is worth remembering that just because a green is free of casts during the dry summer weather or during winter frost does not mean that there are no worms present, it just means that they are inactive under such conditions. Leatherjackets and other insect grubs are again pests which sometimes attack bowling green turf and should not be forgotten as a possible cause of turf weakness.

Other questions which a new greenkeeper, summing up the condition of a green, might ask himself are whether the sward is showing signs of chemical damage—uneven distribution of a past fertiliser application, weedkiller scorch, etc., or does it show signs of mechanical damage—marks left by a poorly set mower or scarring from excessively severe scarification, and so on. Is the turf thin because of shade from nearby trees or the effects of an adjacent excessively tall hedge? Once all surface features have been adequately investigated, the next stage of assessment can be undertaken—this involves a look below the surface.

THE SOIL PROFILE

In a high proportion of cases, the key to the improvement of a particular green and the source of lasting difficulties with playing quality lies beneath the actual bowling surface in the underlying soil profile. This must always be borne in mind when assessing the condition of a green and an appropriate investigation of soil conditions undertaken. Fortunately, for the peace of mind of all concerned, such an investigation of soil conditions need not involve anything as drastic as attacking a green with a spade or hiring a mechanical digger to cut an exploratory trench across from ditch to ditch! All that is needed is either a long sheath knife, a golf hole cutter or preferably a purpose-made soil sampling tool. The aim should be to look at the top 200-225 mm or whatever rootzone depth prevails if there is an underlying stone or clinker layer.

On new greens the situation should be straightforward, namely the presence of a well rooted sward into the rootzone, the latter being homogeneous in texture and condition throughout its depth.

In the case of an old-established green the situation is often much more complex with the soil profile showing stratified layers which are as distinct as the growth rings in a tree trunk. These layers can almost be regarded as representing the archeology of a particular green and can often give a clear indication of the history of that green, at least as far as showing what original construction method was followed and what top dressing materials were used over the years. Examination of a soil core should give information on the following points:–

Rooting depth

Ideally the grass roots beneath a green should extend 125-150 mm below the surface. With older greens this ideal seldom exists as soil compaction, rootbreak layers and the presence of a surface thatch layer all tend to limit rooting depth. Some greens, particularly those showing a distinct thatch layer over a compacted soil, may show not much more than 25 mm of root. A significant percentage of greens invariably show a rather inadequate

50-75 mm rooting depth. Very shallow rooting makes for a weak sward, too dependent on artificial fertiliser for its survival. Shallow rooted swards are also prone to drought damage, suffering very quickly from water loss as the superficial layers of the green dry out. Pulling a soil core apart can often indicate rooting depth quite clearly as the roots hold the top part of the core together, whereas the core breaks apart at the limit of rooting depth. Very often the limit of root growth coincides with some obvious feature of the profile, such as a distinct layer of sand, a dark peat layer or perhaps the remains of a soil layer (different to the rootzone) which formed part of the imported turf during construction. Excessively shallow root indicates a need for more frequent or deeper aeration work in future maintenance. It should be realised that roots grow in air spaces between the soil particles—the root itself needs air to develop. Soil compaction or waterlogging obviously limits the amount of air present in the soil and limits root growth, and hence top growth and the standard of the bowls surface. Aerating allows more air to penetrate the soil and hence encourages healthy root growth. Using aeration equipment can also help break up layers of sand or peat, as described above, which form "rootbreaks" and limit the depth of root penetration.

Thatch or fibre layers

It is most important to decide whether or not there is a layer of organic material between the sward itself and the actual soil surface. Spongy thatch is the most frequent cause of excessively slow bowling surfaces and can also encourage surface waterlogging, moss growth, the spread of annual meadow-grass and other problems. The accumulation of a

An excessive layer of surface thatch creates slow bowling surfaces

layer of fibrous material is a natural feature of turf development and cannot be entirely prevented. Total prevention would in fact be most undesirable as a surface with no underlying fibre would lack resiliency and could easily become thin in wet weather or situations of particularly heavy use. However, when fibre builds up to an excessive degree it becomes a problem. About ¼ in. (6 mm) of matted material would be acceptable on bowling greens while a ½ in. (13 mm) layer would begin to prove troublesome.

Most people who are experienced in turf management will realise that there is more than one form of thatch or fibre. In the past, words like mat, thatch or fibre have been used very loosely and more precise definition of terms would therefore be of value. The following classification could be a guide:–

● **Litter:** A loose and fluffy accumulation of grass clippings and decaying leaf bases and sheaths in between the grass stems at the base of the sward. Litter is not usually seen on intensively used or well managed turf but is more characteristic of old and neglected lawns which are perhaps cut weekly without boxing off clippings and which receive very little additional treatment. It would never be found on a bowling green unless it had been neglected and probably not played on for a number of years.

● **Fibre** resembles coconut-matting, being tough and wiry in texture and brown in colour, and consists of old roots and other organic debris. Fibre usually overlies dry soil, the turf becoming very dry indeed and difficult to re-wet under drought conditions. Fibre is most commonly found under acidic conditions where the sward is bent and fescue with a tendency to invasion by acid-loving weeds like sheep's sorrel, bedstraw and woodrush.

● **Thatch** can be waterlogged throughout most of the year and often smells strongly of decay and stagnation. It is yellow/brown in colour, sometimes with black streaks showing the activity of anaerobic bacteria. The underlying soil is usually wet, compacted and perhaps containing clay with restricted drainage. Annual meadow-grass usually predominates in the sward with perhaps some surviving bent. Thatch can accumulate to layers several inches thick particularly in water-collecting hollows on heavily played parts of a green. Over-watering and over-fertilising are also major factors in the process of encouraging thatch build-up.

As with many other problems, the prevention of fibre or thatch formation is more satisfactory and much less laborious than curing an established problem. If one is starting with a young and fibre-free sward, occasional use of groomer facilities on the mower (if available), occasional brushing or very light scarification should prevent any unwanted thatch build-up. The use of a comb attachment on the mower is also a useful supplement, raising horizontal stems into the cutting mechanism and so preventing build-up.

However, if soil conditions are such that fibrous layers are being encouraged then attacking them by scarification may be a losing battle as scarification does nothing to attack the actual cause of thatch formation. If fibre or thatch can be seen to be building up or if an established layer is present then measures are required to remove its cause and these are likely to be more effective in the long-term than a direct attack on the layer itself by scarification or hollow tining. In practice, both approaches are usually useful.

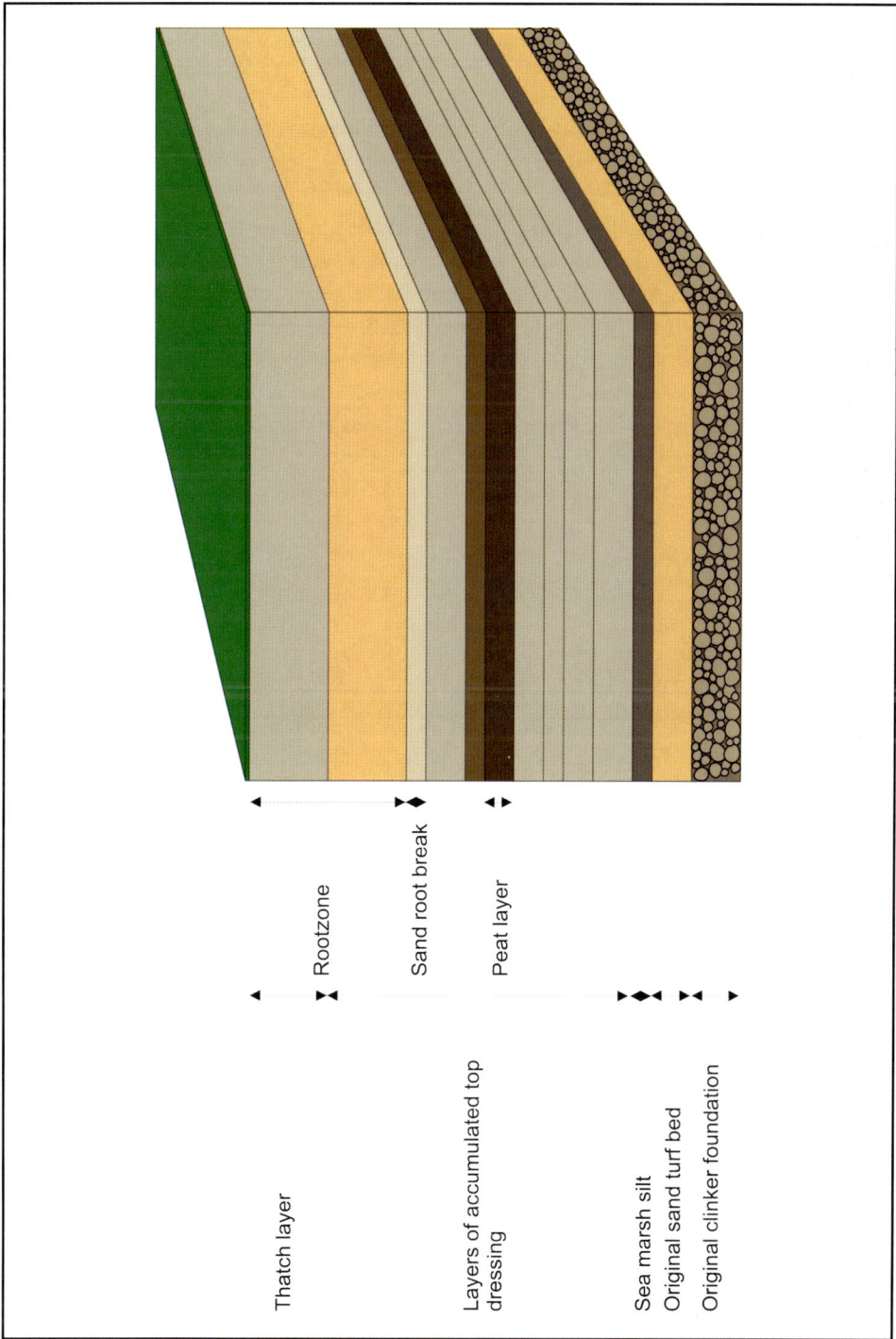

Thatch layer

Rootzone

Sand root break

Layers of accumulated top dressing

Peat layer

Sea marsh silt

Original sand turf bed

Original clinker foundation

Bowling green soil profile showing typical features

Control of thatch and fibre

In the specific case of fibre, as defined above, effective control can often result from frequent aeration work. All forms of aeration allow air into the layer and encourage natural organisms which break down the dead material. Aeration also encourages water penetration into very dry fibre and underlying soil and hence increased bacterial activity. The deep hand forking of dry high spots is particularly important as irrigation water and rain otherwise tend to run down into adjacent hollows. Dry, fibrous high spots often become associated with a fungal condition known as 'dry patch' which exaggerates the contrast between dry, fibrous-looking mounds and the lusher, greener and wetter low areas. Aeration is therefore the primary method of controlling the fibre, with scarification to remove the existing material. If soil analysis shows extreme over-acidity then lime treatment may be advisable, but only with extreme care as undesirable side effects can occur. Lime can easily increase weed, worm and weedgrass populations and encourage the very damaging take-all patch disease.

In contrast, thatch, again as defined above, can be the result of poor surface drainage and any measures aimed at improving water penetration will help dry the layer and promote natural breakdown. Aeration is again of importance but it is essential to penetrate down below the thatch layer into underlying soil layers. Aeration equipment capable of penetrating up to 150 mm or more is particularly useful in this respect. Often the causes of thatch are to be found in barriers to water penetration below the layer itself—peat layers, hydrophobic sand layers or simply compaction are the commonest causes. If slow drainage is being caused by a heavy clay subsoil or by poor initial construction with the whole of the soil profile compacted, then even deep surface spiking is unlikely to prove effective. Complete reconstruction is then likely to be the only answer. Occasionally, special aeration work using deep aerators like the Verti-Drain can be a helpful supplement to more conventional spiking. If carried out when the soil is dry, these operations can produce a cracking effect at a greater depth than the machine actually penetrates.

Thatch is undesirable as it holds water on the surface and makes the turf wetter than it should be. Fertiliser, as well as water, is often held in the surface and roots are confined to the thatch layer, dead roots usually adding to the layer and making the situation worse. Such a wet surface is prone to fusarium and damage from play. Over-watering of course makes the problem infinitely worse. Turf with a thick thatch layer is often very soft and mattress-like and hence easily footmarked giving an uneven surface. Soft thatch may also give a following player an unfair advantage, as he or she can see the indented track left along the surface by the bowl previously played by the opponent. Wet thatch layers tend to discourage the finer turfgrasses and annual meadow-grass increases as it is one of the few grasses which can grow reasonably well under such conditions. On thick thatch layers, however, even annual meadow-grass tends to weaken, particularly in wet winters. Removing the thatch can therefore have many beneficial effects in producing firmer and truer surfaces which are better able to withstand play even under adverse conditions.

Top dressing can be beneficial in firming up and helping the break up of thatch. A very sandy dressing well worked into aeration holes and the thatch makes the layers less spongy. It also helps air penetration and natural breakdown. Regular applications of sandy compost are therefore an essential part of the fight against thatch. Scarification, aeration and top dressing are all essential weapons but victory hinges on identifying and eliminating the prime cause of thatch formation.

In recent years various bio-stimulants (often microbial preparations or products containing mycorrhizal fungi) have been sold as another way forward to encourage thatch reduction. Such bio-stimulants (which can be expensive) are usually used in conjunction with aeration treatments. Variable results have been reported.

Compaction

Compaction in the soil profile may be responsible for slow surface drainage, thus encouraging thatch layers and their attendant ills, and for poor root growth. Look for zones in the soil which resist the penetration of the coring tool and which appear rather structureless with no visible soil air spaces. Many greens have been subjected to heavy rolling in the past, sometimes with vibrating rollers and other machines more suitable for consolidating the foundations of a motorway than for use on a bowling green. Such implements can produce severe over-compaction. Finer textured soil imported with the turf, and then buried by subsequent top dressings, can be compacted by rolling and form an almost impenetrable barrier to water percolation and root growth. Over-compaction can also be

Soil and profile sampling tools

produced by continuous treading by the players themselves as well as by heavy rollers. The compacting effect of the players' feet may be unevenly distributed over a green, being particularly common on the rink ends of a flat rink green.

Layering

An old green, as already mentioned, may show a soil profile with as many varied layers as an expensive chocolate cake. Apart from the thatch and soil layers from imported turf described above, layering is usually the result of top dressing with various materials over a long period of time. Sand or peat rootbreaks are most commonly the result of a heavy top dressing of such materials, subsequently buried by further annual top dressing. Ideally, a bowling green soil profile should remain uniform and homogeneous by consistent top dressing, after preliminary scarification and aeration, with the same type of material from year to year. Aeration work can help break up and mix together the different layers in a profile where they have formed. To avoid the danger of layering, top dressing should be thoroughly worked into a well-aerated green and not simply left lying on the immediate surface. New greens built with a carefully chosen sandy soil rooting medium should be top dressed with an identical sandy mix to preserve uniformity. Once one has decided upon a suitable top dressing mixture therefore, one should be consistent in using it from year to year. The practice of using sand one year, peaty dressings the next, etc. should be avoided. Layered profiles themselves can add to water percolation problems and encourage shallow rooting and are therefore to be prevented if at all possible.

Total soil depth

It is useful to obtain a clear idea of the total topsoil depth which exists over underlying clinker or stone drainage layers. During the process of determining soil depth you should also note the condition of any underlying clinker or stone layer. Is the clinker or stone clean and does it drain effectively (perhaps assessed by carefully pouring some water onto the exposed clinker/stone layer)?

CHEMICAL ANALYSIS OF THE SOIL

After carrying out a visual examination of the soil profile, one should complete one's knowledge of basic soil conditions by having an appropriate chemical analysis of the soil carried out. It is not something which the amateur can undertake for himself—it really requires the facilities of a well-equipped chemical laboratory and the analysis results need to be interpreted by someone experienced in such matters. Some commercial firms involved in the turf maintenance industry offer a service of this kind and some public analysts might be able to help. STRI offers a comprehensive soil testing service. It should be remembered that soil analysis by trade firms is sometimes followed by commercially biased advice.

The sample taken for analysis should be truly representative of the whole green. Most laboratories would require about 0.5 kg of soil, this quantity being made up of sub-samples taken here and there in a random fashion over the surface. A hollow tine fork is an ideal sampling tool or one of the soil-coring tools referred to in the previous section. Fifty or 60 cores should be collected and the core depth should be 125 mm.

A basic soil chemical analysis should produce information on soil acidity or alkalinity (i.e. the pH level), and on two of the three major plant nutrients, phosphate (P_2O_5) and potash (K_2O). The third major nutrient, nitrogen, cannot be meaningfully included in such an analysis as levels in a particular green can change from day to day and any figure obtained tends to have very little significance. Phosphate and potash levels are determined by extraction into weak chemical solutions under standardised conditions. pH is best determined electrometrically using a pH electrode in the laboratory under standardised conditions. Various kits for do-it-yourself pH determination are commercially available but these do not really give reliable results. Chemical testing kits where a coloured soil solution is compared with a standard colour chart can be rather inaccurate, while various battery-operated stick pH meters which give a reading when inserted into the surface of a green are woefully unreliable—the reading for one thing may vary according to how damp the green is at the time.

The pH scale indicates soil acidity or alkalinity, as mentioned above, on a 0 to 14 scale. Soils on bowling greens usually fall within the range 4.0 to 8.0. Figures between 6.0 to 6.5 may be regarded as neutral for practical purposes, 6.0 to 5.5 mildly acid and below 5.5 acid. Similarly, a bowling green soil with a pH of between 6.5 and 7.0 would be mildly alkaline and above 7.0 definitely alkaline. Inland bowling green soils should be within the range 5.0 to 5.5, but it is to be stressed that figures must be looked at with caution and always in the light of the general condition of a particular green. For example, if a green is found to have a very low pH and is therefore theoretically over-acidic, this does not automatically mean that lime treatment is required. A green showing a pH level of 4.5 for example is, strictly speaking, over-acidic but if the sward was healthy and the bowling surface very satisfactory, lime treatment would probably be most unwise. Liming is best regarded as a rather drastic treatment which, if overdone, encourages weeds, worms, undesirable grasses and the very damaging take-all patch disease. It should therefore only be undertaken in situations where the sward is perhaps thin, mossy and fibrous and showing obvious symptoms of over-acidity, and then only with extreme caution and preferably with expert advice. Many seaside greens constructed using local sandy soils are naturally alkaline—in this situation high pH levels should not be a cause of concern.

Soil nutrient figures giving phosphate and potash levels are an invaluable and essential guide to future fertiliser requirements. The question of how much fertiliser is needed will be discussed more fully later, so at this point suffice it to say that fertiliser should not be overdone. Applying too much encourages fusarium patch disease and annual meadow-grass, promotes thatch development and produces heavy lush growth and consequently a slow bowling surface.

Occasionally if there are problems relating to the textural make-up of the soil profile, then tests to ascertain physical criteria can be helpful, i.e. tests to show how much sand, silt, clay and organic matter are present. More specialised laboratories (such as at STRI) are needed for carrying out such tests and the interpretation of the results, together with any subsequent advice, is definitely a job for a consultant agronomist.

Making arrangements for a competent analysis of the soil completes our assessment of the present condition of the green. Such a survey should provide a firm basis for planning future maintenance and should highlight aspects of the green where improvement would not come amiss. Bowling greens are as individual and idiosyncratic as the bowlers who play upon them, so the details of the maintenance programme must be tailored to the specific needs of a particular green. It is, however, possible to lay down general guidelines as to maintenance requirements which are applicable to all greens, whether crown or flat rink.

Setting out such maintenance requirements on a seasonal basis allows one to compile a greenkeeping calendar. For the sake of clarity, maintenance operations are here divided into two categories, Primary and Secondary.

PRIMARY MAINTENANCE consists of those operations which should be performed on *every* bowling green *every* year as a matter of routine. Neglect of any one of them can be expected to result in an at least gradual deterioration in the quality of the playing surface. Primary operations are set out here in **bold** type.

SECONDARY MAINTENANCE covers work required on certain greens at certain times to correct specific faults or to meet an unforeseen problem such as an outbreak of disease or weed invasion.

The timing of maintenance work is often vital for success and it is impossible to be dogmatic on this point as weather and climatic factors vary from year to year. The following calendar must therefore be understood to be a very general guide only.

THE GREENKEEPING CALENDAR

JANUARY, FEBRUARY, VERY EARLY MARCH
(In frost, snow or very wet weather, leave well alone!)

MOWING: Cut if any growth is taking place. Set mower high initially and gradually lower level as growth strengthens.

SWITCHING: Switch or brush green each morning to disperse dew, as required by weather conditions.

AERATION: Occasional careful solid tining if conditions are suitable.

MOSS CONTROL: If necessary, when weather is reasonable.

DISEASE CONTROL: Fusarium can strike if weather favours it. Treat at once.

TOP DRESSING: Supplementary to autumn top dressing—sometimes advisable. Only if weather is suitable with some growth taking place. Material used at this time must be thoroughly and finely screened.

MARCH—APRIL

MOWING: Gradually lower cutting height.

SWITCHING: Continue as necessary.

WORM CONTROL: If required in mild moist weather, or leave until autumn.

DISEASE CONTROL: Fusarium still common. Treat at once.

SCARIFICATION: When growth is taking place and ground conditions are good.

ROLLING: On one or two occasions to prepare surface for play.

FERTILISER: Apply spring dressing if growth is established (ideally before play starts if conditions are right).

PLAYING SEASON COMMENCES (usually Easter)

APRIL—MAY

MOWING: Three times weekly usually necessary.

FERTILISER: Spring dressing when growth is established, if not given before play starts.

GROOMING/RAKING: Use groomers or fit comb to mower. Use throughout growing season when good growth.

RINK MARKERS (flat greens): Move frequently.

WEED CONTROL: Selective weedkiller when growth is strong. Late spring or early summer.

AERATION: Careful micro-tining or use of the sarel roller.

DISEASE CONTROL: Fusarium can still strike.

ROLLING: Light roll for important matches. Keep to a minimum.

SWITCHING: Continue each morning.

SCARIFICATION: Regular light treatments may be useful, perhaps monthly.

IRRIGATION: Commence as appropriate, but apply the minimum. Use wetting agents on dry spots.

JUNE, JULY, AUGUST, EARLY SEPTEMBER

SWITCHING: Continue each morning.

MOWING: Continue frequently.

GROOMING/RAKING: Continuously whilst good growth.

FERTILISER: One or two summer dressings, say at end of June and in late August.

IRRIGATION: As necessary in dry periods.

DISEASE CONTROL: Red thread disease—treat by fertilising or with fungicide.

WEED CONTROL: If weather unsuitable earlier, or a repeat treatment if required.

DRY PATCHES: Fork, use wetting agent.

RINK MARKERS (flat greens): Move frequently.

AERATION: Micro-tining or use of the sarel roller.

SCARIFICATION: Continue programme. Not in drought.

SEPTEMBER, OCTOBER
(Play finishes at some point—the earlier the better from a greenkeeping point of view! Autumn work under reasonable weather conditions is vital)

MOWING: Continue as growth demands, gradually raising height of cut to winter level.

SCARIFICATION: Thorough scarification before growth ceases.

SWITCHING: Continue each morning.

RENOVATION: Seeding, turfing, general repairs. Overall overseeding?

AERATION: Overall aeration of some appropriate type.

DISEASE CONTROL: Fusarium common in damp weather. Treat promptly.

WORM CONTROL: Mild moist weather.

TOP DRESSING: Overall sandy compost dressing (4 tons at least) absolutely essential. More if necessary. Extra on low spots. Spread and work in while weather is still reasonable with some growth occurring, and when the surface is dry.

NOVEMBER, DECEMBER, JANUARY

AERATION AND TOP DRESSING: May have to be completed if not done earlier. Now getting too late.

MOWING: Do not neglect if growth occurs. Winter cutting level.

SWITCHING: Continue if necessary. Keep surface as dry as possible.

RENOVATION: Turfing can still be carried out (up to Christmas).

AERATION: Winter aeration (solid or slit tines) can be useful when weather permits.

MOSS CONTROL: Under reasonable weather conditions as required.

NOTE: On completion of the above, go back to the start and begin the whole cycle all over again.

6 Modern Bowling Green Maintenance: Fertility and top dressing

INTRODUCTION

For bowls, the speed and trueness of the bowl travelling across the surface are probably the most important aspects of the playing quality of the game. Two of the most influential cultural factors in the hands of the greenkeeper that impact upon both green speed and trueness are fertility and top dressing.

Fertility affects not only the health and species composition of the sward but has a large impact on the rate of growth, density, grass cover and fineness of leaf, which also directly influence the roll of the bowl. Adequate growth promotes recovery from disease or stress periods, player abrasion and mechanical treatments, e.g. mowing, grooming, verticutting and aeration.

Of the grass species appropriate to fine turf, fescues offer the least resistance to roll followed by bentgrasses, with annual meadow-grass providing the most resistance. Density, as measured by the number of leaf blades, influences the upward or downward motion of the bowl, a denser sward supporting the weight of the bowl better. While grass cover is fundamental to hold a surface together, soil exposure in between plants creates undesirable bumpy and slow surfaces. Leaf blade width affects resistance and is determined by the species and cultivar, i.e. the narrower the leaf blade the less resistance there is to bowl motion. All of these attributes of the grass sward, i.e. species composition, density and texture, are directly influenced by fertility.

Top dressing's influence on ball roll is in terms of firmness and smoothness of the surface. Top dressing with sandy materials positively influences firmness by reducing the surface moisture content of soil and thatch, particularly under very wet conditions. Smoothness is affected by top dressings, evening out any discrepancies that may deflect the ball either upwards or downwards (deceleration), or that may cause bowls to veer off line.

FERTILITY

Many nutrients are utilised by grasses. Of these, there are two groups based on the relative quantities used by the grasses, i.e. macronutrients and micronutrients. Macronutrients are used by grasses in much larger quantities than are micronutrients or trace elements. The overall quantities of elements required by a plant are very small, often measured in parts per million. In Britain and Ireland, deficiency of any nutrient (other than nitrogen) is unusual on soil-based rootzones and micronutrient deficiencies are rare. However, low levels of potassium and phosphorus can occur, especially on low nutrient retaining sandy rootzones. What would be considered a deficient level of any one nutrient varies between the different sward types, e.g. between bentgrass and annual meadow-grass turf, soil types and on the maturity of the sward.

PLANT NUTRIENT REQUIREMENTS

Nitrogen

This is the nutrient required by the plant in greatest quantities and has the greatest influence on stimulating growth of new leaves. Amongst the responses it evokes are shoot density, shoot growth, leaf width, root depth, drought stress, wear tolerance, thatch build up, recovery and colour. Excessive nitrogen increases leaf width, length, thatch and disease, and a reduction in carbohydrate reserves. Thin and large succulent cell walls brought on by excessive nitrogen may make plants more susceptible to fungal entry and water loss is greater as stomata can close more slowly. Some diseases, e.g. fusarium, are thought to be responsive to nitrogen as they themselves may use it as a nutrient source. Adequate carbohydrate reserves are needed for new root growth, recovery from stress and to give cells a greater hold on water under drought conditions. Also of importance in relation to growth development is the carbon to nitrogen balance in plant tissue.

Over-use of nitrogen may also change the botanical composition of the sward, encouraging unwanted annual meadow-grass, which, by its nature, gives rise to slow bowling surfaces. At the other end of the spectrum, low nitrogen levels often result in stunted growth leading to chlorosis, whereby the oldest leaves turn yellow and may eventually lead to thinning of the turf if allowed to remain untreated.

Potassium

The availability of potassium plays an essential role in stress tolerance, having influences upon drought resistance, wear stress, susceptibility to fungal attack and also on nitrogen up-take by turfgrasses. The benefits on stress tolerance may not always be readily visible.

On low nutrient retention soils, i.e. those with a high sand content, potassium can readily leach and fertiliser input may be necessary. Drooping of leaves and interveinal chlorosis often identifies deficiencies.

Phosphorus

The main turf responses from adequate phosphorous utilisation are enhancement of the rate of establishment from seed and root growth, but there are also subtle effects on drought, heat and cold tolerance. Enhancement of growth when the sward is under drought stress due to unhealthy roots may occur with phosphorous application. Overall there is little visual response to phosphorus input unless available phosphorous is at extremely low levels. Once phosphorous levels are adequate there will be no further plant response to additional supply.

High concentrations of available phosphates are not known to have detrimental effects on grass plants, but may well favour the growth of the undesirable weedgrass annual meadow-grass at the expense of the desirable bent and fescue grasses. Phosphate is not the only factor that can encourage annual meadow-grass but it is an important one; thus avoiding over-fertilising with phosphate is a way of discouraging the spread of this undesirable species. However, the elimination of phosphorous from a feeding programme on the modern sand-based rootzones of high leaching potential can lead to deficiency symptoms, represented initially as stunted growth of dark green colouration developing to a purplish tinge to leaves with spindly growth and eventual root growth decline. Visual deficiencies are sometimes evident during establishment or during cold springs when root growth uptake may be slow.

Other macronutrients

Deficiencies of magnesium, calcium and sulphur are not very common. Such deficiencies may nevertheless occur where very rapid drainage rates have been achieved, e.g. in sandy constructions, or in situations where the rootzone is very acid. In this latter case, if an application of lime is appropriate, then both calcium and magnesium could be supplied by using ground dolomite (magnesium limestone).

Micronutrients

Their role is in cell wall synthesis (chlorine and boron) and as enzyme activators (iron, manganese, zinc, copper and molybdenum). Deficiency of micronutrients is most likely to occur on soils of a sandy texture and with an alkaline pH (except for molybdenum). However, deficiencies are extremely rare because the quantities used by turfgrasses are so small they do not deplete reserves (even when clippings are removed) and/or the quantities used are replaced, i.e. as impurities in fertilisers applied or due to the chemical constituents in top dressing.

Of the micronutrients, iron is the only one applied regularly as it has a number of beneficial effects. Iron, invariably in the form of calcined ferrous sulphate, is used because it has a cosmetic greening up effect on the grass as well as the added benefit of controlling mosses and weeds (through scorching) and worm casting (by acidifying the turf surface). It also has some effect in discouraging fusarium patch disease. However, regular repeated use of ferrous sulphate is not something to do with abandon, as there can be drawbacks due to the extra acidification of the rootzone and inducing drought susceptibility in turf.

NUTRIENT AVAILABILITY, pH AND LIME

To be able to grow satisfactorily, any plant needs to extract suitable quantities of each of the following elements from its environment (the soil solution and air):–

Macronutrients		Micronutrients	
Carbon		Chlorine	
Hydrogen	from air and water	Boron	
Oxygen		Iron	
		Manganese	from soil solution
Nitrogen		Zinc	
Potassium		Copper	
Calcium	from soil solution	Molybdenum	
Magnesium			
Phosphorus			
Sulphur			

Nutrient availability is determined by factors such as the ability of the soil to supply the nutrients and also the plant's ability to utilise the nutrients supplied (roots, temperature, oxygen, etc.). In the soil, clay particles and organic matter hold nutrient elements weakly while others are held as less soluble compounds on the soils solid fraction. The movement of ions into and out of soil solution for root uptake depends on their concentration and soil pH. Nutrient availability is often not a straightforward matter with many complex interactions at work.

However, the following general notes identify the forms in which nutrients occur and their availability.

Nitrogen

Nitrogen is readily available to plants primarily as nitrate (NO_3^-) and, to a lesser extent, as ammonium (NH_4^+) and/or urea ((NH_2)$_2$CO), and is taken up by roots and leaves supplied through rainfall, residual nitrogen in the form of organic matter and applied fertilisers. Nitrate nitrogen has a very dynamic nature in the soil decreasing rapidly due to its high solubility. The ammonium source is slightly less dynamic and is somewhat more difficult for the plant to tap as ammonium becomes attached to the clay and organic fractions in soil, but it is then converted to nitrate in a short time. Ammonium at high concentrations is toxic to plant tissues, however it is broken down quickly. In a natural situation nitrogen is available to grass plants mainly through the breakdown of the soil organic fraction. This process takes place very slowly and is usually insufficient for promoting the grass growth required for the plants to tolerate the intensive wear and maintenance of a bowling green.

Uptake of nitrogen is at an optimum in well aerated soils as the micro-organisms involved in the process of conversion of ammonia to nitrate (nitrification) are not only temperature dependent, but are also oxygen dependent. Oxygen levels below 5% reduce nitrification rapidly. Losses may occur due to leaching, denitrification (waterlogged or compacted soils) and volatilisation (urea under dry conditions and ammonium under alkaline conditions).

Nitrogen is, in many situations, the only fertiliser element required to promote the necessary amount of grass growth on a bowling green. However, if there is an imbalance in the soil of any other nutrient needed for healthy growth of a particular grass species, then the ability of the grass plant to make best use of nitrogen supplied may be affected, e.g. nitrogen is readily translocated to shoots when potassium levels are high but not under high calcium conditions.

Sources of nitrogen

Quick release sources of nitrogen include the relatively inexpensive inorganic salts of ammonium and nitrate and the synthetic organic urea mentioned above. All of these forms are readily water-soluble, give a rapid response and must be applied in low quantities to avoid over-stimulation of growth and fertiliser burn. Repeated long-term use of ammonium sulphate (one ammonium source) may reduce drought tolerance and may lead to over acidification, particularly on sand-dominated rootzones. Included under this category are urea formaldehyde products such as some methylene ureas (depending on the urea/formaldehyde ratio) and triazones (liquids) that give a response similar to urea but are safer to use in terms of burn.

Slow release sources of nitrogen are classified according to their release mechanism, i.e. low water solubility (isobutylidene diurea known as IBDU), microbial activity (natural organics, ureaform and methylene ureas) or coatings that act as physical barriers (sulphur coated ureas, polymer coated sulphur ureas and polymer fertilisers). Water solubility is determined by granule size and to some extent by temperature and pH. Microbial activity is temperature, pH, moisture and oxygen dependent. Release from coated fertilisers is dependent on coating thickness. To overcome potential problems of delayed response, particularly if factors affecting the breakdown of products are not favourable, many slow release preparations will include a percentage of quick release nitrogen.

The advantages of slow release products are that they less prone to leaching, have low burn potential, can be applied at higher rates and provide longer lasting effects but they tend to be more expensive than quick release sources.

Phosphorous (usually measured as phosphate, P_2O_5)

Phosphorous, which is relatively immobile in soils, is taken up by the plant as $H_2PO_4^-$ and HPO_4^{2-}. However, relatively insoluble forms of phosphate held within any rootzone material invariably maintain an appropriate quantity of phosphate for turfgrasses in the soil solution. Often low levels of available phosphorous are related to low levels in the soil or where the soil pH is either too low or too high.

Sources of phosphate

Like nitrogen, phosphate fertiliser is available in several forms. Bone meal is an organic source from which the phosphate is a slowly soluble form only made slowly available to the grass plant. In addition, bone meal contains a small amount of slowly released nitrogen.

This material was frequently used as an autumn/winter fertiliser in times past but this is now rarely the case.

Superphosphate, an inorganic source of phosphate, was used in custom made mixes, which was the case a number of years ago (often referred to as a Bingley mix). Such phosphate was largely soluble in the form in which it was applied but it quickly converts into fairly insoluble forms in soil and in sand. The most common sources of phosphorous used in today's proprietary blends and homogenous fertilisers are monoammonium phosphate and diammonium phosphate.

Potassium (usually measured as potash, K_2O)

Leaching of potassium (plant available K^+ ion in soil solution) is dependent on the clay fraction of the soil; hence in very sandy soils extra potassium is likely to be needed in the annual maintenance programme when compared to turf grown on a loam soil. The amount of potassium supplied annually in fertiliser should be determined by soil analyses and the results related to previous testing to determine the trend of potassium content in the rootzone.

Sources of potassium

A variety of compounds can provide a source of potassium but the three most common are potassium chloride, potassium nitrate and potassium sulphate. Of these, potassium sulphate is easier to handle and store and is less prone to scorching. Potassium chloride is widely used in commercial formulae. They are similar in effect on turf and the potassium is quickly made available.

pH and lime

The pH of a soil is the measure of H^+ ion activity in the soil solution. It has a major influence on nutrient availability by modifying the balance of ions on clay and organic matter sites, chemical complexes in the soil and microbial activity.

Acidity

Nutrient availability is generally most favourable at a pH of 6.0-7.0 on mineral soils. However, grass species composition can be influenced by the intolerance of a species to certain elements. With the primary objective of promoting a fine fescue/browntop bent sward a slightly acid pH of 5.0-5.5 strongly favours these species over annual meadow-grass. It is not so much that the fescue/browntop bent turf favours these conditions but its relative tolerance to them gives it the competitive edge. Invasion of the turf by weeds and moss and profuse development of worm casting are also discouraged under a slightly acidic pH. Under such conditions acidic cations (H^+, Al^{+3}, Mn) become more soluble and start causing plant root toxicity, especially to the more sensitive annual meadow-grass. However, genotypes of annual meadow-grass may vary in their sensitivity.

Below a pH of 5.0 bentgrass becomes increasingly sensitive to the acidic cations, which may result in both root and crown loss. Fe, Mn, Cu and Zn also become less available to the plant at such low pHs forming less soluble hydroxides and oxides, while mineralisation of N and P from organic matter and from fertiliser is slowed. The activity and populations of the beneficial thatch reducing bacteria and actinomycetes also lessen below pH 5.5, particularly under cool, wet soil conditions, resulting in possible increases in organic matter build up. High populations of bacteria and actinomycetes are believed to be responsible for degradation of many soil organic matter compounds.

Conditions leading to increasing acidity include high rainfall (leaching of basic cations), use of acidifying N sources and/or an acidic irrigation water source. Soils differ in their rate of pH change, this being most rapid on sandier soils where the buffering capacity is low. Correction of over-acidity, if problems are occurring, may be made through additions of lime ($CaCO_3$) such as ground limestone or chalk, but treatment should be based on a lime determination test in a soils laboratory. Burnt (CaO) or slaked lime ($Ca(OH)_2$) are slightly more rapid in their effect of correcting soil acidity but are difficult to handle and may cause scorch to established turf. Ground limestone is much preferred but care must be taken to avoid its application within 10-14 days of any ammonia fertiliser in order to prevent any reaction and the release of toxic ammonia gas. A very gradual approach to correction is best if lime is applied to an existing sward, while addition of greater quantities is possible where lime is necessary to correct an over-acid seed or turf bed prior to establishment. Very rapid changes of turf pH values can alter sward composition away from the desirable fescue/bent species to an annual meadow-grass dominated sward. Hence, if the soil becomes over-acid beneath such turf, it must be corrected very slowly. Excess lime encourages not only annual meadow-grass but also worms and weeds like daisies. Liming can also directly lead to attacks by the very damaging take-all patch disease and other turfgrass diseases.

Where routine soil testing every two to three years indicates a decline in pH beyond the desired value, slightly alkaline or neutral top dressing over a period in combination with limiting sulphur-carrying fertilisers can arrest the decline in the first instance. Good results have also been obtained by using some seaweed-based preparations (containing calcium) to correct developing over-acidity.

It is important to realise that a green which is theoretically over-acid but which plays extremely well should not necessarily receive corrective treatment. The low pH should, however, be borne in mind if difficulties in maintaining an adequate sward start developing. It is easy to over-estimate the significance of pH in practice and the pH figure should only be looked at in the context of the characteristics of a particular green as a whole.

Alkalinity

Alkaline conditions (pH >7.0) occur due to an accumulation of basic cations from either irrigation water, fertiliser, over-liming, parent soil material or top dressing. Under increasing alkaline conditions nutritional problems may occur, although root-harming toxicities are rare. Furthermore, the impacts on thatch degrading bacteria, actinomycetes and fungi are much less than with over-acidity. The main nutritional problems that may be experienced are phosphate deficiency (especially if free $CaCO_3$ is present) and iron deficiency and the associated symptom of iron chlorosis.

Correction of alkalinity may well be appropriate in the promotion of fescue/browntop bentgrass if the rootzone is excessively alkaline and perhaps causing nutritional difficulties. Sulphur (S) could be considered to reduce pH but much will depend on soil texture and the initial pH, with greater quantities of sulphur required for clay or organic soils in comparison to sands. Low rates (avoids excessive surface acidity) of sprayer-applied water dispersible granules of high purity elemental S are suitable for established turf. Guard against scorching the turf with sulphur treatments, avoiding periods of stress and ensuring watering in. Ammonium based N carriers and iron sulphate in the fertiliser programme may be enough to counter potential alkalinity increases brought on by small quantities of calcium carbonate in an irrigation water supply without the need for expensive acid to water treatment.

For greens constructed of calcareous ($CaCO_3$) sand or where the only top dressing source is calcareous, pH adjustment may well prove to be uneconomical and impractical given the strongly buffering capacity of the calcium carbonate. Adjustments may be made for sands with up to 2% free calcium carbonate but, even then, change must be viewed in the long term and not without undue expense. A more appropriate approach may be to make fertiliser adjustments through the possible addition of P and foliar applications of micronutrients Fe, Mn, Zn or B (if deficient) rather than attempt to adjust pH.

SOIL ANALYSIS

The nutrient status of soils and ability to supply nutrients can be measured by soil analysis. For soils with some clay content, the frequency of testing could be approximately every three years as major changes are unlikely from one year to the next. For bowling greens constructed of a high sand content, soil analysis is particularly important because changes in low nutrient retention sandy soils can take place far more quickly, e.g. leaching of potassium and magnesium is very rapid in comparison with a soil that contains some clay, and a wider range of nutrients may be leached too. In very sandy constructions, additional nutrients (potassium in particular) will be needed each year for the turfgrasses to make best use of the nitrogen supplied. Hence, in such situations soil analysis might be carried out annually and even more frequently during the "grow-in" phase of a new green.

Nitrogen level is not measured during soil analysis as the soluble forms supplied during fertiliser treatment are very mobile and readily washed through the roozone. The nitrogen status can indeed vary significantly over a 24 hour period, particularly on sandy soils. An appropriate amount of nitrogen is automatically needed each growing season (with maybe two to three times as much nitrogen given to sand-dominated rootzones in comparison to soil-based greens).

A further routine measurement made during soil analysis procedures is that of pH given its importance.

FERTILISER TYPES

Fertilisers supply one or more additional elements that are essential for turf growth. They may be comprised of organic or inorganic substances of natural or synthetic origin. Their formulation varies widely giving the greenkeeper an array of choice to match his needs.

Fertilisers (liquid or granular) may be supplied as *compound*, i.e. comprising at least two fertiliser elements, *complete* containing N, P and K or just simply *straight* containing one element.

Liquids are derived generally from highly soluble materials, a proportion of which is taken up by the leaves. As with granulars, they are available in a wide array of nutrient content. They have the advantage of supplying small amounts without any residue left behind and do not need watering in.

On-site mixing of sources of nutrients can produce fertilisers to suit the requirements of the turf. However, most clubs purchase both liquids and granulars (blended or homogenous) as commercial fertilisers for convenience.

Blended fertilisers come as a mixture of two solid materials. Slow release fertilisers usually come in a blend with quick release granules. Spotty results may appear if the density of the two granules varies and in such cases application with a drop spreader is best rather than with a rotary type.

Homogenous fertilisers produce more equal distribution of nutrients as the elements are contained in one granule.

FERTILISER PROGRAMME

A fertiliser programme has the ultimate aim of supplying sufficient nutrient to satisfy the needs of the turf ensuring sufficient to withstand against wear but without over stimulation of growth (excessive thatch, mowing and disease). It is not about maximum tissue production, nor is a bowling green an ornamental lawn to be admired for its colour. The basic fertilising principles for bowling greens should be to keep it as simple as possible, to provide minimal fertiliser thus promoting quality rather than quantity of grass. Furthermore, to base the programme on mainly nitrogen inputs, but with occasional treatments with products that provide supplementary elements as and when the need exists.

Nitrogen needs and timing

Any programme should be based on the growth of the plant at different times of the year, so understanding growth patterns is fundamental. As soon as some growth is seen in spring, modest amounts of nitrogen fertiliser may be applied to boost density, reduce weed infestation and aid recovery from winter injury or disease scarring. The main spring application should be given when growth is established, usually late March, but later in slow springs and as one moves north up through England into Scotland. During the playing season suitable amounts of nutrient are necessary to maintain density in view of wear. End of summer/early autumn is the key period to return to modest application to ensure the sward has good strength entering into the potentially harsh and slow growing winter period, but avoiding any soft or lush growth (which could be very prone to fusarium patch disease).

The best use of nitrogen is to aim to avoid peaks and troughs of growth. "Spoon feeding" with a little but often approach is often a good strategy if soluble products are used. The desire to achieve fast green speeds also fits the little and often approach during the playing season, in particular the use of very low rates of nitrogen applied as liquids. These frequent applications may also require less fertiliser due to reductions in leaching or fixation

Nitrogen selection and rates

If spring or autumn are characterised by particular local climatic conditions, the careful selection of nitrogen source may achieve the best response for those conditions. Ammonium sulphate is generally used as the granular source of nitrogen in spring on soils due to its ability to be absorbed under cool conditions, while a slow release/quick release combination is generally used on sandy rootzones to provide both quick response and residual nitrogen in such a lowly buffered environment. During wet conditions leaching is a risk for soluble forms on sandy soils, but conversely one should avoid excessive nitrogen levels as these may make the grass grow too fast. In such instances a combination of slow release fertiliser combined with soluble nitrogen (15-25% quick release) may provide the best results, avoiding nutrient release rates that are either too fast or too slow. Under dry conditions, low levels of soluble nitrogen work best as little nitrogen is needed by the plant. Early spring fertiliser treatment, totally or mainly reliant on slow release forms, must be carefully considered if the nitrogen release is dependent on temperature.

A single application of a quick release mini granular fertiliser should contain no more than 2.5 g of nitrogen/m^2, while slow release/quick release that supply 5-7 g of nitrogen/m^2 per application are commonly recommended by manufacturers to minimise losses through leaching and to avoid excessive growth and burn.

During the potentially warmer and drier conditions of summer, rates of 0.5-1 g of nitrogen/m^2 every one to two weeks are generally used for soluble nitrogen sources applied through a sprayer with a spoon feeding approach to sand rootzones. Water carrier levels of 1000 litres per hectare may be necessary to avoid burn in dry weather. The interval between applications may be extended to three weeks on soils with some clay. Soluble liquid applied nitrogen in conjunction with calcined iron sulphate (4 g/m^2 per application) or chelated iron can have the same greening effect as double the rate of nitrogen. Similarly in the non-playing period, low nitrogen analysis autumn/winter granular (soil temperatures above 50°C) may be appropriate in certain circumstances.

Overall programme

Recommended annual application rates of fertiliser depend on soil type and retention ability with the following used as a reliable guide:–

Soil rootzone	N	6-12 g/m^2
	P$_2$O$_5$	0-2 g/m^2
	K$_2$O	0-15 g/m^2
Sand rootzone	N	12-25 g/m^2
	P$_2$O$_5$	0-5 g/m^2
	K$_2$O	0-25 g/m^2

The range of application rates are given as a guide to determine maximum and minimum levels but should be adjusted according to the nutrient-holding capacity of the soil, the local climate, traffic, the grass species, the degree of watering and the mechanical treatments together with experience and observation. Therefore each individual green must be judged separately and there is no one fertiliser programme that can be universally used.

In a grow-in situation on sand rootzones, rates may need to be slightly higher than those used thereafter for the first couple of years until sufficient organic matter has built up to reduce leaching. In addition, one to two applications of complete micronutrient fertiliser may be necessary on new sand rootzones in the first couple of years.

The most valuable time for adding phosphorous or potassium is at the end of winter/early spring. However on sandy soils, phosphorous in conjunction with potassium might be included to regularly give adequate supplies over the growing season given the low retention capacity of these soils and the capacity to buffer against high rainfall losses.

If soil sample analysis has shown that other elements need to be added for the grasses to make best use of the nitrogen supply, then these are usually most effectively included as part of the spring dressing.

STORAGE

Fertilisers should always be stored in dry conditions. Care should be taken to protect bags from sharp points or jagged edges and bags should be laid down flat rather than on their corners. To maintain dry conditions, it is wise to have a platform of duckboard or similar between the floor and the bags and to ensure ventilation around the bags and in the building, though doors and windows should be closed in damp weather. The most convenient arrangement is usually to have the bags stacked in a criss-cross arrangement, keeping the height down to about six bags and certainly not more than ten bags. Always close a part-used bag to conserve the remainder of the fertiliser in good condition.

APPLICATION OF FERTILISER

Uniformity is an essential characteristic for good green performance and it is very important that fertilisers be applied as evenly as possible. Uneven application results in uneven growth and excess applications (such as caused by overlapping) may damage the turf severely (scorching). Ideally, fertiliser should be applied in a dry spell in between showery weather to help remove granules off leaves and avoid potential scorching from high salt sources. If no rain falls immediately after application, where practicable watering should be undertaken to achieve the same end.

Nutrient applicators

Drop-type linear distributors are the more precise applicators of the two spreader types. Spread is quite even within their width, subject to using uniform fertiliser in good condition, evenness of the ground, etc. Drift is reduced as granules have only a short distance to drop, but great care is needed to achieve correct marrying of successive widths (slight overlapping with the wheels) and to avoid difficulties at the ends of runs. The most accurate application is achieved by dividing the fertiliser into halves and applying it in two directions at right angles. A header (one or two widths) is necessary at the end of each run to ensure uniform cover when turning.

Rotary-type distributors complete the job faster than drop types, applying fertiliser in a semicircle pattern. However, these types can apply more fertiliser in the middle of their spread than they do at the outside. Thus to improve the evenness of spread it is wise to again reduce the application rate by half but this time to make each pass in the same direction (not at right angles) at half the width of the normal spread of fertiliser. Marker posts should be laid down at the end of each run to ensure each pass is set at half the width covered by the spinner. This is known as the half width method. The operation of rotary spreaders may require greater headers at the end of each run given the tendency for some spreaders to throw at least 2 metres in front. To avoid misapplication, spreaders of either type should on no account continue to spread when turning.

Liquid applications can be made using pedestrian push type and wheelbarrow sprayers, which have capacities of 25-100 litres and boom widths of 1.50-2.50 metres. Progressively larger sized sprayers are selected according to the number of greens to be sprayed and the frequency of liquid application in the programme. Utility vehicle-mounted (tank capacities typically 200-500 litres) equipment is only likely to be suitable for local authorities or organisations with a number of greens under their control.

Calibration

This refers to the elements that add up to ensuring that the correct amount of fertiliser is applied to the treated area. This includes calculating the correct amount of product, proper mixing and adjusting the equipment to apply the desired rate in a uniform swath.

The factors that influence application accuracy for both sprayers and spreaders include:

- Speed of travel.
- Operating pressure.
- Application height.
- Swath width.
- Nozzle output for sprayers.
- Uniformity of granule distribution for spreaders.

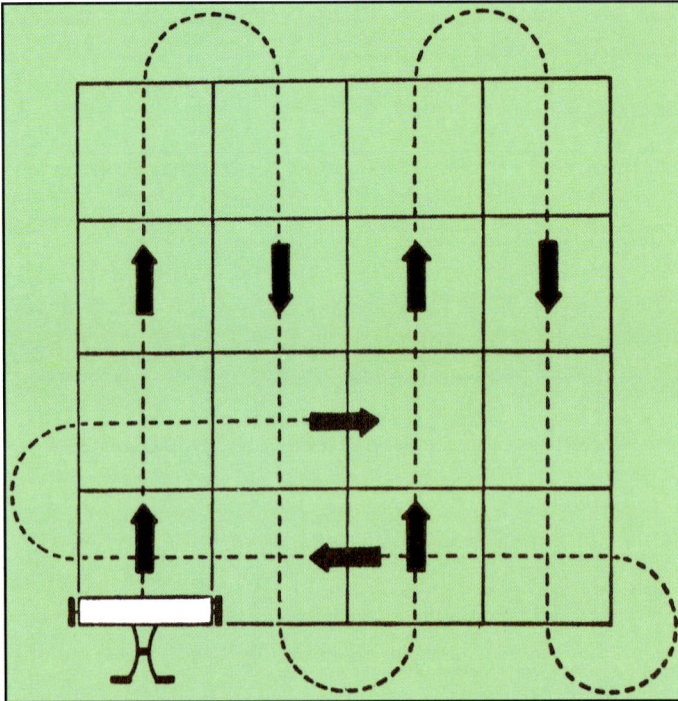

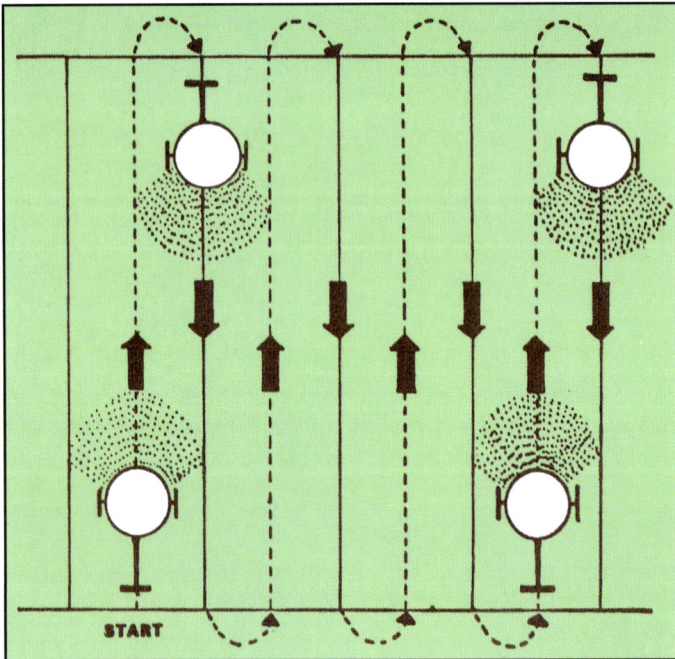

Working patterns for linear (top) or spinner (bottom) fertiliser distributors

Rotary-type fertiliser distributor

Drop-type linear fertiliser distributor

Since solid fertilisers differ in their density and spreadability (even the same fertiliser may perform differently on different occasions), it is wise to regard calibration marks on a distributor merely as a guide and to check the setting of the fertiliser distributor before each use.

Calculation of the output of the spreader can be made by applying product over a known area. Begin by marking out a known area of, say, 50 m². Fill the spreader with the product to a marked level on the hopper. Operate the spreader over the known area. Weigh the amount of product required to refill the hopper to the mark. The amount of product applied is then known for the area covered. The spreader may then need to be recalibrated to supply the recommended rate. An alternative is to spread material at normal working speed and to lay out a 1 or 2 m² area of paper or similar which will receive the fertiliser. Thereafter, weigh the material deposited on the known area.

Sprayer output is determined according to speed of travel, swath width and flow rate of the nozzles so that the values for the following formula can be inserted and output calculated:–

$$\text{Sprayer output (litres/hectare)} = \frac{600 \times \text{Nozzle output (litres/min)}}{\text{Swath width (metres)} \times \text{speed (kph)}}$$

TOP DRESSING

This refers to the application of a bulky material to the surface of the green. The aims of a top dressing programme may be varied and include the following:–

1. The development or retention of a smooth surface and to improve general levels.
2. As an aid in the control of the water-holding, soft and spongy effects of thatch.
3. To help modify the upper rootzone.

These aims are primarily concerned with producing the main objective of a bowling green, which is to produce a uniformly fast, smooth, true and dry surface resistant to wear and compaction. Application to develop a true surface can be two-fold:–

- To reduce minor surface imperfections and prevent the bowl bobbling over the surface and maybe losing speed and direction.
- To improve general levels, especially to build up low spots to create a flatter surface (so important for the flat rink game).

It is a far more efficient method of improving surface levels than heavy rolling which produces soil compaction and a variety of associated problems, as we have already seen. Light rolling may be used occasionally whereby it is introduced primarily for a polishing effect.

Very sandy top dressing can help in the reduction of thatch and provide a better environment for microbial degradation of remaining material.

Top dressing may also be used to improve surface drainage—again sand is particularly useful in this respect to help ameliorate soil types that are relatively slow to drain. Conversely, top dressing may sometimes be used to increase drought resistance by including organic materials such as fine humus. However, this is relatively rare as far more greens in the British Isles and Ireland are too wet than too dry.

Some top dressing materials may have some nutritional value if they contain quantities of soil or organic matter but this is not the primary object of the exercise. Where top dressings contain peat, the peat can influence nutrient retention and release.

CHOICE OF MATERIAL

The material used for top dressing can be straight sand or one of a high sand content mixture. High sand content mixtures may include soil and/or peat or another organic source such as green waste. The underlying soil type, i.e. soil or sand rootzone, primarily determines choice. Sandy composts may be selected where the underlying soil is also sandy and relatively free draining, while heavier rootzones might be ameliorated with pure sand (although this sand needs to be well integrated into the soil by ongoing aeration and not allowed to persist as a separate layer on the surface). New constructions with very sandy rootzones on the other hand should be matched with exactly the same material used in the original rootzone construction for continuity.

Availability influences the decision to buy in or home manufacture. In the past, many bowling clubs mixed their own top dressing using varying proportions of sand and topsoil, sometimes with peat added. In some cases, the soil constituent was replaced by compost manufactured from grass clippings and other available sources of organic matter. Today, most bowling clubs have neither the space, time nor labour resources for the home manufacture or mixing of top dressings, and the majority tend to purchase ready-made top dressings from commercial suppliers. As well as being time-consuming and laborious, home manufacture also has the disadvantage of producing an unsterilised product. Using such material can therefore spread annual meadow-grass and other weed seed.

A mix containing:–

6 parts (by bulk) suitable sand	or	3-4 parts (by bulk) suitable sand
3 parts screened sandy loam topsoil		1 part screened sandy loam topsoil
1 part fine peat		

might be regarded as appropriate for commercial purchase or producing ones own top dressing. For a wet, heavy green the proportion of sand could well be increased and the peat content eliminated. There has been a tendency for too much peat to be used in the past and its use may be adding to the problem of organic matter dominance rather than reducing it. An excess of peat can build up into a soft, spongy, water-retentive layer, in turn leading to a heavy, wet and easily footmarked playing surface. The peat content of dressings should therefore be limited to a small percentage of the whole except in the case of very free-draining sandy greens where drought stress is an ongoing problem. Only then should peat be considered to counter drought and where there is a clear need to increase moisture-holding capacity (this situation is rarely encountered in practice). The percentage of peat should not exceed more than 10% by volume if it its inclusion is deemed necessary. Furthermore, peat should certainly never be used straight but only with sand or soil. There is a tendency to discourage the use of peat for environmental reasons, in that peat bogs are a rare habitat that requires conservation, and alternative organic materials may be sourced if their inclusion in the blend is considered necessary.

Whatever material is chosen, continuity of top dressing material is critical to avoid layering and subsequent rootbreaks and the reduction of infiltration rates. Care should be taken to avoid using fine textured sands/sandy materials over coarser textured underlying rootzones as you may create a perched water table at the surface. Where a close match is difficult, it is better to err on the slightly coarser side. Furthermore, if one is considering changing to straight sand, this should only be undertaken on the understanding that when carried out it is often a mistake to return to sand/soil blends. Any change to pure sand dressings must also be accompanied by the availability of an efficient irrigation system to avoid the potential for severe drying over the mid to long term as sand dominated depth accumulates.

Top dressing is supplied in bulk loads or bagged. The former is significantly cheaper but requires suitable covered storage facilities on site and adequate room for the large delivery vehicles to drop their load.

SAND SELECTION

Ideally sand should have a narrow range of particles with at least 80% in the 0.15-0.75 mm diameter range to reduce the susceptibility of the sand to compact under traffic and to optimise drainage rates. Of critical importance is the clay and silt content, never consider a sand unless the silt content is less than 5% and clay less than 3%. Better still if the sand is free of silt and clay.

Sands of high silica content are most suitable as they are hard and resistant to weathering unlike softer lime-based sands, which are typically available through much of Ireland. Ideally, the sand selected should be free of lime to avoid the problems associated with increasing pH.

In regions where high rainfall is experienced the selection of sands at the coarser end of the range may be best to improve surface drainage, while the sands closer to the finer end may be chosen for drought-prone areas, if available.

RATES, FREQUENCY, TIMING

The rate and frequency are interlinked and are often based on thatch accumulation. The overriding aim is to dilute and integrate thatch accumulation with top dressing so that the rootzone is free of any alternating layers and organic matter. Such layering can slow water percolation and cause black layer (an anaerobic stagnant layer within the profile that can have serious repercussions on root growth and turf performance).

Light applications (0.5 kg/m^2) made on a regular basis throughout the growing season can produce very good results in combination with light scarification to help integration. However, bowling greens (except new greens not yet opened for play) are virtually never

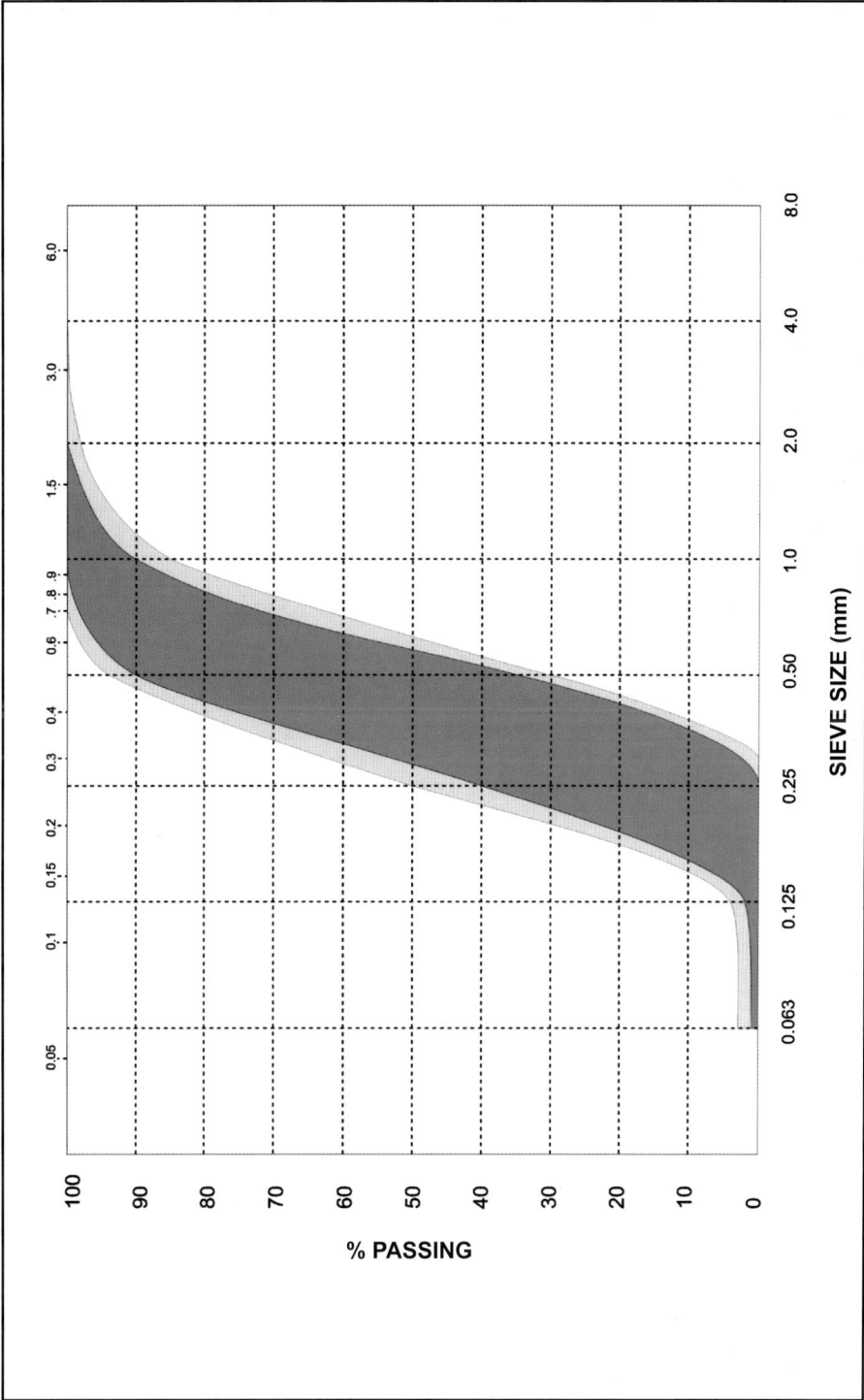

Grading curve defining recommended and acceptable limits of sand size for fine turf

top dressed during the summer playing season due to conflicts with play and sometimes a lack of resources. Material dampened by rain or dew after application would adhere to bowls during play and complaints would be likely. Top dressing is therefore usually an out of playing season practice with the dilution of organic matter build up in between applications, very much dependent on regular light scarification through the growing season.

Top dressing is a crucial autumn operation best timed to coincide with the slightly deeper end of season scarification and aeration work. Top dressing is best applied immediately following aeration as this facilitates working the material into the surface—much material drops into the tine holes, particularly after hollow tining. Rates of 2-2.5 kg/m^2 are required after slit or solid tining, whereas 3-3.5 kg/m^2 would be needed after hollow tining. Top dressing material must be dry for ease of application and must also be applied to a dry surface to facilitate working in with a drag brush or mat (also perhaps carrying out some work with a long lute to locate low spots and commence the process of depositing dressing in such low spots). Equally important is that top dressing is undertaken while good grass growth is still taking place to allow the grass to grow through the dressing and not to sit on the surface and possibly smother the grass.

The playing season must therefore not be permitted to drag on too long or vital autumn work will suffer and there is a danger of the bowling surface deteriorating for the subsequent bowling season. Timing of the close of play is often a point of contention between bowlers and the greenkeeper, so it is to be stressed that ceasing play in reasonable time is in everyone's long-term interest. The timely completion of the autumn renovation programme will go a long way towards determining the quality of the playing surface the following year.

A supplementary spring top dressing may also be necessary to restore levels after frost heave, footprinting from mowing or disease scarring. Such a dressing can also form part of a programme to clean out any organic debris that has built up over the autumn and winter months. The spring dressing should be given as soon as reasonable weather occurs, with some growth taking place, but before play starts. The rate of any spring top dressing application must be carefully considered (usually significantly less than in the autumn), so the material has been completely lost from the surface by the time play starts.

In addition to overall autumn and spring top dressing, it can often be useful to give extra quantities to particular parts of a green, i.e. low areas, scarred or scuffed patches, or areas of the green which have been returfed or reseeded. The technique would be to give the overall top dressing first and, when this has disappeared into the surface, to give extra quantities where required. This process can be repeated as long as the weather remains good with some growth still taking place. Frequent, light dressings to help true-up the green might be undertaken on a rink-by-rink basis through the bowling season, or green-by-green to multiple green sites where it may be possible to rotate temporary closure.

APPLICATION

Clubs which look after the green themselves invariably spread the top dressing by hand using shovels from a barrow, or from bagged material placed at convenient points over the green surface. Purpose-designed top dressing spreaders are also available, both pedestrian-operated machines and vehicle-mounted ones, and are commonly used by contractors who want to complete work quickly and efficiently.

After initial spreading over the surface, the top dressing should be worked in. The material should not be left lying on the surface in quantity as it can smother the grass, with the ultimate development of bare patches. Grass covered with an excess of top dressing is also prone to severe fusarium patch disease attacks. Such problems are often more prevalent if the work is left too late in the autumn.

There are several ways of working in top dressing, but at most clubs it is by drag mat or brush. Attachment of the brush or mat to a domestic tractor-mower mechanises the operation. For dispersal work, old-fashioned birch besoms, fibreglass switches or small lutes are used. Hover-type rotaries (with the blade removed) may also be employed to force the top dressing (even when damp) into the sward while at the same time very coarse particles may be pushed to the side for collection. A compact tractor operating a series of oscillating brushes on a frame are sometimes used by contractors to speed up the working-in process.

For flat rink bowling greens however, where there is a need to produce truer levels (unfortunately this is usually the case), there is one very important implement which should be considered for distributing an overall top dressing. This essential flat green top dressing tool is a large rigid-frame lute, although a long straight edge is a possible alternative. Lutes have the advantage of scraping material off high spots and depositing relatively more on low areas of a green, hopefully producing a gradual level improvement. Lutes can be obtained in various widths but for flat greens, the wider the implement, the better as long as operation is physically possible and practical. A flat rink greenkeeper who does not use a large lute is possibly not doing his job properly. For surface level improvement, top dressing should be worked-in in several directions.

Hollows needing extra top dressing are best located by means of a green survey. The location of puddles after heavy rain photographically recorded, and long straight edges or strings laid taut across the surface can also be used to indicate low spots.

It is essential when top dressing to try to avoid forming the layered soil profiles described earlier. Shallow spiking using a Sarel roller and solid or slit tining will aid the mixing of sandy material into the top of the rootzone and help dilute any layers present.

Where annual meadow-grass is a problem and it would be an advantage to improve botanical composition, it is often useful to mix bent and fescue seed in with the top dressing. The sowing rate could be 15-30 g/m^2. New seed can germinate in spike holes or in the compost mulch provided by the top dressing. Overseeding must, however, be a part of a general management programme designed to favour the better grasses if it is to stand a chance of achieving significant results.

Drag mat

Drag brush

7 Modern Bowling Green Maintenance: Mechanical Work

WHAT IS MECHANICAL WORK?

A simple definition of mechanical work would be treatments that affect the growing medium and grass cover to a green which do not involve the application of a material. This would include mowing, scarification and aeration; a triumvirate of vital treatments that, barring the weather, have the greatest influence on the quality of the playing surface. Let us consider these major maintenance inputs in turn.

MOWING

Mowing is the act of clipping grass, which maintains the height of the turf and has a direct effect on density of the sward.

Frequency and height of cut

At the correct setting, with sharp blades, increasing the frequency of mowing generally produces a finer textured turf and improves the density of the sward. A bowling green should be cut at least three times a week through the growing season, never neglecting mowing over the winter months when there is grass to be taken off. Quite often, one of the simplest means of improving the presentation and playing quality (notably the pace) of a green during the summer is to mow it more often. The evenness of cut, which is critical to turf quality, is determined by the number of cuts made by the mower per metre of forward travel, with the best modern machines giving up to 240 cuts per metre with 11-bladed reels. At the close cutting heights expected these days, a cutting rate of much less than 200 cuts per metre with 11-bladed reels or less than 140 cuts per metre with 10-bladed reels will tend to produce a slightly less fine finish. This can also happen if machines are poorly set or trying to cope with grass that has been allowed to grow excessively long between cuts.

The height of cut is a vital aspect of the operation. Setting up the mower is critical to the standard of finish and this should preferably be done with a purpose-made mower gauge. Mowing height is defined as the vertical distance between the cutting edge of the fixed bottom blade (or sole plate) of the mower and a straight edge placed across from the front and rear rollers. Every time the mower is set, the height of cut should be checked at both ends and to the centre of the sole plate to ensure that the height of cut is going to be consistent along the length of the bottom blade. The setting height is altered by adjustment of the front roller, which is accomplished in slightly different ways depending on the mower. The thickness of the sole plate will affect the finished cutting height. The mower should be serviced regularly (at least once a year) and part of this service should be to replace the bottom blade. In addition, the greenkeeper should routinely check the cylinder reel and bottom blade for flaws and notches, which, if present, will impair the quality of the finished cut. When setting the mower, the cylinder reel moves down to the bottom blade. This should not actually touch, as this will increase wear, resulting in tearing rather than cutting of the grass. If there is a whirring or knocking noise coming from the mower then the reel and bottom blade may well be set too tight to one another. Check the finished setting by cutting a blade of grass at various sites across the width of the sole plate to ensure that the mower will give a clean cut. The ideal setting between the cylinder and bottom blade is one that is obvious once achieved but not an easy setting to describe.

Mower gauge

One should also be aware that the bench setting height of cut on the mower does not necessarily match the finished height of cut to the green. Pedestrian-operated cylinder mowers are relatively heavy units that will settle into the turf, more so if the surface is soft due to, for example, excessive thatch accumulation.

The general guidance for mowing height is for it to fall within the range of 4-6 mm through the growing season, rising to 6-8 mm over winter. Through the summer, the higher end of this range should be employed during periods of extreme drought. Cutting closer to 3 mm is permissible for major events when that extra bit of pace is desirable, but should only be done for short periods and only when the turf is strong and healthy. The exact mowing height should be determined by many factors, including sward composition, softness of green, and prevailing weather and growing conditions. If the cut is set too tight then scalping may occur, not uncommon on any ridge that has formed 0.5 m or so into the green when edges start to fall away. The fine, wiry fescue grasses tend to be least tolerant of very close mowing and cutting your green at 4 mm or even closer throughout the playing season will only promote the annual meadow-grass in the turf. If you have a lot of fescue in your turf and you want to keep it, never cut less than 5 mm. Interestingly, a wiry, dry fescue turf with minimal thatch content will bowl noticeably faster than a lusher, thatchy annual meadow-grass turf cut at 3.5 or 4 mm. Mowing height should never be varied significantly over a short period. Gradual adjustment, say no more than 1 mm at a time, is the way to prevent stress to the turf and to achieve the desired quality of cut. There is a basic rule of thumb that no more than one third of the length of the grass leaf should be removed in a single cut.

In addition to setting up or checking the mowing height every time you cut the green, it is also important to prepare the turf for a cut. This should involve removing all surface debris that might interfere with or damage the mower and clearing dew or any other source of surface moisture. You will get a cleaner cut, with more efficient collection of clippings, by mowing dry, rather than wet, grass.

Effects on the turf

Except in special circumstances, clippings should always be boxed off when cutting a bowling green. Allowing clippings to fly increases the threat of more rapid thatch accumulation and can spread weed seeds (notably those of annual meadow-grass). The increase in organic content of the turf may enhance disease activity and there is the obvious concern, from the bowler's point of view, of debris on the surface when clippings are allowed to fly. Research has shown that boxing off clippings decreases the incidence of worm casting. Only when turf is under severe drought stress can a case can be made for letting clippings fly temporarily.

Grass does not just grow in an upright fashion and occasionally procumbent growth can develop (some grass species being more prone than others). Flat growth can influence the run and speed of the surface. The use of a fixed rake or comb attachment to the mower, usually positioned behind the front roller, can help lift procumbent grass leaves into the cutting unit thereby giving a more effective cut and better bowling surface.

Speed and patterns

The speed at which a green is cut, assuming the quality of machine and setting is to the same standard, will depend on the width of the cutting unit. These vary from 46 cm to 66 cm width, but most greens will be cut with a machine with a 51 or 61 cm wide bottom blade. This will allow an average sized green to be cut within 1 hour and 45 minutes. The width of the cutting unit will affect the quality of cut on more undulating surfaces. The narrower the unit, the more tightly it will follow contours thus reducing the risk of scalping.

The "wheelbase" of the mower, namely the length between front and rear rollers, may also be relevant on undulating surfaces. Furthermore, fixed or floating heads on the mower may be another consideration to take into account

The mowing pattern carried out on the green is another important aspect of the operation. The ideal is to vary the direction of cut as much as possible to prevent the development of any nap or grain. Washboarding, a mowing fault that on some uneven greens can result in further surface undulations, is another symptom of repeated cutting in the same direction. In practice however, this has to be compromised to limit the effect of any single mowing operation on the bias of the bowls. For this reason, flat rink greens should never be cut along the line of play but always cut diagonally during the playing season. Vary this as much as possible. Flat greens can be safely cut along the line of play on occasions during the close season. As the crown green game is played in all directions, there is more scope to mow parallel to the sides of the green, again changing the starting direction with each cut, producing what is often termed a "Union Jack" pattern of mowing.

Each mowing operation will usually be completed by making a clean-up or perimeter cut of one or two widths of the mower, although this could also be varied to three or four perimeter cuts on occasions if turning the mower after cutting across the green can be brought in from the edge by several feet. Varying the mower turning points from time to time and then taking the necessary perimeter cuts can help reduce wear on the edges, so often a problem on some greens. There may be a place for leaving a slightly longer fringe round the edge of the green which can be achieved by missing out the perimeter cut now and again or, a better practice, to have a back-up mower set to a higher cut. This, however, is unlikely to be acceptable where championship bowls are to be played.

Mowing in a straight line is a desirable skill, not only in terms of presentation but also to achieve an even cut with minimal overlapping. The trick to straight line mowing lies on keeping one's eye on the end-point of the run rather than on the mower itself or the stretch of grass immediately in front of it.

Obviously, mowing is such a frequent operation that every club must posses a pedestrian cylinder mower of suitable quality. It is also very useful to have a back-up mower in case the main mower breaks down or has to go away for servicing. It is also sensible to use the back-up mower for cutting the green for several days after applying top dressing, rather than wearing down the blade on the premier machine. If contemplating buying a new mower, always keep the existing one rather than trading it in, provided it is still capable of cutting the green. There are mowers on the market that can perform a variety of maintenance functions through interchangeable cassettes, e.g. verticutting, brushing and spiking reels. These may be an answer for clubs working to a tight budget but if the mower breaks down you may lose out on the ability to perform some mechanical treatments.

SCARIFICATION

This term encompasses all raking operations to the green, i.e. scarifying, verticutting and grooming. They all involve the use of vertical rotating blades that remove lateral growth as well as more intense operations that lift litter and thatch lying at the base of the turf. Spring

Dennis mower with cylinder cassette

Dennis verticutter cassette

tined wire rakes are also available but their employment on bowling greens is generally limited to local work to attack coarse grasses, patches of moss and creeping weed.

Whilst one can still see some old hand-operated rake-type heads on frames at the back of some greenkeepers' sheds, powered pedestrian-operated rotary scarifiers are the preferred option for bowling green work. Professional machines are petrol-engine driven but there are scarifiers on the market that are run off mains electric. These are strictly for the domestic lawn and are not built for the rigours of bowling green work. As mentioned previously, there are also some cylinder mowers available that have interchangeable reels with optional verticutting cassettes.

Conventional scarification

Thorough scarification treatment, which is usually a vital component of a green renovation programme, necessitates the use of tough, tempered steel blades as they are expected to cut into the thatch that lies at the base of the turf. Invariably, conventional scarifiers can penetrate no deeper than 6-8 mm into the thatch, any deeper and the machine will struggle or the operation will rip out a lot of the grass cover as well. Intensive scarification must be left for the end of the playing season but completed whilst there is enough growth for recovery. It is the ideal preparation for top dressing and seeding, producing parallel grooves in the turf invariably at quite close spacing. Several passes can be made if thatch is a real problem but, if this is done, each pass must be angled across the previous one by some 15-20 degrees. Never make a second pass with the scarifier at right angles to the first as this will result in cubing of the turf, often resulting in damage to the surface. In many situations, end of season scarification is not severe enough, the operator being frightened by the amount of material that can be removed. This is a destructive operation intended to clean out the thatch, so be bold!

Deeper scarification

Conventional scarifiers can only safely work to several millimetres depth. However, with the comparatively recent introduction of tungsten tips to scarifying blades, there are now machines that can work much deeper. The Graden and the Sisis Rotorake 600 scarifiers claim to be able to work to 45-50 mm depth without causing extra disruption to the surface. This ability could prove invaluable, as the most problematic thatch to deal with is that which lies in layers to the top 50 mm or so of the soil profile. This thatch has accumulated over the years, a bit like tree rings, with each year's fresh thatch development buried by top dressing rather than being scarified out. The units can take 1, 2 or 3 mm blades and the latter are considered the most appropriate for renovation work as a preparation for top dressing. Such severe scarification has been shown to be more efficient than hollow coring as a means of removing thatch, with up to 14.1% area impacted using the 3 mm blades compared to only 4.91% with 12 mm coring tines set to produce a 50 x 50 mm hole pattern. One must be careful, however, when using such robust machines. For example, the turf has to be in relatively good vigour for rapid recovery and top dressing must be worked in soon after treatment, particularly with the larger width of blade if employed to any depth to resolve a deep and serious thatch problem. Without doubt, deep scarification treatment does bring a tremendous amount of debris to the surface, so be prepared for a massive clean up operation if using such a machine. As part of the renovation programme, experience suggests that coring or deep tine aeration is best completed before deep scarification.

SISIS R600

A gentler touch; verticutting and grooming

Less severe scarification in the spring is good preparation for the growing season, cleaning out any litter and organic debris that has built up over the winter. The same sort of blade as employed at the end of the season could be used but a single pass at a much shallower depth often suffices at this time. This operation should be timed to take advantage of any previous moss control measures, the scarification lifting out any dead moss. It might also be seen as a precursor for any light spring top dressing.

Verticutting is the term used for gentler scarification treatment, which should be ongoing through the growing season. This term originated from the golfing world where verticut reels are an attachment to ride-on triple green mowers. The finer blades on a verticut reel, which are set close together, are used to lift procumbent growth, a partner to mowing if you like, with the "vertical mowing" action of the scarifier complementing the horizontal cut of the mower. With regular operation, at least once a month and perhaps even weekly, verticutting can prevent excessive thatch accumulation through a season, which may mean less of a need for severe scarification later in the year. Removing lateral growth also encourages the grass to tiller, producing a denser turf with a more upright growth habit. The result is often greater pace to the surface. As with mowing, passes with the verticutter should be as varied in direction as possible though, again, across the diagonals on a flat green. The scarifying marks or "tramlines" from a single treatment should grow out within two or three days of the operation. If not, the unit is set too deep.

Obviously, all debris brought to the surface when scarifying should be boxed off or swept up on completion of the exercise.

Grooming is the final refinement within the family of scarification treatments. Another introduction from the golfing fraternity, pedestrian cylinder mowers can be purchased with a groomer reel attachment. The reel consists of a row of closely spaced blades, much thinner steel being used, as the purpose of the groomer is simply that, to groom the turf. The reel, sited in front of the cutting unit, rotates very fast and has the dual action of cutting off leaf tips and lifting the grass up so that the cutter following close behind takes off more of the leaf than it might otherwise. Consequently, more grass is removed when mowing with a groomer reel attachment. This means that you can achieve the same pace to the green at a slightly higher cut, reducing turf stress. Overuse of grooming reels can, however, add to turf stress. This is especially true during spells of drought when all scarifying operations should be postponed. Invariably, the groomer units are set to operate about 1 mm below mowing height.

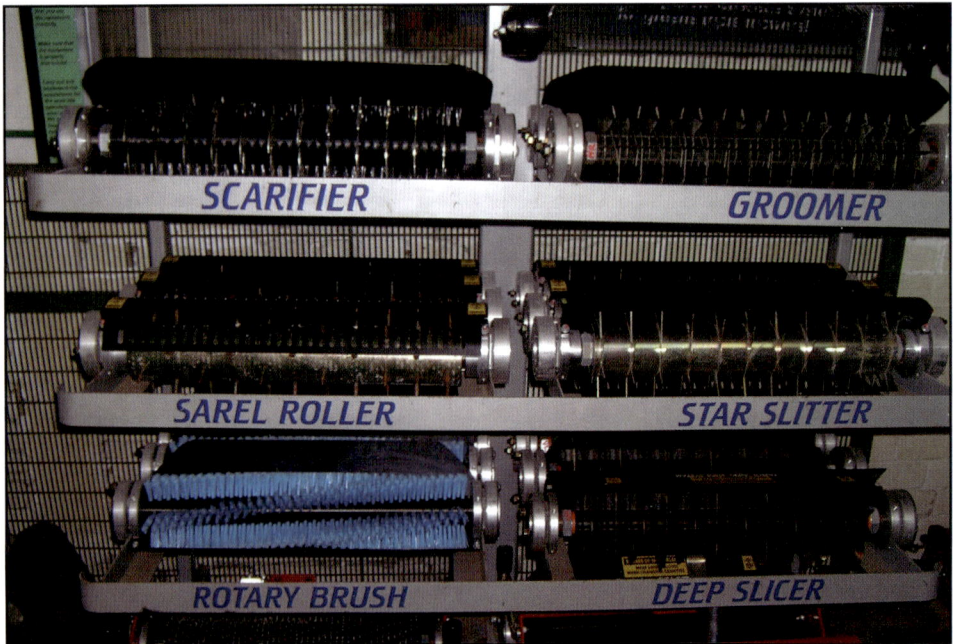

Various cassette heads for the Greentek Supa-System

Brush and comb which fit behind the front roller on some mowers

Groomer unit (between the grooved front roller and the cylinder)

All scarifying treatments should be undertaken in a straight line. Never turn the machine on the surface with scarifying reels in operation, not even the fine groomers, as this will cause severe scalping.

Machinery maintenance is important if the best results are to be achieved. With scarifiers, the most common fault is using worn blades. The tines to the reels wear down with use, though the manufacturers of tungsten-tipped models claim that this does not happen to their reels. Worn, rounded blades are inefficient and increase surface disruption, so replace reels as often as is necessary to achieve the full benefit of the operation.

AERATION

To achieve good grass growth, the growing medium needs to provide an anchorage with ample air space to allow for root development, drainage and nutrient up-take. In a healthy growing medium, air needs to make up for approximately 50% of its volume. Compacting forces at the surface, e.g. play and maintenance equipment, squeeze this pore space thus limiting the potential for root action and water movement. Compaction leads to shallow-rooted, easily stressed turf, an increased rate of thatch production and possible waterlogging. It is a wholly undesirable condition and one that can be combated and reversed through aeration techniques.

Aeration is a mechanical means of increasing porosity to the soil. This is achieved through the use of hand forks or pedestrian-operated or tractor-mounted aeration units which have tines that penetrate into the turf and soil. There are many different aeration techniques, most of which will have a role in bowling green maintenance. It is important to consider aeration as a package, a programme of different techniques designed to improve soil condition to the full so that the turf growing in the soil is as healthy as it can be. Only by achieving this end goal will you have the quality and density of turf on which to perform other management operations such as mowing, scarifying and fertiliser treatment.

Common forms of aeration

There are three basic forms of aeration operation:–

● **Slit or chisel tining** where knife-like blades slice through the soil. The aim when slit tining is to achieve penetration from 75-150 mm depth, introducing air and cutting into the thatch. The rotating action of most slit tining units will help push sandy dressing material through the thatch and work some of it deeper into the soil profile, perhaps reducing the risk of layering. As with all forms of aeration, improved root action is seen, indeed slit or chisel tines are sometimes called root-pruning tines. Slitting is also a form of aeration that can be completed very frequently, it has not been unknown for fine turf to be slit tined every couple of weeks through the winter months. This degree of repetition may not be necessary or desirable, as too many slit marks across a surface can produce a rippling effect. Slit tining should be postponed over the winter during periods of frost, snow or extreme wet weather. More harm than good will be done if working on a soft of frozen surface. It is important to recognise that this form of aeration is usually confined to the close season as slit marks can open under dry spring and summer conditions, which could seriously affect the playing quality of the bowling surface. On flat greens, successive passes with the slitter should be made along the same line or, at most, a slight angle to this. Cubing and breaking up of turf is possible if slit tine marks cross at right angles. There are punch-action aeration machines that can take chisel tines and these produce a much narrower surface slit than the rotary units

- **Solid tining.** Solid tines quite simply produce a round hole in the ground as a consequence of pushing the tine into the surface. Revolving drum-type aerators are the most frequently seen aerators owned by bowling clubs and these are acceptable for shallow to moderate depth work (say up to 100 mm). Solid tining is the best option for summer aeration treatment as a means of relieving compaction and perforating the surface for maximum irrigation performance. Whilst not particularly deep, there is also a place for the spiked or Sarel roller, particularly along highly trafficked rink ends where 14-28 day treatment during the playing season is advisable. The mowers with interchangeable cassettes previously mentioned can have a spiked roller option. However, punch-action solid tining machines are the favoured means of undertaking this operation as they produce a cleaner hole often to greater depth and closer spacing. It will take a couple of passes with a revolving drum-type machine to achieve the 50 x 50 mm hole spacing that is one of the common set patterns for a punch-action machine. Deeper solid tining, often referred to as Verti-Draining, even though this is the make of an actual machine, is quite popular on bowling greens these days, though one has to be careful when starting deep tining as shallow-rooted turf can lift like a carpet with more intensive treatments. This lifting effect can actually apply to the commencement of any aeration regime, as even slit tining will cause plucking if aeration has been previously neglected. The range of punch-action machines available today allows for penetration from 50 to 300 mm with tines ranging from 6 to 18 mm diameter. Narrower diameter tines would be best for summer work, leaving the wider ones for the post-playing season when the soil profile needs to be opened up to fully relieve compaction through depth. In recent years many fine turf areas such as bowling greens have benefitted from small diameter 6 or 8 mm solid tines, sometimes called pencil or micro-tines. There is minimal disturbance with such tines and they can be invaluable for keeping the surface uniformly "open" during the summer. However, solid tines need not be round in cross-section. A few new shapes, such as star and cross-shaped tines, are available for some machines. The holes produced by these tines are claimed to remain open for longer than those from conventional solid tines. Most punch-action tiners have enough vibration to them to shake the soil about a bit during the aeration operation but it is only the Verti-Drain and its cousins, such as the Soil Reliever and Terra-Spike, that can give a "kick" on achieving full penetration. In effect, these deep spikers are merely replicating the action of deep, prising hand forking, though on a bowling green any significant heave should be restricted to the end of the season on greens suffering from severe compaction and drainage problems, as this action can lead to disruption of surface levels. Hand forking still plays a role in greenkeeping, notably as a supplementary treatment to overcome compaction on rink heads. The deeper and more intensive solid

Hand fork with hollow tines

Aerator with sarel roller

SISIS Arrow
punch aerator

SupaTurfman drum aerator

Sarrel roller

tine aeration operations will, generally, be confined to the end of season renovation programme, following conventional scarification but preceding deep scarification and top dressing. It is not unknown, however, for such a unit to be used in an emergency during the playing season, say to promote rapid surface drainage during a particularly wet summer so that the season's fixtures can be completed. In such a scenario, it is vital to bring in a very experienced operator to minimise injury to the turf.

● **Hollow coring**, when a plug of soil is actually removed. This is an operation that is of value in removing poor quality material, e.g. thatch or heavy soil, so that a good quantity of quality top dressing can be worked in. The same machines are used for hollow coring as for solid tining and the same quality issues in terms of working depth and hole spacing apply. Coring can be carried out with tines of 6 mm ("micro-cores") up to 20 mm ("Jumbo cores"), though 12 mm diameter tines are the ones most commonly used. Generally speaking, the narrower the core the closer the spacing. For example, it is possible to achieve a 38 x 38 mm pattern with micro-cores whereas a 100 x 75 mm pattern is probably the best that might be attained with Jumbo cores. The 12 mm or larger diameter tines are usually the ones used for autumn renovation as it is easier to work top dressing into the larger holes. The micro-coring tines can serve a very useful purpose in opening up the bowling surface coming out of the winter without the threat of disrupting the turf or levels for the start of the playing season. Indeed, these small diameter cores might even be used to treat locally compacted or dry areas through the summer. The smaller tines can usually only remove a core to around 50 mm depth, 12 mm diameter cores can be taken to 125 mm depth and the Verti-Drain can remove 200 mm plugs. These deeper coring tines may be useful if there is a need to reconnect the surface to an underlying ash or stone drainage carpet. There are few greenkeepers who still hollow tine locally using a hand fork, but not to hollow tine the entire green! It can take three weeks or so of body aching effort to hand core an average sized green, when a machine can do a similar job in hours. There can, however, be good reason for carrying out limited hand hollow tining to deal with specific problems. For some time there was an attitude that hollow coring should be undertaken every three years on a bowling green. Nowadays, coring is considered an operation that should form part of an aeration programme, to be seen to as often or as little as is necessary to keep on top of thatch and compaction. It is possible to over hollow tine core, which can produce a softer surface due to the presence of excess air pockets near the turf surface, an effect similar to that of a cushion mattress. Hollow coring is also seen as a means of redressing minor discrepancies to surface levels. Coring high spots in conjunction with judicious top dressing of depressions can gradually true up a surface but only if the degree of adjustment is slight.

Slit, solid and hollow coring tines wear with use, so it is necessary to replace worn tines if the aim is to achieve the maximum depth of penetration. There may be times when the use of worn tines is actually desirable, e.g. for shallow spiking in the summer. It is also advisable to "run in" new tines on an area of turf off the green as new tines can pull up turf and it is best to take off the shine for a clean result on the green.

Other aeration operations

There are other forms of aeration which, though not widely employed, may play a role in the upkeep of the green.

● Most of these implements that take the appearance of pneumatic drills force a long probe into the ground, at which point compressed air is blasted out of a notch at the end of the probe. The released air creates fissures in the soil which work their way to the surface. This is a technique that has been used to create a series of miniature drainage sumps in poorly draining areas, when the main hole produced by the probe is backfilled with an appropriately sized aggregate. This works best when the probe makes contact with a free-draining layer. This form of aeration may have some value in certain situations but you also have to watch that such treatment does not affect surface levels. Recently, however, Sisis have produced a more conventional tine with the capability to exude air, such tines being fitted to their more traditional aerators and facilitating quick, efficient aeration in the top 100 mm.

● Drills. These are not a new innovation, indeed some greenkeepers have been known to use ordinary electric hand drills to extricate soil out of ground suffering from bad compaction or severe dry patch. There are machines available which can complete this task.

● Water injection technology arrived on UK shores in the form of the Toro HydroJect, though there are other machines around which perform the same technique. Essentially, this involves injecting water at very high pressure into the turf which, if making repeated pulses, can achieve up to 40-50 cm penetration. The thin streams of water leave nothing more than pin pricks at the surface, so this form of aeration often finds favour with bowlers and committee members. Water injection is certainly a most effective means of tackling dry patch but the cost of the machinery means that hiring-in is the best most bowling clubs can manage and there is some debate over the aeration value of this technique if carried out on an infrequent basis.

Having the machines to do the job

Mowing, scarification and aeration are the main mechanical operations undertaken on a bowling green on a regular and routine basis. It is therefore felt that every bowling club should posses the machinery to complete these three fundamentals, not only because of the frequency of use but also to ensure that the equipment is available when it is most appropriate to use. For this latter reason, sharing these vital pieces of machinery is not a good idea. Every partner will probably want the aerator or scarifier at the same time and you can guarantee that no-one will accept responsibility for damage to the machine. Specialist contractors invariably undertake occasional more specialist aeration operations such as intensive coring, Verti-Draining and water injection. If hiring, make sure the hire company supplies a machine with new tines of the type you need. A representative of the company should run through the operation of the machine if it is a unit-only arrangement. If it comes with an operator, ascertain how much experience the operator has had with bowling green work as operating large, especially tractor-mounted kit in the confined space of a green requires a fair degree of skill.

OTHER MECHANICAL WORK

Mowing, scarification and aeration may be the most important mechanical operations undertaken on a bowling green but they are not the only ones. There are other operations that could be considered under the heading of surface care.

Rolling

Rolling is a valuable operation for smoothing turf and minor surface discrepancies but we see many agronomic problems, notably soil compaction, thatch and weak rooting, that can be put down to the use of too heavy and too frequent rolling over the years. This has been recognised for many years and there are few who still fall into the trap of believing that a fast, true surface depends on rolling. A dry, firm, true and densely grassed green will provide an exceptional playing surface, whereas a green suffering from compaction due to over-rolling will present, at best, a highly inconsistent playing arena. It is wrong to believe that heavy rolling will produce a more level green. Such rolling merely provides an even compacting effect and on a thatchy green the firming effect is very short lived as the thatch soon springs back into place.

There is a place for rolling a bowling green, but remember that the turf is rolled every time you cut it with a pedestrian cylinder mower. Coming in at around 100 kg, the mower is not an inconsiderable roller given that it is employed at least three times a week during the playing season. For bowling greens, there should be no place for a roller weighing

Rolling with the Sisis Trulevel

more than 250 kg. Every green should be rolled with such a unit two or three times in different directions (with the line of play as well as diagonally on flat greens) to provide an even firming effect in the weeks running up to the start of the playing season. This will help settle any frost heave.

Additional rolling through the playing season might be necessary to "polish" the surface for an important fixture or championship. If undertaken for this purpose, on a flat rink green roll at right angles to the line of play to be followed during the days immediately after rolling. This should only be seen as an occasional occupation and not a frequent event which could lead to surface compaction. The green may also benefit from rolling after an intensive aeration operation such as coring or Verti-Draining if there is a need to settle the surface, though any major tears or lifts should be repaired by hand first.

Rolling should never be carried out when the turf is wet or soft, as this will increase the compacting effect of the treatment. When rolling, take care to cover the green uniformly and to avoid damage to the surface when turning at the ends. The old-fashioned narrow pulled rollers should be set aside for units such as the Sisis Trulevel or the motorised ride-on turf irons.

Turf Iron

Switching/brushing/drag mats

Switching or brushing are important operations, mainly aimed at preparing the surface to get the best out of some other task, e.g. mowing. The switch is a long, flexible rod that is used in a vigorous side-to-side motion, progressively working across the entire surface. Traditional bamboo switches are still available but the most common type in use these days consists of a metal tubing handle with a fibreglass extension. The drag brush is usually a 122-182 cm wide brush with synthetic bristles which is simply dragged behind the greenkeeper.

The switch or brush should be used prior to cutting a green to clear surface debris, e.g. worm casts, grass clippings or twigs. The main aim is to clear morning dew or other forms of surface moisture so that a clean cut is achieved. Even on days when the green is not being cut, switching or brushing the surface will result in a cleaner, drier and faster bowling surface. The "dew roller" performs the same task when dragged over the green. This has very light, narrow rolls which spin rapidly to disperse water and works best on flat greens with good surface levels.

Daily switching or brushing is the ideal through the playing season but these operations should not be neglected during the close season, primarily to retain a clean turf surface. Clearing dew in the autumn will also help reduce disease incidence as the most common turf disease in the UK, fusarium patch, thrives in cool, moist conditions.

Brushing also acts as a very mild form of scarification, lifting creeping growth that can then be taken off by a mower. This can be a valuable thing to do in droughty conditions when the more severe forms of scarification, such as grooming, have to be postponed. Brushing can also be a useful means of lifting the flowering seed heads of annual meadow-grass prior to mowing so that they are more effectively removed.

A drag mat is a very good tool for working in top dressing, although, as it is flexible, it tends to follow ground contours (therefore not the ideal levelling tool). It can also be used for dispersing dry worm casts as well as dropping dews.

8 Modern Bowling Green Maintenance: Water and Irrigation

The average rainfall for Britain is about 1090 mm but there is tremendous variation, e.g. East Anglia is less than 640 mm, whilst rainfall in wet, mountainous areas of Wales is over 2030 mm.

The potential loss of moisture by evapotranspiration during the summer may be between 60 and 100 mm per month on average, according to district. Thus, in dry areas in dry months, when the rainfall may be down to 13 mm or less, the soil is very likely to dry out to the point where grass roots are unable to obtain sufficient moisture to make up for evapotranspiration losses. There is thus a need for artificial watering if colour, appearance, texture, growth and suitability for use are not to suffer. This is particularly true on bowling green turf which usually has shallower rooting than less intensively maintained turf and therefore is dependent on a smaller volume of soil for its moisture supply.

Apart from the direct benefits to the turf of ensuring sufficient supplies of moisture to prevent deterioration, an efficient irrigation system facilitates other aspects of management, making it much simpler to arrange fertiliser application, weedkilling, scarification, etc.

To maintain satisfactory top growth and colour in turf there must be sufficient soil water in the rootzone. A deficiency of water results in stress and if this is allowed to persist for more than a few days, wilting may occur and the turf can develop brown patches. In time, some of the grass could die, but such extreme circumstances are rare in the British Isles but, with possible climate change effects, such concerning scenarios are likely to occur more often.

Stress occurs whenever the rate of water loss by transpiration from the leaves exceeds the rate of water intake through the roots. Thus, stress may indeed occur when there is a reasonable supply of water in the soil but uptake by a poor rooting system is insufficient (not uncommon in very dry, hot weather). Paradoxically, shallow rooting can be related to management practices, including over-watering. Root growth depends on the soil conditions, including drainage, grass species, mowing practice, irrigation management, aeration, etc. Irrigation management which keeps the soil near saturation constantly will restrict soil air supply and rooting depth. Then, the grass roots will tend to develop mainly in the mat or thatch above the soil surface because of the better aeration there. When a large proportion of the grass roots are in the mat, the turfgrass may require watering every day in drought conditions. This means, in turn, constant wetness and more surface rooting—the problems feeds upon itself. As these conditions encourage root growth in the mat or thatch, the depth of fibre increases and becomes a distinct problem in overall turf management.

When soil physical conditions are favourable, roots will penetrate deeper if irrigation management provides water only as needed, without excessive applications, and where there is time in between waterings to allow partial drying.

Some bowling clubs may have been persuaded to part with considerable sums of money to improve and update irrigation facilities because of a marked lack of drought resistance of their greens in situations where this was not primarily due to a lack of water per se, but due to an excess of fibre (or thatch) and shallow rooting. In view of these remarks, it is clear that if we have a fibrous mat problem to begin with, watering may make it worse, especially since the mat itself is water-holding and tends to impede percolation of water down into the soil. With or without a watering system, it is still necessary to eliminate the excess of fibre and obtain better rooting.

Some grasses are known to be more drought resistant than others; fine fescue is relatively resistant to drought, whereas annual meadow-grass is drought susceptible. Constant heavy watering is likely to reduce the proportion of fine fescue in a turf and to increase the annual meadow-grass content.

IRRIGATION MANAGEMENT

Whilst grass roots need moisture at all times, a slight deficiency and some degree of stress is not always a bad thing—it allows air into the soil and encourages the roots to grow deeper, which is highly desirable. Moreover, a deficiency reduces the risk of a subsequent excess from possibly unexpected natural rainfall.

As far as most bowling clubs are concerned, just when to water is essentially a matter of knowing the green. The greenkeeper uses his experience—he may find help from probing the ground or from taking core samples to a depth of 150 mm (6 in.) to examine the soil, but often he will base his judgement on keen observation of known sensitive spots, which show up shortage of water before the rest of his turf and before anybody else has spotted that anything is wrong. There are, however, more scientific ways of assessing when watering is required and indeed how much is needed when necessary. The use of weather stations (especially in conjunction with an automatic pop-up irrigation system) collects information such as evapotranspiration losses, temperature, precipitation, solar radiation, wind speed, etc. which is fed into a programmed computer which can then calculate when and how much to water to apply through the sprinklers to achieve optimum moisture content for the soil and turf characteristics.

At the vast majority of clubs, however, where such expensive technology is unavailable, one normally considers that the amount of water given at any one application should aim at moistening the top 100-150 mm. In drought conditions this may need to be applied at, say, two to three day intervals (longer intervals in less droughty conditions), allowing a period between for the surface 50-75 mm to dry out slightly and let in air. The frequency may have to be greater on light, freely drained soils than on heavy, poorer drained soils. Soil type, as on would expect, has a great influence on the need for irrigation. Frequent light watering may also be necessary to bring on areas seeded during renovation and "syringing" is sometimes useful during extremely hot weather to keep the grass cool, if a pop-up system is available to allow this to be carried out.

It is crucial that the rate of application of the water should not exceed the infiltration rate of the turf, water will penetrate quicker into sandy soils than into clay soils and quicker into uncompacted soils than into compacted soils. There is also the question of the mat or thatch, which can at different times be very water-repellent or water-holding. Where there is difficulty in ensuring adequate penetration of irrigation water (or rainfall), spiking before watering can be of assistance. On some areas of turf there may be patches which, after drying out, take water with great difficulty and on these areas spiking is particularly important. In some cases a suitable wetting agent may be used to assist moisture penetration.

Watering during the heat of the day is likely to lead to greater evaporation losses during application. In addition, a dry surface during the day also usually means more suitable playing conditions and a reduction in the compaction effects of traffic.

There is a fairly common belief that turf which is irrigated needs more fertiliser, particularly nitrogen. This may be true where over-watering and heavy leaching take place, but with good watering practice, irrigation losses should be very low and it should only be necessary to increase fertiliser rates very slightly to make good losses from increased growth.

When watering bowling greens, it must always be borne in mind that the needs of the grass cover are not the only consideration—the amount of watering carried out also has a direct effect on the characteristics of the playing surface. Wet greens, as a general rule, play heavier and lack pace when compared to dry greens (although sometimes one finds that a very light slick of surface moisture has, in fact, the very opposite effect on the speed of the surface). The needs of the grass sward are therefore not the only consideration as far as water management is concerned—the needs of the bowlers must be catered for as well. The two aspects of the situation are of course interrelated and the interests of the grass plant and those of the bowler often coincide—no player would be happy where areas of the grass cover had actually died from water loss, for example. On the other hand, there is a tendency for some greenkeepers to water with the primary object of maintaining the appearance of the green, sward colour and lushness taking precedence. It should always be remembered that the green is primarily a bowling surface—some loss of sward colour and growth rate in summer drought is neither here nor there providing the process is not allowed to go too far with the grass actually dying back. Some degree of drought stress can actually temporarily improve the quality of the surface and if the appearance of the green suffers in such a situation it should not be regarded as too important. Ultimately, a balance must be struck between the players' point of view and the requirements of the grass sward. One thing is clear enough—over-watering is to be condemned from both points of view. A permanently wet green is not only unacceptable from the bowlers' viewpoint, but will also suffer from annual meadow-grass invasion, soil compaction, shallow rooting and thatch development—all undesirable as far as sward health is concerned.

WETTING AGENTS

Wetting agents are detergents (materials which reduce the surface tension of water), the use of which assists the penetration of water into soil. There are a number of proprietary turf wetting agents on the market, mainly in liquid form although some granular preparations are available.

Wetting agents can be used on a routine basis on turf areas subject to dry patches at intervals throughout the summer months. They can be of particular value as spot treatments on high areas where water tends to run off. The point of using them is simply to make the watering that much more effective in sustaining uniformity of the turf area.

For further comments on this point, see the discussion of 'dry patch' in the Turf Diseases section of this book.

WATERING EQUIPMENT

Most bowling green watering systems work off mains supplies. This is often the most convenient water source but liable to be restricted or cut off entirely when most needed. Bore holes, rivers and streams are sometimes a possibility—permission is usually needed from Water Authorities to take water from such sources and it is wise to make certain the supply is not going to run dry in drought conditions. The source should be free of injurious pollution and soft water is preferable (in other words, lime-free). It is always worth having a sample of available water tested from time to time, particularly if from a non-mains source. The STRI laboratory tests large numbers of water samples each year.

The available water pressure should be between 1.4 and 4.2 kg/cm^2 for most manual types of watering equipment.

The simplest type of watering equipment (apart from hand-held hoses which still have a place even where sophisticated automatic systems are operational to cover troublesome dry patches) is the rotating or oscillating sprinkler. The latter is usually preferable for bowling greens as a squarer watering pattern is obtainable—an advantage for a turf area which is itself square. Such sprinklers are inexpensive but have to be moved frequently and are hence labour intensive and can interfere with play to an irritating extent. Rotary sprinklers may be better than nothing but tend to over-water some areas and under-water others.

Perforated hoses, oscillating lines or fixed spray-lines (water squares) are preferred by many clubs and are a commonly encountered type of watering equipment for bowling green purposes. The latter consists of a number of 5 m lengths of 32 mm diameter aluminium spray-line, fitted with brass nozzles in a carefully designed pattern to apply a gentle even 'rain' over a strip of up to 12 m in width. Each length applies up to 540 litres of water per hour (0.54 m^3/hr) at operating pressures of 2.1 kg/cm^2. The spray-lines are connected by flexible quick-action couplers and mounted on swivel ball-carriages so that they can be moved in any direction without uncoupling and without damaging the turf.

For the flat rink game, sprinklers of the spray-line variety have the advantage of allowing the whole surface of a single rink to be watered at the same time—the pipe-line should of course always be laid out along the current direction of play and not at right angles to it. This maintains uniformity of pace along the rink as a whole—watering only sections of a rink or different sections at different times produces variations in green speed which affects the run of the bowl.

Spray line

A number of the more affluent clubs have now installed automatic watering systems with fixed sprinkler heads buried in the green surround. Such systems are costly but permit efficient night-time watering with no expenditure of extra labour and minimal interference with play. A typical system for a single green would consist a 9000 litre storage tank with accompanying pump to deliver water to eight pop-up sprinklers, four in the green corners set for 90° operation and four in the centres of the sides set for 180° water throw. Sometimes corner sprinklers are omitted except in the case of particularly open sites where wind problems can affect the evenness of water distribution and hence make the four corner sprinklers mandatory. Each of these would come on automatically in turn. Connecting pipework and various valves are electronically controlled, invariably through some form of computerised system.

Automatic watering system

The advice of a specialised irrigation contractor with experience of bowling green watering is absolutely mandatory if the installation of a system of this kind is being contemplated.

MAINTENANCE IN DROUGHT

With climate change appearing to take place, the experts are predicting hotter, drier summers with warmer, wetter winters. Certainly, recent years have seen greater extremes of weather with records continually being broken and there is understandable concern, particularly in some parts of the country such as the south east, about water availability during dry years. Water restrictions in future in some parts of the UK are a real threat.

If watering restrictions are imposed, the following actions should be considered to address the drought conditions and their effects:–

- Raise the mowing height to 6-7 mm (with a very dry surface, the green should still play reasonably well).
- In very long, hot dry spells consider allowing the clippings to fly occasionally, i.e. do not box off.
- Suspend all mechanical treatments such as veticutting, which could place additional stress on the grass.
- Consider providing a very light compost dressing, which could act as a mulch and help conserve moisture. Great care will be required as the last thing that is needed is applying an abrasive material.
- Suspend all chemical treatments such as weedkilling, wetting agent treatments, etc. (although early wetting agent will be an important part of post-drought maintenance).
- If there are any dews, switch the surface to drop the dew. Hopefully, this small amount of moisture will be useful rather than letting it evaporate away.
- Spread wear and tear as much as possible.
- Consider buying in water in desparate situations.
- Close the green if conditions are bad and deteriorating (perhaps acting sooner rather than later).
- Prepare a programme to renovate the green when the drought ends.

9 Modern Bowling Green Maintenance:
The Control of Weeds, Moss, Pests & Diseases

INTRODUCTION

The maintenance work covered in this Chapter consists of secondary operations which are not automatically necessary on every green every year, but may be required on occasions to combat a particular threat to the general condition of the green or the quality of its bowling surface.

Weeds, pests and diseases not only reduce the aesthetic appearance of a bowling green but also disrupt the playing surface. For example, the symptoms of take-all patch include a slight depression of the turf surface which often has little or no bentgrass growing in it and numerous broad-leaved weeds. A bowling green with take-all will not have the same playing characteristics as a bowling green with no take-all patches and a bent/fescue sward.

INTEGRATED PEST MANAGEMENT

Weed invasion is such a common occurrence that the majority of greens usually need some form of weed control work every year, even if it only consists of hand lifting the odd daisy or plantain. Occasionally, a pathogen may attack the green which will require control and insect pests are becoming more numerous on bowling greens. However, it is always better to have a maintenance plan that discourages the weeds, pests and diseases and may lead to greens that do not require regular applications of plant protection products to produce the optimum playing surface. This type of maintenance plan is usually referred to as an Integrated Pest Management strategy (IPM).

The first step to a pest management programme is to produce a sward that is as healthy as possible by appropriate maintenance procedures. Overall, a sward that is growing healthily will be much less susceptible to infection by pathogens and weed ingress. The turf should be adequately (but never excessively) fertilised at the right time of year. It should not be over-watered nor should the grass be stressed by drought. Thatch should be controlled to prevent excessive levels building up. Aeration procedures should be implemented to produce an aerobic rootzone. The cutting height should be appropriate for the grass species present and airflow over the green should be encouraged. All of these factors will encourage healthy turf and reduce the chance of pests, weeds and diseases becoming a problem.

However, even on well-maintained greens, pest, weed and disease problems can arise. The most important operation is then the precise identification of the problem. Only by accurately achieving this can one put in place the most appropriate management plan. If you are unsure, contact your local adviser or STRI for help in identification. Management will then depend on the nature of the specific problem.

WEEDS AND WEED CONTROL

What are weeds?

A weed can be defined quite simply as a plant growing in the wrong place. Thus, a petunia or a potato would definitely be a weed if growing in a bowling green. In the UK, turf for bowls surfaces should ideally consist of only two grass species, bents and fescues. In such swards all other plants are weeds that may spoil the appearance and playing quality of the sward, compete with the desired turfgrasses and harbour diseases or insect pests.

Weeds may occasionally serve a useful purpose by indicating turf faults or inappropriate management practices. Examples include excessively low soil pH, bad drainage or lack of nutrients. Some weeds are particularly associated with each of these problems. When this is the case, it is essential to pay attention to the underlying fault. Unless this is corrected, no amount of chemical weed treatment will be effective. If the fault is corrected, the weed may disappear without any specific treatment but simply because conditions no longer favour it. This approach is central to the concept of IPM.

Broad-leaved species

Broad-leaved weeds can be categorised into three different types:–

1. **Annuals**—plants which flower and seed in one year. These are generally found in new seed beds but tend to mow out once frequent cutting starts, e.g. common chickweed.
2. **Biennials**—plants which grow and flower over a two year cycle, e.g. ragwort.
3. **Perennials**—plants which usually flower and seed over more than two years, e.g. dandelion. Perennial weeds are the major problem in amenity turf.

Weedgrasses

Weed control in swards of fine turfgrass will also mean the control of undesirable grasses. These may include perennial ryegrass (*Lolium perenne*) or Yorkshire fog (*Holcus lanatus*), which are seldom considered acceptable in fine turf, and annual meadow-grass (*Poa annua*), which is best considered a pernicious weed in turf and not an essential turfgrass.

Discouraging weed ingress

Weeds are distributed in the various ways (listed below) as seed or as plant fragments (for example pieces of rhizome or underground stem):–

1. Wind.
2. Flooding.
3. Birds and animals.
4. From weed-infested banks or surrounding lawns.

5. Contaminants in grass seed.
6. Weed-infested, unsterilised compost or other top dressing.
7. Equipment (particularly mowers) and shoes.
8. Use of poor quality turf.

These sources of contamination should be constantly borne in mind by the greenkeeper, especially those that are under his or her control, and particularly the last three.

Construction/establishment phase

Weeds from soils and rootzones

Seeds can remain viable in unsterilised soil for many years, although their actual longevity is determined by the species and the soil conditions that have prevailed. After preparing unsterilised soil for sowing with turfgrasses, weed seeds almost invariably emerge from this source. These can consist of grasses and broad-leaved species and they may be annual plants, biennials or perennials.

The standards expected of a bowling green are such that virtually no weed species should be present in the developing sward. This means that the soil or rootzone material that forms the surface should be sterile, a condition that can be achieved by raising its temperature to one which kills any living material within it. Of the processes involved in the construction of a new bowling green, this is usually accomplished by the specialist supplier of the soil or rootzone material.

Fortunately, once cutting of a newly seeded area begins, many weeds die out. They are unable to tolerate the close mowing regime. Nevertheless, problems can arise if a weed-ridden sward is not mown early enough as fast-growing broad-leaved weeds can prevent the successful germination and establishment of those grass seeds nearby. The most troublesome circumstance is, however, the occurrence of weedgrasses in the developing sward. Many of these are able to tolerate the close mowing and examples include perennial ryegrass, annual meadow-grass and Yorkshire fog. As well as being able to tolerate close mowing, at the moment these weeds cannot be controlled by chemical means and hand weeding is the only option.

Weeds in seed and turf

Grass seed mixes can also be contaminated by weed seeds. For this reason, only certified seed from reputable suppliers should be used when establishing a bowling green in this way. Standards of seed quality are such that serious problems arising from this form of contamination is comparatively rare.

Most new bowling greens are established from turf. The Turf Growers Association have defined standards of quality for turf and these include reference to its weed content. For the resurfacing of a bowling green however, it is not unreasonable to ask for new turf to contain no visible weed species at all on delivery. The best approach is to arrange for someone suitably qualified to examine and approve the turf at the turf farm before it is actually placed on order.

Even then there is still the possibility that weed seeds originating from the turf farm may germinate and establish on the bowling green soon after the turf has been laid. Unfortunately, the extent to which this can occur is almost impossible to predict. Liability for this is also difficult to allocate. The best approach is usually to plan for the prompt removal by hand weeding of weed species as they emerge.

Cultural practices on established greens

Any process that results in a scarred or weakened surface can provide conditions in which weeds may thrive. Although these problems generally cannot be avoided if the turf is to fulfil its purpose as a bowling green surface, it is usually possible to minimise damage or preparations can be made to deal with foreseeable problems.

Controlling play

The manner in which the turf responds to the intensity of play is very much related to its general health but spreading wear over time and over the surface of the green is always effective. On flat rink greens this involves regular rink marker movement and changes in the direction of play. A commonsense approach to allowing play to continue in unsuitable conditions is also necessary. Bowlers should also be encouraged to step down onto the green at varying points around the green's perimeter.

Mowing

Height of cut affects weed population. Allowing grass to grow very long and then shaving it very closely will encourage weeds by weakening the grass. In fact, any treatment which weakens the grass will encourage weeds; for example, excessive scarification or careless fertiliser application can leave bare patches which may then fill up with weeds.

Fertiliser

Weed species can thrive in both over and under-fertilised greens so it is vital that the appropriate fertiliser programme is followed. This is discussed elsewhere. Many weeds are associated with particular soil conditions and the choice of fertiliser can often be used to adjust these conditions in order to reduce the tendency for weeds to establish.

Irrigation

Regular light watering can create a surface that encourages the germination of weed seeds. Irrigation is discussed elsewhere but in addition to adopting a generally austere use of water, the heavier, less frequent approach to its application is usually to be preferred.

Top dressing

Like soils and rootzones used in new constructions, and for similar reasons, top dressings should always be sterilised prior to application. Usually they can be bought in this condition.

Overseeding
Maintain a strict control on the seed that is applied to the green for the renovation of worn areas, etc. All too often, patches of perennial ryegrass develop due to the careless inclusion of this species in a seed mix.

Earthworms
A plentiful earthworm population results in a large number of casts; each of these smothers grass and provides a seed bed for weeds. For this and other reasons, it pays to limit earthworm numbers and further discussion of this is provided below.

Hand weeding
Regular hand weeding is the cheapest and simplest method of weed control and the only really reliable one at present for grass weeds, though it must be done effectively, cutting weeds out at root level rather than just pulling up the leaves.

Chemical weed control

With the range of chemicals now available, most broad-leaved weeds of turf are fairly readily controlled. Chemicals, however, are only one means of achieving control and should form only one part of a good general management strategy aimed at maintaining a first-class turf surface.

The 'ingredients' of weed control chemicals
The term 'weedkiller' is best restricted to proprietary products, sold under trade names. It is the active ingredients in these products that are usually described as 'herbicides'. For example, three different proprietary products or weedkillers 'x', 'y' and 'z' might have in common the same active ingredient (a.i.) or herbicide, for example 2,4-D or mecoprop-P. Some weedkillers may contain two or more active ingredients.

The proportion of active ingredient often varies between products. Two firms may sell weedkillers with the same active ingredient but one may formulate its product with 20% a.i. while the other with 30% a.i.

Products also differ due to the various additives that may be incorporated such as wetting agents, colourants or perfumes. Usually these additives affect the specificity of the product with regards to what it is actually intended to do. Very often, a range of products will contain the same active ingredient but only a few of these are designed for use on bowling greens. Individual products are only suitable for use on specified crops or surfaces. Only those products approved for use on fine turf should therefore be used on a bowling green.

Once turf is well established, numerous herbicides for controlling broad-leaved weeds can be used. A few can be used at an earlier stage in a sward's development. Manufacturers provide detailed information on the weeds controlled by their products, how and in what circumstances they should be applied. The product label provides most of this information and so this should be carefully consulted to determine the best product for a given situation.

Use and types of herbicides

Herbicides may be placed in two broad categories: non-selective and selective. We are concerned chiefly with selective herbicides.

Non-selective herbicides

These are also known as total herbicides and include such well-known active ingredients as paraquat and glyphosate. They will kill all green material that they come in contact with and are often used to 'clean' areas of vegetation before re-establishment. Some non-selective herbicides will be used for controlling weeds in the hard standing areas around the green and in the car park, etc.

Selective herbicides

These products kill the weed plants but do not damage the desirable plants. In the case of bowling greens, they would kill the weeds but not damage the grass. They achieve the kill by imitating and corrupting the action of naturally occurring growth regulators ('hormones') within the plants. After being taken into plants, chiefly through the leaves and also to a small extent through the roots, they act to destroy susceptible species, upsetting normal metabolic processes and distorting growth. The effects can be seen in the twisting of leaves and 'freakish' growth within a day or two of application, although the weeds may not actually die for four to eight weeks. Resistant species either take in less, for example because of the angle and type of leaf, or avoid the poisoning effect in other ways.

Selective herbicides commonly used in turf include 2,4-D, mecoprop-P, dicamba and MCPA. Products may consist of a single active ingredient or a mixture of two or more. The efficacy of each product will depend on the mixture and the amount of each active ingredient. For example, MCPA is better against mouse-ear chickweed than 2,4-D but possibly worse against daisy, while MCPA in mixture with mecoprop-P is particularly useful against clover.

When and how to apply selective herbicides

Selective weedkillers based on growth-regulator herbicides may be applied at any time from spring to early autumn, but late spring applications usually give most satisfactory results. The best conditions are fine, warm weather when the soil is moist and growth is vigorous. Catching the right weather and growth conditions is the key to success. Treatment in late autumn or during drought may damage turf. Heavy rain shortly after application can reduce effectiveness while wind brings the risk of drift.

Make sure equipment is calibrated and in good condition in advance. Don't leave this until the last minute.

It is often beneficial to give a nitrogenous fertiliser 10-14 days before applying growth-regulator herbicides which act best when both weeds and grass are growing vigorously.

Weed control work can thus be linked in with the normal spring/summer fertiliser treatment.

Leave turf unmown for a period after spraying to allow intake of herbicide from foliage before it is mown off. An interval of two to three days is preferable, but at the very least leave one clear day before mowing. It can also be useful to leave one to two days growth before spraying so that there is a little more weed leaf to take the herbicide spray.

Growth-regulator herbicides are very powerful and can affect plants even in minute doses. Risks are very real where plants other than grass and cereals are grown nearby. Do not treat areas of turf near valued plants in flower beds, etc. except on a calm day. If contamination of such plants is suspected, wash them down copiously with clean water. Clean out equipment thoroughly after use and dispose of all washings safely (see later section on pesticides).

Iron sulphate

Calcined sulphate of iron is a slightly different 'herbicide' that is often included in fertiliser mixtures for turf. It helps to keep weeds out of clean turf and to reduce their numbers in weedy turf. A lawn sand consisting of 1 part calcined sulphate of iron, 3 parts sulphate of ammonia and 20 parts (by weight) sand or compost applied at 140 g/m^2 will help to eliminate, or at least control, many weeds including some like parsley piert and speedwells which are difficult to control with other herbicides. Sulphate of iron is also used against moss (see later section on moss).

Common weeds and their susceptibility to herbicides

The first requirement for successful weed control is the correct identification of the weed or weeds occurring on a particular green. It is outside the scope of this book to provide instruction which would allow the identification of all the weeds likely to be found in bowls turf. An inspection of the green in company with an experienced greenkeeper or other expert is probably the best way in which the amateur can learn weed identification, but a Flora of the British Isles (with colour illustrations) can be helpful. As with the grasses however, the appearance of a weed can be rather different when it is in close-mown turf. Broad-leaved weeds are at least easier to tell one from the other than the grasses.

Weedgrasses

This subject has been covered elsewhere in this book, but it is appropriate to reiterate here that at the moment there are no recommended selective herbicide treatments for annual meadow-grass or coarse weedgrasses in turfgrass swards. Various herbicide treatments developed for agricultural grassland or grass seed crops are either unsafe or still untested for the conditions of intensive turf management and use.

The best prescription for avoiding annual meadow-grass in turf is to prepare a clean seed bed, sow good cultivars of the required species and then manage the turf to favour them rather than the annual meadow-grass.

Daisy, a common weed susceptible to selective weedkillers

The moss-like weed pearlwort is one of the commonest and most troublesome of bowling green weeds

Mouse-ear chickweed can be troublesome, particularly early in the bowling season

White clover is a common creeping weed which can be weakened by scarifying and combing

All speedwells are very difficult to eradicate with selective weedkillers but are fortunately not all that common in bowling surfaces

A clump-forming weed, toad rush, can commonly be found on bowling greens.

In the absence of herbicide treatments that can be recommended for turf, scattered plants of weedgrasses are best dealt with by hand weeding (pulling or cutting out) young plants as soon as they are noticed. Always take care to remove the whole plant. "Mowing out" is a slow and often unreliable process, although much improved by the use of the grass comb or groomer on the mower.

Yorkshire fog is often a special problem. In newly sown areas, remove young plants by hand. Once plants become well-established, they may be weakened by slashing by hand with a knife across the patch, coupled with raking during mowing, or by scarification or grooming. The only certain treatment, however, is to cut plants out at the roots and, if necessary, replace the turf with new sod.

MOSS AND MOSS CONTROL

Mosses are weeds like any other, but are distinguished from the broad-leaved weeds covered previously in that they are members of a group of relatively primitive non-flowering plants, the Bryophyta. Selective weedkillers are not effective against mosses and a persistent moss problem is often an indication that the grass cover is weak in some way and cannot therefore compete vigorously enough to keep moss patches out of the sward. In such a situation, strengthening the grass cover is the long-term answer—using mosskillers is merely disguising the problem and has a purely temporary effect, doing nothing to counter the underlying causes of moss invasion.

Mossy green

A number of management factors can encourage moss—low fertility, over-acidity, excessively close mowing and so on, and such conditions/malpractices must be corrected if moss trouble is to be eliminated. The golden rule is therefore to cure the cause of the moss and not to simply apply a mosskiller unthinkingly. On the other hand, even the most skillfully maintained greens can develop moss patches at times, often as a result of poor growing weather weakening grass competition. In such circumstances, prompt use of a mosskilling chemical is all that is required and the moss disappears once the weather moderates and grass growth picks up.

Mosses found in British bowling greens may be considered to fall into three groups:–

● **Type 1**: Fern-like, usually trailing: *Hypnum* and *Eurhynchium* ssp.

Present in many types of turf but often overlooked. Characteristic of moist, rather spongy swards where there is a soft surface mat. Such mosses are often a problem on neglected greens.

● **Type 2**: Tuft, mat forming: *Ceratodon purpureus, Bryum* spp.

A very troublesome type of moss especially on acid soils. *Ceratodon purpureus* is common and is the so-called "winter" moss since it appears to die out in spring when active growth starts, only to reappear in the autumn. It tends to become progressively worse each winter unless checked.

● **Type 3**: Upright: *Polytrichum* spp.

Most commonly found on the dry mounds of an undulating green. Not normally very troublesome, except occasionally under acid conditions.

Moss prevention and control

Moss soon establishes on thin swards where there is a lack of competition from vigorous turf. Most mosskillers are palliative—the moss soon returns unless the factors responsible for a thin sward are removed. A strong, healthy turf is the best answer to moss, as stated above.

The following factors can favour the growth of moss:–

1. A moist turf—poor drainage encourages the fern-like and tufted mosses.
2. A very dry soil, e.g. over drains, on mounds and ridges—inadequate watering or over-drainage encourages the upright type.
3. Cutting too closely.
4. Poor surface levels—scalping.
5. A soft, spongy sward with a thick fibre layer.
6. Low fertility, e.g. deficiencies of plant foods, lime, etc. or insufficient soil depth.
7. Over-consolidation of the soil—compaction.
8. Shade.

As already mentioned but worth restating, the cultural control of moss depends on finding the underlying cause and then correcting the factor responsible. Chemical control works well in the long-term only if it is combined with cultural control.

The traditional chemical for moss in turf is sulphate of iron, applied in the calcined form, with or without sulphate of ammonia.

Sulphate of iron gives a fast kill and is cheap but is not long-lasting. It can be used alone bulked with a carrier such as sand, especially in winter, but is more often used for spring/summer application in lawn sand, e.g. a mixture of 1 part sulphate of iron : 3 parts sulphate of ammonia : 20 parts (by weight) carrier (sand or compost). This mixture is used at 140 g/m^2. Such formulations are available from most fertiliser stockists.

Other chemical mosskillers are available. They are fairly quick acting and moderately persistent. Moss on paved areas or non-grass paths around bowling greens can also be controlled using products applied at the makers' recommended rates.

For currently available products refer to the *'UK Pesticide Guide'* which is published annually or the Pesticide Safety Directorate website **www.pesticides.gov.uk**. This publication covers all the pesticides used in turf management.

ALGAE AND LICHENS

Bare ground in turf areas is often quickly covered by a green scum which may be a mixture of algae and moss protonema (filaments from which the adult moss develops). Once grass is established on the bare ground, the algae growth usually disappears. Occasionally algae form black or very dark green jelly-like masses in turf during autumn or spring.

Cultural control should always be attempted by improving grass growth and taking steps to dry the surface—spiking and sanding are often useful. Chemical control involves the use of sulphate of iron at approximately 50 g in 8 litres of water/4 m^2.

Lichens, which are a combination of alga and fungus, can occur on walls, tree trunks, soil, rocks, etc. They also occur on damp turf areas or in dry, acid situations where grass growth is weak. They are rarely as troublesome as moss in the bowling green situation. Cultural control is best, by improving grass growth. More adequate fertiliser treatment and liming may be required. Lawn sand used at the rate recommended for moss is effective if chemical control proves necessary.

PESTS

Introduction

Pests often cause problems on bowling greens. Insect pests can restrict the growth of grass species by chewing and severing the roots, leading to increased susceptibility to drought. They may also encourage birds or mammals which can destroy areas of turf searching for the food source. Mammalian pests can dig holes, excavate tunnels and leave loose soil on top of the sward surface.

Earthworms

Earthworms play a key role within the ecosystem, being major decomposers of plant and animal material within the soil. Earthworms break down litter, recycle nutrients and develop soil structure.

Earthworm biology

Each worm is both male and female but cross fertilisation is necessary. Mating takes place on the surface at night at any season of the year, providing the weather is damp and mild: eight to 16 eggs are produced in a cocoon and take from four to 20 weeks to hatch. The young worms resemble their parents except in size, and mature in 40 to 70 weeks.

Casting

Only a small number of the 25 or so different species of earthworm found in Britain produce casts on the surface, these are generally the deeper burrowing species although other species also produce surface casts in compacted soils.

Casting produced by the worms can cause an enormous headache for managers of fine turf. Machinery and players alike smear the casts to produce an unsightly muddy surface which also provides ideal conditions for the establishment of weeds and annual meadow-grass. The effect of casts on surface levels is also a problem, particularly in bowls where interaction between the ball and turf is critical.

Avoiding earthworm problems

Earthworms cannot tolerate very acid conditions but thrive where there is lime: therefore do not use lime unnecessarily. The less acidic, organic and most slow release fertilisers can encourage both earthworms and weeds. Ammonium sulphate-based fertilisers tend to acidify the turf and reduce casting activity.

Earthworms tend to prefer more organic soils. Reducing the organic matter content of soil can be difficult but keeping thatch under control and avoiding the accumulation of organic material should be central to the management programme. Avoid applying organic matter in top dressings and prevent grass clippings from being returned.

Controlling earthworms

Worms are most active in moist warm weather which usually occurs in the spring and autumn. In cold, frosty weather and in dry weather they burrow deeper into the soil. Control measures should therefore be taken in spring or autumn when they are near the surface.

Worm control can be achieved by managerial methods and/or chemical control.

1. Inhibition—management of turf areas to discourage worm activity. Avoid creating limy conditions, using excessive amounts of organic materials, or allowing clippings to fly.

2. Chemical control—these products are claimed to "kill" only surface-feeding, casting species, leaving unharmed earthworms which live deeper in the soil and which cause no damage to turf. For currently available products refer to the current '*UK Pesticide Guide*' or the Pesticide Safety Directorate website **www.pesticides.gov.uk**.

Insect pests of turf and their control

Crane fly (*Tipula* spp.)

The leatherjacket is the commonest and most troublesome insect pest of bowling greens

Adult crane fly

The most common insect pest of British turf is the leatherjacket, which is the larva of the crane fly or 'daddy long-legs' (*Tipula* species). The adults are active and fly in the autumn when they may be attracted to lights in houses. Eggs are laid in grassy places and the larvae hatch within ten days to feed either on plant tissues or decaying vegetable matter in the soil. Their feeding increases in the spring as they develop and grow. When they are fully grown the leatherjackets are about 5 cm long, grey-brown, legless and without obvious heads. Pupation occurs below ground but just before emergence the pupa pushes itself out of the soil.

Leatherjackets feed throughout the autumn and winter during mild weather, causing damage to established turf and to reseeded grass, especially later-sown turf. They feed particularly voraciously in the spring. Leatherjackets can attack young plants, biting off the stems at or just below ground level. The cut ends of the plants have frayed edges. Leaf tips may be eaten or even pulled below the soil surface. Leatherjackets are usually found near to the damaged plants or, if conditions are mild, close to the soil surface. Autumn-sown grass will usually show signs of damage by early April, although occasionally this will be seen in the autumn (November-December).

On heavily infested established turf areas, bare patches appear where the plants have been destroyed. These may quickly be covered with weeds or weedgrasses. However, in other cases the first signs are either straw-coloured areas of grass debris or the turf being pecked by birds. Often attacks remain undetected until the flush of spring growth reveals patches of greatly reduced vigour in the turf.

If poor, weak areas are seen in the early spring, with accompanying bird activity, leatherjacket damage should be suspected.

Where visible signs of damage are evident and where leatherjackets can be easily found then insecticidal control measures are justified. Insecticides should ideally be applied in the autumn/early winter when the larvae are small and before a lot of damage has occurred. For currently available products refer to the current *'UK Pesticide Guide'* or the Pesticide Safety Directorate website **www.pesticides.gov.uk**.

Fever fly (*Dilophus* and *Bibio* spp.)
Similar in their habits are the grubs of the fever fly (*Dilophus* and *Bibio* spp.). These look like small leatherjackets with shiny brown heads and occasionally appear in definite nests

Fever fly larvae are occasionally found in nests on bowling greens

in bowling green turf. There are currently no insecticides with label recommendations for the control of fever fly.

Frit fly (*Oscinella* spp.) and hessian fly (*Mayetiola destructor*)
The larvae of the frit fly or the hessian fly have occasionally been found on bowling greens. First generation adults emerge in April/May and lay eggs onto grass seedlings or new tillers. The larvae can be found at the base of the grass plants between leaves. They are creamy yellow/white and 2-3 mm long. They turn brown as they pupate. A second generation of adults emerges in June/July and a third generation in August/September. The larvae from the third generation overwinter. Damage is often not noticed until spring when the first fertiliser is applied and the grass does not respond. By this stage the overwintering larvae will have pupated and control may not be effective. For currently available products refer to the current *'UK Pesticide Guide'* or the Pesticide Safety Directorate website **www.pesticides.gov.uk**.

Frit fly larvae are found between the leaves at the base of the plant

Chafer beetles

Cockchafer larvae

Adult male cockchafer

The grubs of five species of chafer beetle are also pests of growing importance in Britain, although rare on bowling greens. The species which are the most widespread and the most troublesome in grassland are the garden chafer (*Phyllopertha horticola*) and the cockchafer (*Melolontha melolontha*). The adult garden chafer is about 9 mm long with a metallic-green head and thorax and reddish-brown wing cases. The grubs are white and about 18 mm long when fully grown. The cockchafer is the largest species. Adults have black heads and reddish-brown wing cases. Cockchafer grubs take three years to mature and can grow up to 48 mm in length.

The life cycle occupies one to three years depending on the species. Adult beetles swarm during June and July, feeding on a variety of plants. Eggs are laid in the soil, usually in the same area where the beetles emerged. Thus, infested turf is regularly re-infested each summer, although the areas with obvious damage are often different each year. Grubs feed from the summer until late autumn, when they either pupate, emerging as adults the next year (garden chafers with a one year life cycle) or they move down the soil profile and emerge the next spring to resume feeding when soil temperatures increase (the cockchafers with a three year life cycle).

Damage appears in September and October and the severity depends on the numbers of chafer larvae in the soil. Generally, more than 50/m^2 must be present before damage becomes obvious.

Usually, poorly growing patches become obvious and these turn brown in dry weather. The grubs can be found immediately below the surface. Soil in these areas is often fine in texture and 'fluffy'. This is due to the grubs actually ingesting soil as they feed on roots.

Severely damaged areas are usually sharply defined, and because the roots are severed, the turf can be rolled up like a carpet. Frequently, birds and mammals cause the most damage to the turf as they rip up the grass whilst searching for the grubs. For currently available products refer to the current '*UK Pesticide Guide*' or the Pesticide Safety Directorate website **www.pesticides.gov.uk**.

Scarification may help physically remove the small grubs when they are near the surface. Aeration treatments and water injection may also help reduce their numbers.

Rabbits and their control

Rabbits live in social groups in burrows. They can cause damage to bowling greens by grazing the grass, leaving droppings on the green surface and burrowing.

A combination of control measures is recommended. The best results are obtain in November-March, when the rabbit numbers are low due to natural mortality and before the breeding season.

1. Cage trapping
2. Ferreting
3. Shooting
4. Gassing

Methods 1-4 will be best left to trained professionals. Approved pest control can be found in the Yellow Pages.

5. Fencing: Can be effective in keeping rabbits out of bowling greens.
6. Repellents: Can give unsatisfactory results.

The mole and its control

Irish and Manx greenkeepers can of course skip this topic as their native islands are free of moles. In fact the mole is not all that serious a pest of bowling greens in mainland Britain as the presence of paths, banks and ditches around greens tends to act as a barrier to their burrowing activities—certainly moles are a more serious pest on other types of turf area. Occasional trouble with moles is, however, sometimes reported by bowling clubs and where it does occur it can be extremely damaging.

Of the following four methods of control, the first two are recommended by the government.

1. Trapping: Probably best dealt with by a professional mole trapper.
2. Poisoning by baits: Poisoning can only be done by an approved operator. Approved mole catchers can be found in the Yellow Pages.
3. Electronic: A device generating sonic vibration is claimed to clear an area up to about 1000 m².
4. Removal of worms: Moles feed almost entirely on earthworms so wormkilling can indirectly control moles.

TURFGRASS DISEASES

Introduction

Good general bowling green management is undoubtedly the best way of avoiding disease problems. Fungicides are only part of an integrated disease control programme and their ready availability must not reduce the attention paid to those cultural practices that reduce the risk of disease.

Identification

When disease appears on a green the first problem is to identify the pathogen. An incorrect diagnosis can lead to wasted (and costly) fungicide applications. Disease identification is not easy in practice, especially if more than one disease is present but reference to the descriptions given in the following pages should help. If in doubt, contact your local adviser or STRI for help in identification.

Use of fungicides

With regard to individual diseases, appropriate cultural practices that can bring about control are described in the following sections although these are most effective as a means of preventing a disease outbreak. In many cases, it will be necessary to apply fungicide as soon as symptoms become apparent. This will of course require that the turf receives regular inspection as some diseases may cause substantial damage in short periods of time. However, fungicides should not be applied as a preventative method of control in the absence of relevant symptoms.

There are three principal reasons why preventative spraying is to be discouraged. Firstly, the repeated, often unnecessary application of fungicides can be expensive, both in the cost of material and the labour required. Secondly, several fungicides have been shown to kill not only the fungus responsible for the disease but also other, beneficial organisms, some of which may help to prevent disease. This may be the reason for the observation that disease attack may be more severe after a course of fungicidal treatment has ended than if no applications had been made at all. Thirdly, repeated exposure to a fungicide increases the risk of selection of strains of the pathogen which are resistant to its toxic effects.

The following diseases are those most commonly occurring on bowling green swards.

Fungicidal control

For currently available products refer to the current 'UK Pesticide Guide' or the Pesticide Safety Directorate website **www.pesticides.gov.uk**.

Available fungicides fall into two groups. Systemic products are actually absorbed into the grass plant during growth and tend to last for some weeks—growth must be occurring for this process to take place. They often affect one physiological process within the plant and so are termed site-specific fungicides. They can usually protect the plant from infection and, because they are taken up into the plant, they can attack fungal mycelium within the plant and so cure established infections. In the winter months when no grass growth is occurring it is therefore preferable to use one of the alternative group of products, the contact fungicides.

The contact fungicides may be site-specific or may have multi-site activity (where more than one physiological process is affected). Contact fungicides remain at the site where they landed during application. They can protect against pathogens that are trying to infect the plant by forming a barrier at the leaf surface. However, they cannot cure an established infection or affect fungal mycelium that has already entered the plants.

MICRODOCHIUM PATCH	
Other names	Fusarium patch.
Causal fungus	*Microdochium nivale* (formerly *Fusarium nivale*).
Importance	The most common and damaging disease of fine turf in the UK.
Season	It can occur at any time of the year if conditions are favourable. Most often seen in spring and autumn.
Symptoms	First appears as small, green/brown water-soaked or orange circular spots. These may increase in size and number very rapidly to produce patches of dead grass. The diseased grass may be wet and slimy. Diseased patches may have a dark brown ring around a paler centre. Sometimes fungal mycelium (appearing white or pink) can be seen around the edges of patches, often matting dead leaves together.
Grasses and turf types affected	Most troublesome in fine turf, particularly if types affected are managed intensively. Annual meadow-grass (*Poa annua*) is the species most severely affected. Other grasses are also attacked.
Conditions under which the disease is likely to occur	The disease is favoured by humid atmospheric conditions and a moist turf surface. Excessive nitrogen applications, particularly the organic type, applied in the autumn often lead to rapid disease development. Top dressings applied at too high a rate or not worked in properly will smother the grass and render it liable to attack. An alkaline turf surface will also favour the disease.
Integrated disease control	Moisture control to avoid humid surface conditions will do much to prevent disease attack. This can be achieved by attention to drainage, ensuring free movement of air over the turf surface by not siting fences or walls too close and by switching to remove dew. Aeration and careful top dressing with a sandy compost make the surface less moisture retentive. Reduction of moisture-holding thatch is also beneficial, as is limiting irrigation supply to avoid excessive water in the rootzone.
	Nitrogen fertilisers and lime should not be applied during periods favourable for disease development. Cuttings should be boxed off, as returning them can favour the disease. Good turf management practices, to minimise the annual meadow-grass content, should be deployed.
	Under very favourable environmental conditions for disease development these preventive measures may not give satisfactory disease control. If the need arises, outbreaks can be fairly easily controlled with fungicides provided they are used correctly. Most fungicides sold for turfgrass use will control the disease. Systemic fungicides are most effective in the growing season as they need to be absorbed into the plant. Contact fungicides will control attacks in late autumn and winter when grass growth is slow.
	Preventative spraying on a routine basis is rarely justified, as a well-timed fungicide spray applied at the first signs of the disease will usually give satisfactory disease control. A repeat fungicide application may be necessary under prolonged conditions favourable for disease development.

RED THREAD	
Other names	Corticium disease.
Causal fungus	*Laetisaria fuciformis* (formerly *Corticium fuciforme*).
Importance	Very common disease. Mostly superficial but severe outbreaks may kill the grass but, generally, infected areas will recover from attack. Often occurs together as a disease complex with pink patch disease.
Season	During summer and autumn. May persist into winter if conditions remain mild.
Symptoms	Patches of damaged grass which often have a pink or red appearance. This is due partly to the presence of red "needles" which stick out from diseased leaves. These needles are the survival phase of the fungus. They may be straight or branched, brittle and up to 25 mm long. In severe attacks pink "candy floss" pustules may develop. The size and shape of infected patches vary from 20-50 mm up to 350 mm in diameter. Commonly, unless grass growth is poor and the attack serious, the appearance is of a fairly superficial damage to the leaves, which die back from their tips. Such patches do not have a very distinct margin and live, green leaves exist within them.
Grasses and turf types affected	May be found on any type of turf. Red fescue (*Festuca rubra*) and perennial ryegrass (*Lolium perenne*) are the species most often affected but other species are attacked occasionally.
Conditions under which the disease is likely to occur	Low fertility, particularly insufficient nitrogen.
Integrated disease control	The disease can be prevented by the selection of cultivars that are less susceptible to the disease, especially if they are to be grown in low fertility situations. During summer, applications of nitrogenous fertiliser should be made if sufficient moisture is available. This will assist grass growth and reduce the severity of the disease. However, care is needed as excessive nitrogen applications can encourage fusarium patch disease, especially where there is a large percentage of annual meadow-grass present. In situations known to be susceptible to fusarium patch disease, it may be better to rely on timely fungicide applications together with judicious applications of nitrogenous fertilisers. Systemic and contact fungicides are generally effective for control.

DOLLAR SPOT	
Other names	Sclerotinia dollar spot.
Causal fungus	*Lanzia* spp. and *Moellerodiscus* spp.
Importance	Usually a disease of slender creeping red fescue turf in the UK. It has also been observed affecting annual meadow-grass.
Season	Summer and autumn.
Symptoms	The patches of dead grass formed are usually small, typically about 50 mm in diameter, are very distinct and often circular. They give an infected area a spotty appearance. In severe attacks, individual spots may coalesce to form larger patches. Within the patches, the dead grass is usually dry, bleached white or straw coloured.
Grasses and turf types affected	In the UK certain types of red fescue and annual meadow-grass are susceptible. Slender creeping red fescues are very susceptible. The disease is seen usually only in fine turf. In other countries, the host range of dollar spot may be much wider and may not necessarily correspond with the UK situation.
Conditions under which the disease is likely to occur	Dollar spot is favoured by the presence of susceptible grasses and low fertility, particularly low nitrogen.
Integrated disease control	The disease can be prevented by choosing a more resistant cultivar. Good attention to fertiliser requirements, particularly nitrogen, is also required. Also try and keep the leaf dry, so with automatic irrigation systems use them in the early morning rather than late at night so that the time that moisture is on the leaf is minimal.
Note:	On red fescue, dollar spot may occur at the same time as red thread/ pink patch. In such cases, the red stromata of red thread disease are seen easily and diagnosis is assumed to be complete. If the fescue is susceptible to dollar spot, careful examination is essential. If in doubt, get expert advice.

TAKE-ALL PATCH	
Other names	Ophiobolus patch.
Causal fungus	*Gaeumannomyces graminis.*
Importance	Under suitable conditions for disease development, it may cause severe damage.
Season	Most active in summer and autumn but infected patches may remain all year round.
Symptoms	A ring of dying bent, from 0.1 to 1.0 m across, may be seen which is the result of a fungal attack on the roots which become discoloured. The centres of the patches tend to be occupied by grass species not suscep-tible to the disease, e.g. fescue and also by weeds.
Grasses and turf types affected	Bent (*Agrostis* spp.) is usually the grass types affected. Annual meadow-grass may also be affected.
Conditions under which the disease is likely to occur	Wetness and surface alkalinity increase the likelihood of attack and the disease occurs often when wet acid greens are limed. Take all may occur on new turf areas which have been sterilised prior to seeding and also on greens made using very sandy topsoil mixes. The susceptibility of these areas to take-all is due to the absence of antagonistic fungi and bacteria in the soil.
Integrated disease control	Once the disease has become established it is very difficult to control. It is better to prevent a disease outbreak by good management. Wet condi-tions can be alleviated by ensuring good drainage. Ideally, turf should be maintained so that lime applications are not required but if liming is essential, this should be done in autumn and followed in the spring by an acidic fertiliser, e.g. ammonium sulphate, to counteract the effect of the lime in the surface layer. Surface alkalinity may also be increased by alkaline sands used for top dressing, and irrigation water from boreholes often has a naturally high lime content. Take these factors into account when considering the management of surface alkalinity. Manganese can help prevent the onset of take-all and should be applied before symptoms are observed in May/June. Iron can also be used to suppress attacks and should be applied in August and September. Fungicides are available to control take-all and should be applied at the first sign of symptoms.

ANTHRACNOSE	
Other names	Colletotrichum basal rot.
Causal fungus	*Colletotrichum graminicola.*
Importance	A fairly common disease if conditions are suitable. Severe attacks will cause significant damage.
Season	Usually in late summer and autumn.
Symptoms	The leaves of infected plants turn yellow. Often the youngest leaf on the plant is red. Diseased plants can easily be removed and the black rotted base can be clearly seen, a highly characteristic symptom of anthracnose. On the base of the shoot, black reproductive structures (acervuli) can be seen if old sheaths are removed. Often occurs in patches but individual plants in a sward may sometimes be affected.
Note:	Leaf yellowing in annual meadow-grass may also be due to a physiological stress reaction.
Grasses and turf types affected	Annual meadow-grass is particularly susceptible to this disease, but other grasses, such as creeping bent (*Agrostis stolonifera*), have also been reported to be affected.
Conditions under which the disease is likely to occur	Usually occurs when growing conditions are poor, particularly when soil compaction restricts air supply to the grass roots and where soil fertility is inadequate.
Integrated disease control	Long lasting control can be achieved only by rectifying the pre-disposing condition, i.e. attention to fertility and relief of compaction. It is sufficient usually to improve the growing conditions. However, fungicides are available that will help to prevent the spread to other plants.

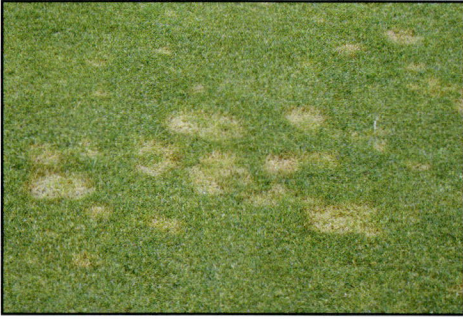
Fusarium patch disease (general view)

Fusarium patch disease (close up view)

Red thread (general view)

Red thread (close up view)

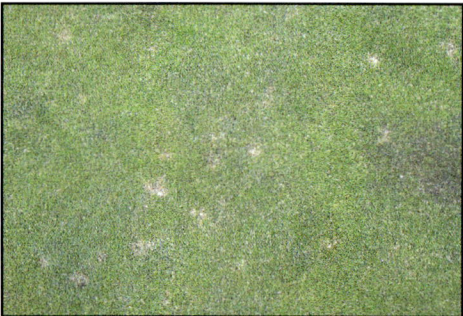
Dollar spot (initial infection)

Dollar spot (severe infection)

Early symptoms of take-all patch disease

Take-all patch bent/fescue sward (close up view)

Fungal diseases

Anthracnose basal rot

Type 1 fairy ring

Type 2 fairy ring

Type 3 fairy ring

Superficial fairy ring

Dry patch

Algal slime or "squidge"

Crow damage due to insect larvae feeding

Fungal diseases. Algal squidge and leatherjacket damage are shown for comparative purposes

TYPE 1 FAIRY RINGS

Other names	Fairy walks, fairy dances, fairy courts.
Causal fungus	Usually *Marasmius oreades*.
Importance	Not often seen on bowling greens.
Season	Rings may persist for many years but symptoms are most obvious during dry weather in the summer.
Symptoms	Type 1 rings are those that kill the grass or badly damage it. Two rings, arcs or ribbons of stimulated and darker green grass growth are seen. Between them there is a ring of bare ground. There are several ways in which *M. oreades* is able to kill the grass in this bare zone. The most important way is that the fungus creates extremely hydrophobic soil conditions, thus droughting plants out. Beneath the ring are large masses of white mycelium which has a characteristic musty smell. Small tan-coloured mushrooms may be seen in the outer ring any time between early summer and autumn.
Grasses and turf types affected	May occur in any type of turf.
Conditions that favour development	The conditions that favour the original establishment of rings are not understood fully but surface moisture may be important. Rings may be found on all soil types but are most noticeable on light sandy soils.
Integrated control	Several possible methods are available for the suppression of rings but complete eradication is difficult to achieve. An effective method of control is the laborious one of digging out **all** of the soil from an infected area.
	Wetting agents can be applied to help prevent soil becoming hydrophobic and the plants dying due to drought. Spiking before application will assist penetration. However, the mycelium of *M. oreades* is very difficult to wet effectively.

TYPE 2 FAIRY RINGS	
Other names	None.
Causal fungus	*Agaricus, Lycoperdon* and *Scleroderma* spp.
Importance	Seen commonly on many fine turf areas. Cause little actual damage to the grass.
Season	Symptoms are usually most noticeable during the summer and autumn but the fungi are present all year round.
Symptoms	Rings, arcs or ribbons of stimulated grass which is darker green and faster growing than that nearby. No actual damage is done to the grass. Occasionally fruiting bodies (toadstools, mushrooms or puff balls) are associated with the stimulated grass.
Grasses and turf types affected	Many types of turf may be affected. Most noticeable on bowling and golf greens.
Conditions that favour development	Not known. Symptoms are most marked when nitrogen is deficient.
Integrated control	No method of preventing type 2 rings is known. As the grass is not damaged, rings are often tolerated but they can spoil the appearance of fine turf. As described for type 1 rings, it is possible to dig out type 2 rings but this is rarely thought worthwhile. During the growing season the symptoms can be disguised by giving extra nitrogen to the whole area. Applications of sulphate of iron will also mask the rings by generally darkening the area.

TYPE 3 FAIRY RINGS	
Other names	None.
Causal fungus	Many basidiomycetes, e.g. *Hygrophorus* spp., *Psilocybe* spp.
Importance	Very common. Usually no effect on the grass.
Season	The fungus is present all year round but the ring is seen only for a short period, often in autumn but, depending on species, sometimes in spring or early winter.
Symptoms	Fungal activity is indicated by a ring or sometimes a less distinct pattern of fruiting bodies (toadstools or puff balls).
Grasses and turf types affected	Found in most types of turf but are not usually seen on heavily worn areas.
Conditions that favour development	Not known.
Integrated control	Control is attempted rarely as there is no change to the grass. To prevent rings from spreading to other areas, fruiting bodies are sometimes picked by hand to stop the liberation of spores. Fruiting bodies can also be removed by mowing.
Note:	As well as forming rings, fruiting bodies of basidiomycete fungi may occur also on turf areas and be seen as solitary specimens arranged apparently in a ring or circular fashion. Some of these fungi may be true lawn fungi whilst others may be colonising buried debris such as twigs or tree roots. The "magic mushroom" (*Psilocybe*) is known to occur in this manner on a wide range of amenity turf surfaces. This can present problems due to members of the public trespassing to pick the mushrooms for their hallucinogenic effects. No chemical control method is available as yet but the fruiting bodies may be destroyed using a mower or a hand brush.

SUPERFICIAL FAIRY RINGS	
Other names	Superficial basidiomycetes, thatch fungi.
Causal fungus	Many non-sporing basidiomycetes involved such as *Coprinus* spp. and *Trechispora* spp.
Importance	Common problem which seems to be increasing. Most severe forms may kill the turf. Some implicated in the dry patch condition.
Season	May be seen at any time of the year.
Symptoms	Intense fungal activity in the thatch layer of the turf, often invading grass sheath bases. Dense white mycelium is visible frequently and the thickness of the thatch layer may be reduced. A mushroom smell is often associated with the mycelium. Grass in infected areas is often greener than that on adjacent areas but may sometimes turn yellow or bleached. Various patterns are formed, including circular patches, complete rings, parts of rings and irregular narrow lines.
Grasses and turf types affected	Any type of turf may be affected. Particularly troublesome on fine turf areas where a deep thatch layer is present.
Conditions that favour development	The presence of a marked thatch layer.
Integrated control	Reduce the thatch layer by turf management practices such as aeration and mechanical thatch removal.

DRY PATCH	
Other names	None.
Causal fungus	Strictly speaking, dry patch is not a disease. However, certain types of dry patch may be of fungal origin. Certain superficial fairy ring fungi have been implicated.
Importance	Becoming increasingly common in fine turf. In severe cases, large areas of damage may be caused.
Causes	Mounds, slopes or undulations in turf are more prone to drying out in drought conditions. These areas may be levelled or aerated and watered by hand using a wetting agent. Compacted soils due to foot traffic or the extra mowing around the perimeter of the green can also cause water-repellent areas of turf. Additional aeration and watering with a wetting agent should relieve the problem.

Barren patches in fescue/bent turf can also be hydrophobic. Dead shoots accumulate and, if not removed, choke out live green growth. This leaves a fibrous surface that may become compacted and consequently very difficult to re-wet. The drier the thatch, the more water repellent it becomes. Once this process has started, it is very difficult for new growth to disrupt the barren surface.

Dry patch can also be caused by type 1 fairy rings. *Marasmius oreades* produces waxy mycelium which is water repellent. This creates localised drought which will account partly for the death of grass.

Water-repellent conditions may be produced by intense fungal activity in the thatch and rootzone where waxy materials may be deposited on sand or soil particles immediately below the thatch layer. The condition is worse in coarse sands and often sand particles may be bound together in a completely impermeable layer.

The water-repellent effect is intensified if an area is allowed to dry out completely so this should be avoided if possible. Prevention of the problem may be achieved by localised spiking and hollow tining and watering supplemented with a wetting agent. |

PESTICIDE LEGISLATION

Pesticides or Plant Protection Products (PPPs) are commonly used to control weed ingress, pest infestations and disease outbreaks on bowling greens. However, they should be used as a last line of defence as part of an Integrated Pest Management programme.

Remember that under current legislation, it is only permissible to use approved products and the conditions and restrictions on the label must be strictly observed. A guide to approved products can be found in the annually produced *'UK Pesticide Guide'*. A list of approved products can also be found on the Pesticide Safety Directorate website **www. pesticides.gov.uk**. All products should be applied according to the manufacturer's recommended rates as stated on the product label.

Always follow the product label instructions carefully and ensure that all Control of Substances Hazardous to Health (COSHH) Regulations are applied. All PPPs are potentially dangerous to the user and some are very dangerous indeed. Always be careful in measuring out and mixing concentrated herbicides: avoid inhaling the spray and store and dispose of containers carefully. If appropriate, use gloves, protective clothing and a face mask. Above all, read everything on the label before opening the container. This is now a legal requirement and all pesticide users should therefore be familiar with the Food and Environment Protection Act (1985), Part 3: the Control of Pesticides Regulations (1986) and the Plant Protection Products Regulations 1995.

Users of pesticides should be suitably qualified and hold appropriate certificates of competence. The most appropriate certificates for pesticide users on a bowling green would be PA01—The Foundation Module and PA06—Hand Held Applicators. Information on these certificates can be obtained from The National Proficiency Tests Council, Avenue 'J', National Agricultural Centre, Stoneleigh, Warwickshire, CV8 2LG (**www.nptc.org.uk**).

THE APPLICATION OF PESTICIDES TO TURF

Herbicides, fungicides and insecticides are generally formulated as liquids for application by sprayer or by watering-can.

There is a wide range of spraying equipment available. For comparatively small areas like bowling greens, a knapsack sprayer may be adequate but even better are "knapsacks on wheels" or other pedestrian equipment. A horizontal boom with several nozzles is essential if even coverage is to be achieved.

The volume of liquid applied by a sprayer depends partly on the machine itself (e.g. pump output), partly on nozzle size, and partly on speed of movement over the ground (see "Calibration of equipment"). The generally accepted definitions of the various volumes of application are as follows:–

Low volume	–	55-225 litre/ha
Medium volume	–	225-675 litre/ha
High volume	–	675-1125 litre/ha

Knapsack sprayer

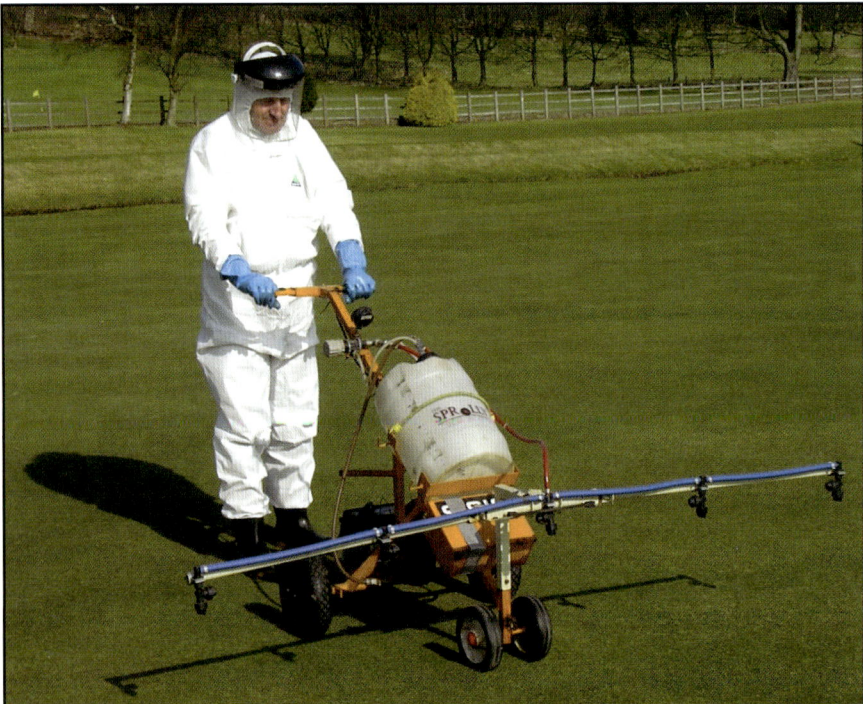

Pedestrianised sprayer

Low volume applications require greater accuracy, have greater drift risks because of finer spray, and are often less effectively taken up by weeds. High volume spraying entails more water-carrying. Medium volume, about 450 litre/ha, is normally best. Higher volumes are usually recommended where the sward or weed growth is dense. Product labels will give recommendations as to the water volume and spray quality required.

For small confined areas near flower beds, or other places where drift must be avoided, a dribble bar or an ordinary watering-can rose should be used, or a no-drift application machine with a fluted roller.

It is important to ensure uniform coverage and to avoid overlapping. To ensure success, one should use strings or pegs as guide lines. Grass is resistant to recommended rates but not to over-application. A very skilled and knowledgeable operator may be able to make successful spot treatments with a hand sprayer or watering-can but scorch is the most common result. Aerosol cans or weed-sticks are a safer method of spot treatment but the risk of grass scorch is by no means eliminated.

To spray or not to spray

In the case of weeds and pests this will be dictated by the numbers present. If there are just a few daisies on the bowling green it will be best environmentally and economically to hand weed. However, an even coverage of daisies would merit a herbicide application. Similarly with pests, when the numbers present are showing symptoms of pest damage it will be appropriate to apply an insecticide.

Diseases, however, pose a different problem. A pathogen will only infect when the environmental conditions are conducive. If the weather is mild and wet in the late autumn, fusarium patch may occur. If small disease patches in moist or wet turf are observed, a decision must be made as to when to apply a fungicide. If the weather is becoming drier or a frost is imminent, fungicide application may not be justified as the conducive conditions for fusarium patch are changing and the growth of the pathogen will be suppressed and damaging blemishes may not occur. However, if the weather forecast is for continued wet weather and the disease looks active, fungicide application will be required before the pathogen spreads, leaving large fusarium scars.

Conditions for plant protection product application

Plant protection products should only be applied in a certain set of weather conditions. The product label will indicate these conditions for that specific product. In general PPPs should not be applied when rain is imminent as the product may just be washed through the profile. They should not be applied in frost. Some products can be more phytotoxic on hot, sunny days. Windy days can cause the PPP to drift which may damage adjacent desirable plants. Some granular herbicides may need to be irrigated into the turf if no rain occurs for a couple of days after application. The advice is always to read the label and observe all precautions printed on it.

Typical pedestrian sprayer at a bowling club (hopefully not spraying anything too nasty for the operator!)

CALIBRATION OF EQUIPMENT

The following procedure will allow accurate calibration of small spraying equipment. The volume of application depends on:–
1. Walking speed
2. Nozzle output
3. Swath width

1. Walking speed

Walking speed should be timed over a given distance of ground similar in conditions to those where the actual spraying will be done. Protective clothing should be worn and water should be sprayed out from the tank. Ensure you maintain a consistent rate of pumping. Mark out 100 metres and record the time taken to walk this distance three or four times. The average should then be used.

Record this information here; seconds per 100 m

e.g: 90 seconds

The speed is measured in km hr^{-1} = 360 ÷ time in secs to walk 100 m
e.g: Speed of walking = 360 ÷ 90 = 4.0 km hr^{-1}.

Record your speed here

2. Nozzle output or flow rate

Select the pressure you wish to use for spraying. Keep the pressure as constant as possible. Select the most suitable nozzle for the operation. Even spray flat fan nozzles are appropriate for the application of fungicides, insecticides and selective herbicides to bowling greens where good cover is essential. To determine the nozzle output, water should be sprayed into a measuring jug for one minute. The nozzle output should be recorded in litres.

e.g: Nozzle output = 2.2 litres per minute

Record your information here

3. Swath width

The swath width should be measured by holding the lance in a comfortable position, walking slowly forward while spraying water onto a dry area of concrete or tarmac. The width should be measured in metres.

e.g: Swath width = 1.3 m

Record your width here

So, now we know the following, e.g:

a. walking speed   =   4.0 km hr⁻¹
b. nozzle output   =   2.2 litres
c. width of spray (swath width)   =   1.3 m

Record your information here

Walking speed [   ] km hr⁻¹

Nozzle output [   ] litres

Swath width [   ] m

4. Volume of application

The next step is to discover the amount of water which will be sprayed out over 1 hectare. Do this by calculating the following:

600 x nozzle output ÷ walking speed ÷ swath width = litres per hectare, e.g:
600 x 2.2 ÷ 4.0 ÷ 1.3 = 253.85 litres per hectare,
rounded up to 254 litres per hectare.

Record your information here

600 x [   ] ÷ [   ] ÷ [   ] = [   ]

rounded up to [   ] litres per hectare

5. Dose rate

The dose rate per hectare will be given on the product label. For this exercise the dose rate is assumed to be 5 litres ha⁻¹ which needs to be added to the amount of water shown in Section 4.

e.g: 254 litres.

If the tank holds 20 litres, find out the number of tanks full per hectare.

e.g: 254 ÷ 20 litres (size of tank) = 12.7 tanks.

Now, find out amount of chemical concentrate per tank full

e.g: $5.0 \div 12.7 = 0.39$ litres per tank full.

Record your rates here:

Litres per hectare

Capacity of sprayer (tank)

No. of full tanks per hectare

Concentrate per hectare

Amount of concentrate per tank

If we assume a standard bowling green of 40 x 40 m = 1600 m², then

The number of tanks to treat the green = 12.7 tanks $\div$ 10,000 m² (1 ha) x 1600 m² (green size) = 2.03 tanks

Record your rates here:

Size of bowling green

Number of tanks to treat green

10 Modern Bowling Green Maintenance: Miscellaneous Work

To complete our survey of modern bowling green maintenance techniques, it now only remains to consider various greenkeeping tasks not covered by the previous chapters. It should not be assumed that the topics covered in this section are of only minor importance because they have been left until last—many are vital if the required standard of bowls surface is to be achieved.

RENOVATION AND REPAIRS

Worn areas evident at the end of the bowling season will need renovating and thus the question arises, should one seed or turf worn areas? Perhaps the general answer to this question is best expressed as follows:–

- If there are bare areas at rink ends, returfing would tend to be most appropriate.
- If there are thin areas, overseeding could be undertaken if the work can be done early in the autumn.

There are, however, a number of important points to bear in mind when renovating.

Overseeding

Only use proven cultivars of bentgrass, slender creeping red fescue and Chewings fescue seed obtained from a reputable seed house. The thin areas of turf should be adequately pricked, forked or lightly raked to provide a suitable surface in which to overseed, the seed could perhaps be mixed with a little top dressing before working in. An alternative would be to employ a dedicated overseeding machine. The necessity to do this work early in the autumn cannot be overstressed if the technique is to prove successful. Make sure during the overseeding work that levels are not upset.

Turfing

If possible, aim to use turf which matches that already on the green—this is when a turf nursery on site can be so useful. If turf has to be imported, make sure that the soil in which the turf is growing is not of a heavy nature but a free-draining, sandy loam material.

One of the most common mistakes made by amateur greenkeepers is obvious when inspecting their turfing. Turf introduced into worn areas is usually left proud to allow for settlement. The latter invariably never happens or at least not to the extent expected, consequently during the first close cut the next season the area is scalped and the problem begins all over again. When returfing worn patches one should:–

1. Remove the turf to the thickness of the new turf being introduced.

2. Thoroughly fork over underlying soil, particularly if there are layers of sand, soil, peat, etc.
3. Re-firm the cultivated soil, perhaps by heeling and raking if possible to ensure an evenly firmed turf bed condition.
4. Lay the new turf on to the prepared surface so that it is flush with surrounding ground, not proud in anticipation of settlement. Top dress lightly.

There should be no settlement problem if the turf bed is properly firmed, but if the odd turf does sink a little, levels could be made good with light top dressing.

Although turfing can proceed much later into the autumn than seeding, it is still good policy to try and finish the work as soon as possible, and certainly before the worst of the winter weather arrives. One final word about turfing, particularly on rink ends; make sure the turf is mature and contains a high proportion of the desirable bentgrass. Turf dominated by young fescue grass may not be particularly tolerant of close mowing or heavy play the following season.

Levels

The advantages of obtaining an accurate survey of playing surface levels have been stressed earlier. This is of considerable help if remedial work on surface levels is being contemplated as a part of autumn renovation and repair work. With such information available, contour lines can be drawn on to the plan and a clear indication of exactly where and how big low or high areas are. It is surprising how many times people have tried to fill in a 'valley' whereas in fact the correct course of action would have been to have lowered the 'hills'.

With an accurate survey, exact remedial work can proceed. If level discrepancies are, say, ± 18 mm then remedial top dressing work over a period of time could correct low spots, whereas hollow tining on several occasions over two to three years could lower high areas. If the low or high spots are in excess of ± 18 mm it is worth contemplating more extensive work, i.e. removing the turf, adjusting soil levels as necessary and returning the turf. Such levelling work is of a specialist nature and should only be undertaken by a skilled and confident greenkeeper if the area to be covered is of any size. Large scale returfing of a major part of a bowling green's total area is probably best left to a specialised and experienced sports ground contractor. The major recontouring of either flat or crown greens is a very skilled task and the inexperienced turfer could well end up with a surface even more uneven than the one he was attempting to correct.

Raising the edges

Besides general discrepancies within the body of the green, a particular concern at many clubs is a situation where the edges of the green tend to fall away. In such instances the problem can be solved by cutting the turf into strips about 300 mm wide at right angles to the green and carefully slicing under the turf with a turf float to create a turf which can be rolled back towards the centre of the green. The turf should obviously be rolled back a sufficient distance to allow levels to be made good. Extra sandy loam soil should be bought in to make up any deficiencies in levels, ensuring that this imported material is properly firmed before unrolling and re-laying the turf to the required level. Again, it is important to be aware of the dangers of leaving the edges proud in anticipation of settlement.

If the actual edge of the green has to be raised 25-50 mm, it is not a bad idea to lay a narrow inverted strip of turf with a heavy soil right on the edge of the green upon which to eventually re-lay the rolled up turf. This technique at least produces a very firm edge to the green (due to the heavy soil)—problems can be encountered with crumbling edges if there is any significant build up of sandy soil over the inner kerb edge.

Spring renovation

Autumn renovation work is always preferable as this leaves a longer period for establishment and recovery before play starts once again. Not infrequently, however, some renovation must also be completed in the spring—in a situation, for example, where a green has been vandalised or damaged by disease over the winter months. Winter moss control can also leave bare patches where dead moss has been raked out. If moss control is carried out late in the off-season it can be wise to leave patches of dead moss undisturbed. These will slowly disappear and the grass grow in, causing less disruption of the playing surface than if the moss is raked out to leave bare spots at the start of the playing season.

Sometimes hand operated rakes can be useful on small areas

Great care must be taken if renovating in the spring to avoid adding to problems with disrupted surface levels. Success is also dependent to a great extent on the weather—in late springs no growth may occur before play starts and overseeded patches may not germinate and establish before they are overtaken by play. Spring renovation must therefore start as early in the year as possible, as soon as the weather is at all reasonable. Light top dressing, at least of damaged patches and possibly of the whole surface, can sometimes be appropriate at this time to speed germination of seeded patches and to maintain good levels. The use of some germination sheets may also be very useful.

Turfing can be most useful in the spring, particularly for the minor patching of small scars. Again, great care must be taken with levels, avoiding the practice of leaving new turves standing proud against the surrounding surface. Turf patching tools which cut square or circular turf plugs and which allow them to be fitted into identically sized holes cut in the green with the same tool are particularly useful for spring work. Similar work may sometimes be necessary during the actual playing period but the need for playing surface renovation when play is proceeding should be avoided if at all possible. It is difficult to ensure that seed germinates satisfactorily or that turf establishes successfully when the green is being cut low and renovated areas disturbed by the players.

Turf Doctor

The success of renovation can sometimes be improved by confining play to healthy areas of the green while damaged patches are attended to. It is relatively easy to close one rink on a flat green early in the autumn or late in the spring to allow for renovation, but even on crown greens something similar can often be arranged if players co-operate.

RINK MANAGEMENT

It is hoped that the crown green fraternity, to whom of course the subject is of no interest, will bear with us for a moment so that the importance of rink changing in flat green management can be stressed. The subject has been touched upon earlier, but is worth considering in more detail as it is often the cause of arguments in many clubs, with certain bowlers taking it as a personal affront that the greenkeeper has moved markers off a favourite rink position.

For a flat green the ideal to be aimed for is a completely uniform surface with constant playing characteristics over all parts. This theoretical ideal is probably never achieved in practice but it is essential to attempt to approach it as closely as possible. Any factor which tends to concentrate play and wear on certain areas of the green is hence undesirable and tends to work against surface uniformity. Where play is concentrated on popular rinks, very significant differences between used and unused parts of the green can appear in time. Worn areas tend to show a higher annual meadow-grass content, more soil compaction, shallower root growth and variable thatch than areas not played upon, which in contrast can tend to become soft, mossy and matted. Surface uniformity of playing characteristics is hence lost and it is worth remembering that a uniform surface is a key factor in separating a good green from a poor one. Changes in surface level are also a result of concentrating on a limited number of rink positions, heavily used rinks becoming gutter-shaped in time with consequent deleterious effects on bias and the quality of the game.

For the long-term welfare of a flat green therefore, it is essential to move rink markers as much as possible and to encourage bowlers to use as high a proportion of the total available area as possible. It is impossible to give hard and fast rules as to exactly how this should be done in practice as greens vary in overall size. The permissible variation for Bowls England and English Bowling Federation greens is 34 x 34 m to 40 x 40 m. There are of course many non-standard greens, some in the shape of narrow rectangles, where play is only possible in two directions rather than four. In the case of greens where the dimensions permit, variations in rink position can be achieved by:–

a. Varying the width of rinks. For the game played under Bowls England rules, rink width may be varied between 5.5 m and 5.8 m. Federation rules are more flexible, the permitted variation in this case being 4.8-6.4 m. Narrower rinks are permissible for friendly play, this being 4.3 m minimum on Bowls England greens.

b. Varying the position of rinks. Six rinks are normal for a standard sized green and fit well within the limits set by the 40 m length of the green sides. Remember, a margin of at least 0.6 m must be left between the the end rink and the adjacent parallel side of the green. Six 5.8 m rinks take up 34.8 m plus two 0.6 m margins = 36 m. This leaves 4 m spare on a full size green for varying rink positions by increasing or decreasing the width of the side margins.

c. Varying the number of rinks. The maximum number of rinks is a necessity when the green is busy, but in slacker periods it may be possible to reduce the number and hence vary positioning even further.

This question of varying playing positions can become extremely complex, so most clubs settle on a simplified system, having coloured marks along the inner ditch kerbing representing perhaps three alternative rink positions. In addition, wear should be further spread by changing the direction of play through 90° at least once a week and preferably more than once a week in wet weather or periods of poor growth.

One can never entirely escape the problem that end rinks are unpopular as they run along the worn rink ends caused by play in the other direction. All that can be done is to minimise wear as far as possible on all rink ends, bringing us back to the basic argument that play must be as evenly spread over the green as far as this is possible. The co-operation of players is a main requirement and all club members should be made aware of the long-term problems caused by the over-use of favourite rinks.

It is in fact possible on most greens approaching standard size, by the sensible positioning of full width rinks or by the use of narrower rinks for casual play, to maximise the size of spare areas of the green surface running between the outside of the end rink in play and the ditch of the parallel side. This allows the greenkeeper to work on these spare areas, which of course include the worn heads of rinks running at right angles. Spiking, hand forking and surface pricking can all be performed without interfering with the area in play. During the playing season as a whole therefore, considerable extra work can be carried out on all rink ends and it is these areas where damage is concentrated in the flat rink game. Judicious rink positioning can also allow the centre of the green to be covered during such extra work but this part of a flat green takes far less wear than the ends, so additional treatment is not often essential for the centre area of the green. This is a most important point in the maintenance of flat greens which is overlooked by many green-keepers who do not realise how much of a green's surface is not actually being played over at any one time.

The use of mats can be helpful in minimising wear. They may be particularly appropriate for use at the end of the season, say early September onwards, when major competition play has usually ceased and when greens tend to be wetter/softer and hence more easily scarred. The open-weave nylon mesh type of matting is to be preferred to denser textured materials. On the other hand, the use of mats should not be employed to play a game on occasions when really conditions are such that the green should be closed.

THE CARE OF DITCHES, BANKS AND SURROUNDS

Although the highest proportion of the greenkeeper's time will be spent on the actual playing surface itself, ancillary surrounding features of the green too need regular attention if they are to remain in satisfactory condition.

Ditches

To consider ditch maintenance first, Bowls England rules state that the surface of the ditch infilling material should be no less than 50 mm or more than 200 mm below the level of the green itself—this should be checked periodically. Requirements are much less rigid for the Crown or Federation codes.

A variety of materials are currently available as ditch infilling. A list can be presented as follows, with the possible advantages and disadvantages of each. Remember that requirements are much more exacting in the case of the EBA game where a bowl is not necessarily "dead" when in the ditch and where any lateral movement of the bowl along the ditch must be prevented.

a. Sand: grade is important—medium sands of even particle size are probably best. Coarse particles, if present, can scratch bowls whilst a proportion of silty fines can lead to packing and hence poorly drained ditches. Sand-filled ditches are somewhat prone to weed growth. Total weedkiller may be used in such situations but great care must be taken during application to avoid contaminating the edge of the green and killing the grass. Non-residual weedkiller only should be used, either a contact material such as paraquat or preferably a systemic herbicide like glyphosate. Bowls or the soles of shoes may become contaminated with the material immediately after application and hence transferred to the playing surface—the work is therefore best done when play is not taking place. In wet conditions after rain or irrigation, sand tends to adhere to bowls causing some annoyance to players. Sand is reasonably effective at killing the motion of a bowl, providing it is kept reasonably loose and not allowed to pack down too hard.

b. Pebbles: the most commonly encountered ditch infilling material is smooth, rounded pebbles, usually between 12 and 18 mm in diameter. Such pebbles are usually considered suitable for the purpose, although they are by no means perfect as some scratching of bowls can occur. An alternative material is Lytag of 10-12 mm grade. Pebbles are effective at preventing lateral bowl travel, but vandals can throw handfuls onto the green perhaps causing damage to mowing equipment, etc.

c. Corks: old wine-bottle corks can be obtained cheaply in some localities. They are excellent at preventing damage to bowls and kill motion quite well. Their main disadvantage is that they can float out onto the green in very wet conditions, or even occasionally blow out of the ditch in very high winds.

d. Wood chips: advantages and disadvantages are similar to those for corks.

e. Rubber chips: nodules of hard rubber are excellent ditch fill material, killing bowl motion very effectively and being heavy enough to stay in position. It is interesting to note that in trials comparing various ditch materials held at Worthing in preparation for the 1992 World Bowls Championships, rubber chips were preferred by players and officials. A cheap source of supply are sporting goods manufacturers—if available mis-shapen reject shuttlecock heads are also ideal for the purpose.

The above materials might all be described as loose aggregates—most become soiled in time and need to be removed and washed periodically, this usually being a winter task for the greenkeeper. Our listing can be continued to cover more rigid ditch liners.

f. Industrial belting: old mill pulley belts or strips of mine conveyor belt are traditional ditch topping for crown green ditches, usually laid as a cover over gravel or sand. Almost indestructible, such material remains popular but does not stop bowls moving along ditches and is hence unsuitable for flat rink greens.

g. Battens: ladder-like sections of wooden battens are sometimes used for both crown and flat green ditches. As an alternative in recent years, some clubs have used plastic duck-boarding as a final ditch surface with great success. This consists of a vinyl lattice of strips at right angles, actually manufactured as floor covering for changing rooms, etc. It is available in various lengths 600 mm wide, so it has to be cut down into strips corresponding in width to the bowling green ditch width. The material is placed in the ditch so that the strips of the lattice which are uppermost run across the width of the ditch, longitudinal strips being underneath. This ensures that bowls falling into the ditch do not move laterally along the ditch, as they are held in the groove between lattice strips running across the ditch. Use of this material appears to be an ideal method of eliminating scratching problems without creating any other disadvantages, and it is easy to lift for cleaning, but does not prevent weed growth in underlying sand or gravel.

h. Specialist ditchfill: seen as a dimpled black rubber material with a surface resembling an egg-box. It is easy to lift and hose down and eliminates damage to bowls. It may, however, allow some lateral movement of bowls on rare occasions, particularly if the bowl is spinning rapidly. Weed growth in underlying material is obviously eliminated, but the material is relatively expensive.

i. Artificial turf: supplied commercially by a number of firms. The only problem with such materials hinges around whether they kill bowl travel along ditches completely effectively.

BANKS

As for the green itself, mowing is of course the most frequent operation for grass banks. The traditional hand shears are still used for this purpose, usually at weekly intervals during the growing season. Spinning filament mowers of the strimmer type are now also widely used, with a considerable saving of time and labour as compared to the use of hand clippers. Rotary mowers of this type must be used carefully, trying to cut at an even 12 mm or so. Over-close cutting on bank faces is all too easy and will in time weaken the grass and encourage bank erosion.

Operations such as moss and weed control are sometimes necessary on banks and should be carried out using methods and materials advised earlier for the green itself. Weedy banks are not only unsightly but are also a source of infection, seed being easily transferred to the bowling surface. Bank renovation is usually required periodically as bank faces can erode or subside. Turfing is usually the best method of repair, pegging new turf in place as described earlier for initial green construction. Difficulties in maintaining a strong turf on bank faces is often the result of summer drought—banks tend to dry out very rapidly. Hand watering should therefore not be neglected if required; one usually finds that south and west facing banks dry out first.

Wall surrounds and high-backed purpose-made ditch units minimise maintenance work but such constructions are not completely maintenance-free. Striking boards and battens need replacement at times. If artificial turf is used as a facing, it is very easy to damage it when mowing around the edge of the green. Adhesive should be kept in stock so that sections torn by the mower can be glued back or replaced.

SURROUNDS

It is hardly necessary to say that, although a well-kept playing surface is the heart of a bowling club, required maintenance work extends further than banks or ditches. Pavilions, flower beds and other features also require regular attention and pleasant and well-kept surroundings can add a great deal to the pleasure of the game.

Of perhaps more relevance here is the fact that some features of the green's surroundings can have a definite effect on the quality of the surface. Take the case of perimeter fencing, and particularly hedging, for example. Walls, solid fencing such as larch-lap as well as hedges should be at least 3 m from the green to minimise shade effects. Shelter makes playing conditions more pleasant on windy days and a strong wind across a green can make accurate bowling doubly difficult, if not impossible. A compromise must obviously be arrived at—windbreaks should be as far from the green as is practicable and should not be excessively high. Hedges should not be allowed to grow more than 1.5-2 m high.

A further problem with hedges, particularly if they are too close, is root growth under the playing surface or into perimeter ditch drains. Turf weakness near the edge of a green can occasionally be attributed to this cause—strong growing hedge plants like conifers and privet are particularly troublesome. In certain circumstances, it may prove necessary to sever roots—usually this involves trenching around the outer edge of the path surround and infilling with broken stone (plastic sheeting to create an unbroken physical root barrier may also be appropriate) to try and prevent reinvasion.

Trees near the green can also create the same problem of drought-stricken and starved-looking areas of adjacent turf. Roots may again have to be pruned and their regrowth blocked. Overhanging branches too should certainly be pruned to minimise shade and autumn leaf fall onto the green.

Tall trees close to the green can be a nuisance

Path surrounds should be kept in good condition. As with banks, moss and weed growth can be a source of infection for the playing surface and suitable herbicides should be used if necessary.

A common query is whether footbaths of fungicide or disinfectant should be provided to prevent fusarium and other disease spores being carried from other outside turf areas onto the green. This, on the face of it, would seem a wise precaution but is in fact almost totally pointless. A cupful of soil from virtually every green in the country will contain huge numbers of disease spores and these will develop to produce symptoms if conditions are favourable to the development of the fungus. Cross-infection from one green to another is usually not a significant factor. Disease is best combated by the methods outlined earlier, i.e. maintaining a healthy disease-resistant sward and using fungicide when applicable.

Other points in the general management are to vary the point of entrance to the green to spread the wear caused by players constantly stepping onto the green at the same place. Mowers and other equipment should also be taken onto the green by varied routes, usually by means of a moveable ramp over the bank and ditch. One can also mention draining the pipework of irrigation systems to prevent winter frost damage, and examining silt pits and inspection chambers of the green's drainage system to ensure that water flow from drains is as it should be, clearing silt deposits and rodding drains, etc. as necessary.

SHADE

Parts of the green that are in regular shade for long periods are at greater risk of suffering poorer, less dense turf from time to time as well as being more susceptible to a moister, softer surface more prone to disease outbreaks and algal growth. Where permanent structures such as surrounding buildings are the cause of the shade there is little that one can do, other than to give the shaded areas a little more attention to minimise problems and create the best possible turf and surface in the circumstances. Where it is possible to reduce or perhaps eliminate shade from tall hedges or trees, then every effort should

Shade can cause turf problems

be made to reduce heights of hedges or lop off offending tree branches (although care and thought will have to be given to tree thinning or maybe removal). Sometimes it is a brutal choice between trimming/removing surrounding vegetation or accepting ongoing inferior adjacent turf.

Besides surrounding vegetation producing shade, there is also the likelihood of reduced airflow over the surface, which in turn may well mean areas of the green being a little softer as a consequence of the turf drying out more slowly. More persistent moisture on the leaf from poorer air movement will increase the risks of disease problems, especially fusarium patch disease. Shade and lack of air movement will also most certainly increase the risks of algal growth at the base of the turf.

From the management viewpoint, shaded turf with reduced air movement will need some additional aeration, particularly in terms of sarel rolling. It is also likely that shaded areas will need less irrigation than sunnier, more open aspects.

TURF NURSERIES

A well-maintained nursery of suitable replacement turf is of great value for the repair of areas damaged by wear, disease, accident or vandalism. It is appreciated that a suitable space is not always available, but wherever it is possible to have one, the value of a turf nursery should not be overlooked.

The preferred position is one that is easily accessible and within reach of irrigation, possibly adjacent to the storage sheds used for machinery and materials. The site should be well prepared and have a cover of stone-free soil to facilitate lifting of the turf. Sometimes turf is brought in to form a new turf nursery but where possible seeding is undertaken as it is cheaper.

In practice, preparing a turf nursery is a relatively straightforward matter but there is sometimes difficulty in ensuring regular first-class maintenance, which is so essential if the nursery is to serve its purpose of providing good replacement turf at short notice.

Usually, nursery turf established from seed needs about two to three years before it is entirely satisfactory for replacement purposes so that a suitable size for a nursery is twice the estimated annual requirement plus an amount for emergencies. For a single green, a nursery of about 100 m^2 is probably adequate. Maintenance should involve, at the very least, weekly cutting, spring fertilisation, occasional scarification and weed, worm and disease control as required.

Appendix A

Reprinted from *The Journal of the Sports Turf Research Institute,*
Vol. 61, 1985

TECHNICAL NOTE
A SURVEY OF pH, PHOSPHATE AND POTASH LEVELS IN SOIL SAMPLES TAKEN FROM GOLF AND BOWLING GREENS

By D.M. STANSFIELD
The Sports Turf Research Institute, Bingley, West Yorkshire, BD16 1AU

SUMMARY

Results are presented of pH, phosphate and potash levels of some 1800 individual golf greens and 225 individual bowling greens sited throughout the United Kingdom and Ireland and sampled between 1978 and 1981. The summary of results shows 55% of golf greens and 25% of bowling greens have pH's less than 5.5. The phosphate levels show that 58% and 90% of all golf greens and bowling greens respectively have a P_2O_5 content of greater than 150 ppm. The potash levels show 28% and 20% of all golf greens and bowling greens respectively have a K_2O content greater than 150 ppm. In general the results show excessive amounts of potash and phosphate, particularly the latter, present in the rootzone material of golf and bowling greens.

INTRODUCTION

As a service to its subscribers, the Sports Turf Research Institute (STRI) undertakes chemical analysis of soil samples taken from turf areas used for sport. While a complete analysis can be made, as a routine mainly pH values and the levels of extractable phosphate and potash are measured. The results obtained are used as an aid to making recommendations for appropriate fertiliser programme(s) to clubs which subscribe to the STRI Advisory Service. The survey presented shows the results from tests on soils taken from 1800 individual golf greens and 225 individual bowling greens, sited throughout the UK and Ireland, between October 1978 and November 1981.

The clubs concerned receive advice on turf management from the STRI but all do not necessarily implement this fully with respect to fertiliser treatments. Also, some of the results have come from clubs which had only recently entered into membership of the STRI and in these cases the fertiliser programme applied prior to this will have affected the values obtained. No records are available which detail the various fertiliser programmes which have been applied and obviously this reduces the value of the results as a scientific survey. Similarly, there is no strict control over the sampling technique (samples are collected by individual clubs along guidelines provided) and as the timing of each sampling will vary within a given year this means there are important variables which have not been controlled. The results presented here are simply to provide a record of the values obtained during routine soil analysis in recent years. In the future it is hoped to expand upon this work by carrying out more surveys of results obtained and thereby present a picture of the true value of the soil sample analysis to advisory work, that is the identification of trends in the availability of phosphate and potash, and changes in pH levels both within a given year and over a number of years.

MATERIALS AND METHODS

1. Sampling technique

Samples are usually collected by the clubs themselves. The recommended method is to randomly sub-sample a whole green where conditions are reasonably uniform, or to take separate bulk samples from each area where distinct differences in the turf are evident on a single green. Sub-samples are taken using a hollow tine fork and the cores raised bulked together to form a minimum 0.5 kg soil from a green or each area of a green. Sampling depth should be 100-125 mm.

Samples are air dried, crushed, then passed through a 2 mm mesh sieve prior to testing.

2. pH determination

20 g soil is mixed with 50 ml distilled water and allowed to stand for one hour with occasional stirring. pH is determined by means of a glass electrode and a direct reading meter.

3. Extractable phosphate

2.5 g soil is shaken with 100 ml N/2 acetic acid for one hour. The suspension is then filtered and diluted by a factor of ten. The phosphate content of the filtrate is determined by spectrophotometry using the molybdenum blue method, employing stannous chloride as the reducing agent.

4. Extractable potash

5 g soil is shaken with 25 ml Morgan's solution for one hour. The suspension is then filtered. The potash content of the filtrate is determined by flame photometer.

RESULTS

To give definition to the results presented, a soil reaction value of less than pH 5.5 is considered significantly acid, i.e. sufficiently acid for this to have some effect on the quality of the turf. For extractable phosphate and potash the dividing lines are at levels of 60 ppm and 150 ppm. Below 60 ppm there may be a theoretical deficiency of either of these nutrients. While above 150 ppm there is considered to be an unnecessarily high supply of phosphate and potash. Without further dilution, the maximum readings are: P_2O_5 330 ppm; K_2O 210 ppm.

Categorisation within the above groups is given in Table 1 and the overall findings are presented as histograms in Figures 1 and 2.

Category	Percentage no. of golf greens	Percentage no. of bowling greens
TABLE 1. Groupings of the percentage number of golf and bowling greens above or below "significant" dividing categories		
(i) pH less than 5.5	55.2	24.7
(ii) P_2O_5 less than 60 ppm	5.2	2.9
(iii) P_2O_5 greater than 150 ppm	57.6	90.3
(iv) P_2O_5 greater than 330 ppm but included in (iii)	25.4	75.0
(v) K_2O less than 60 ppm	6.9	17.5
(vi) K_2O greater than 150 ppm	27.6	19.5
(vii) K_2O greater than 210 ppm but included in (vi)	9.4	8.9

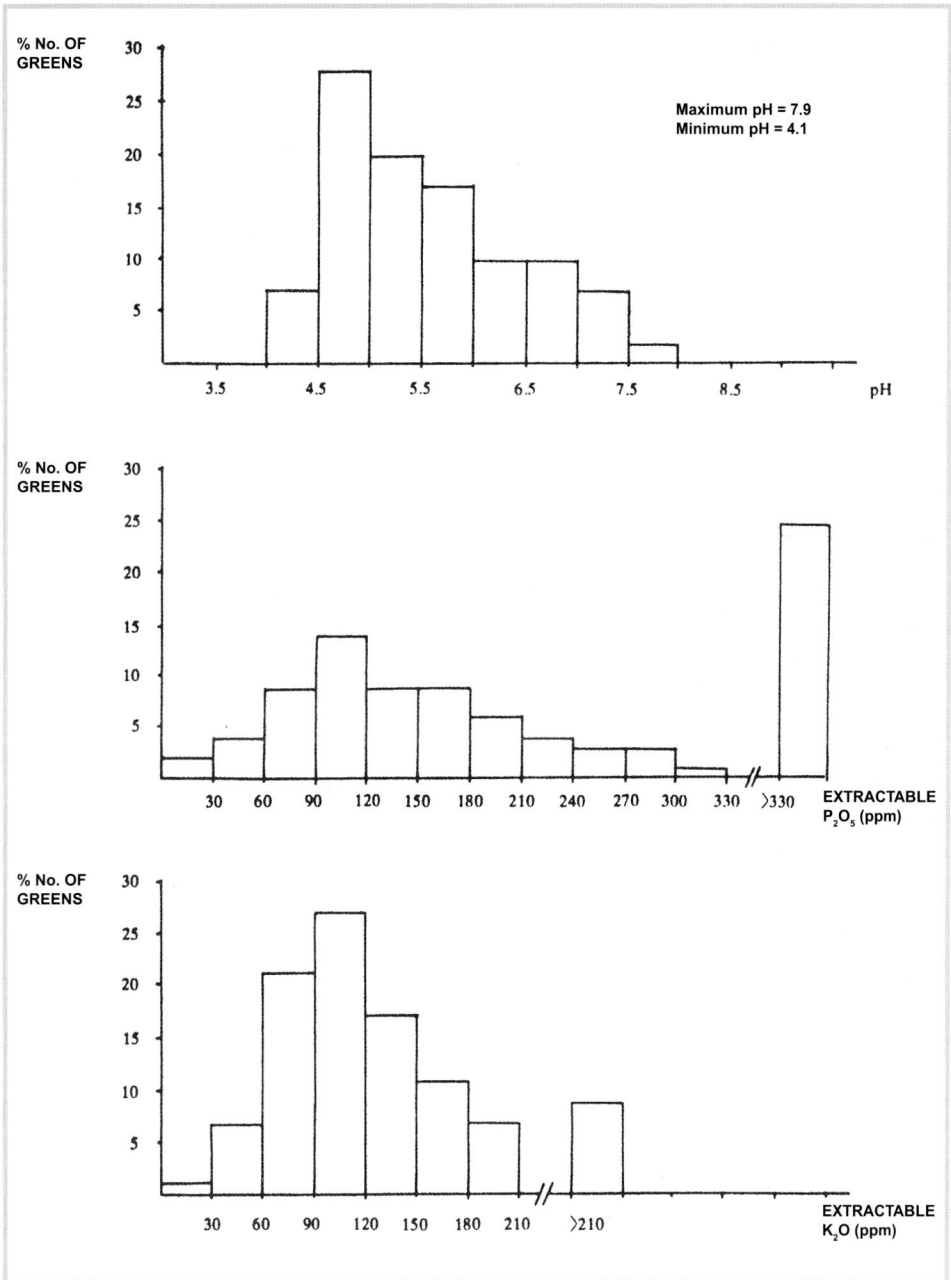

FIGURE 1. Distribution of pH, extractable phosphate and extractable potash in soil samples taken from golf greens.

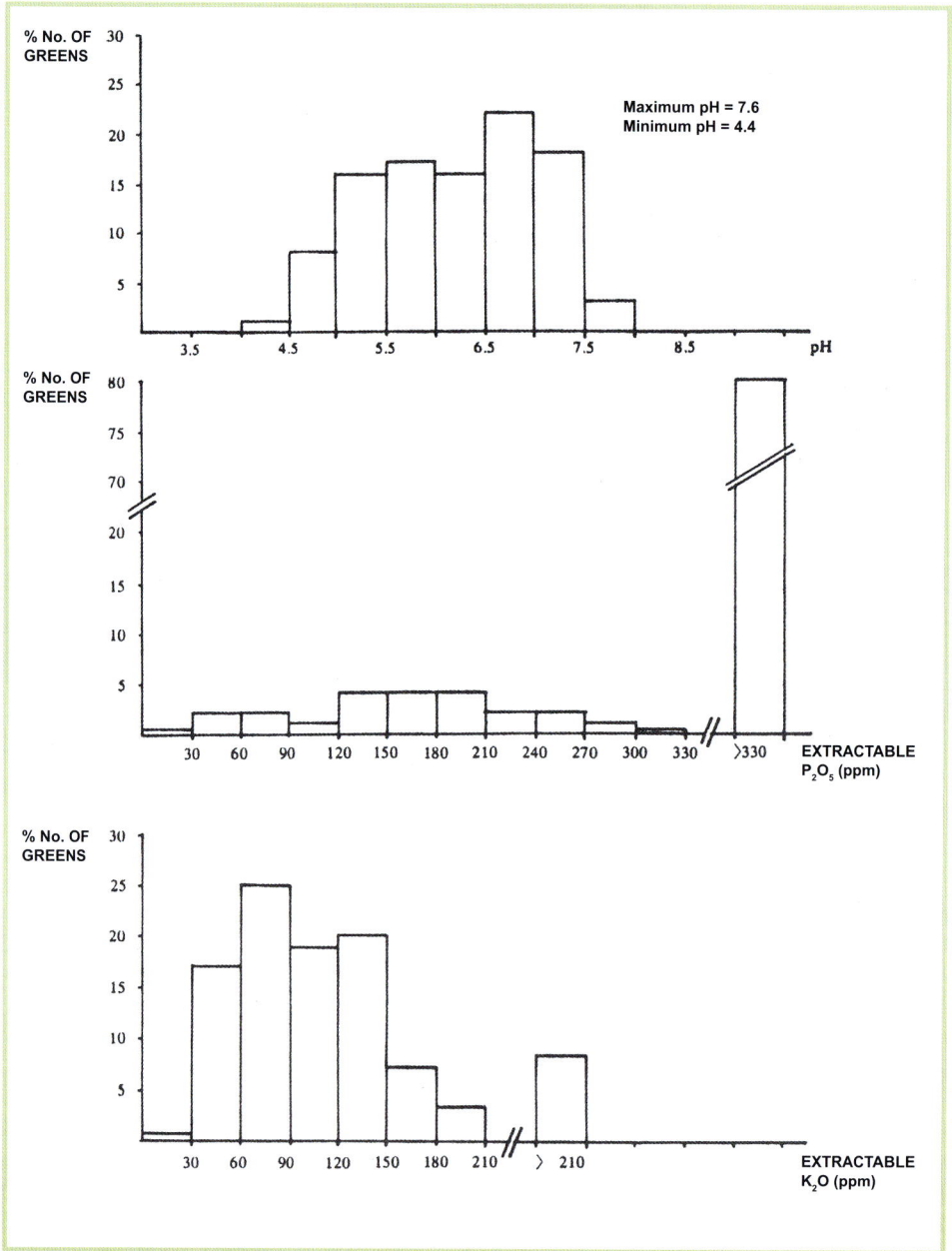

FIGURE 2. Distribution of pH, extractable phosphate and extractable potash in soil samples taken from bowling greens.

DISCUSSION

The primary aim of soil analysis is to be an aid to advisory work and the analysis was not intended to be part of a scientific survey as such. Hence, while individual advisory officers (who interpret the data) will have been aware of the condition of the turf, soil type, the timing of the sampling, previous fertiliser treatments, etc., these have not been recorded for posterity, but just used as tools when offering practical advice. So a meaningful interpretation in chemical or biological terms cannot be presented because there are so many unknowns. For example, the extractable P_2O_5 greater than 330 ppm and extractable K_2O greater than 210 ppm groupings may represent heavily skewed distributions or those clubs who unthinkingly have applied complete fertiliser just before taking samples. Further work is now in progress which may assist with better interpretation of this data but, again, the main intention here is to provide a record which can be used for the identification of trends when comparable results become available in the future.

The information presented here is indicative of frequency of the occurrence of situations which are thought to have a bearing on the condition of fine turf, in particular the type of fine turf one would wish to find on golf greens and bowling greens, i.e. composed predominantly of species of *Agrostis* and *Festuca*, and suffering with a minimum of weed invasion and worm casting. For example, it is generally considered that, on the majority of inland sites, an acid soil favours these desirable grasses. This is by no means the only factor involved, but only 55% of golf greens and 25% of bowling greens are on soils which could be considered significantly acid, i.e. less than pH 5.5. Further to this, only 1% of soils from bowling greens are at a pH level which may be detrimental to good turf growth, while a more evident proportion of golf green soils, 7%, have been found in this very acid state. The number of areas within these two small groupings which may require some corrective measures as a last resort will be even smaller because the overall condition of the turf and the general trend of pH readings are more important than one reading at one point in time.

It is at the low end of the range of results for extractable phosphate where the values obtained could give advisory officers useful information for recommended fertiliser programmes, and it will be noted that in only 5% of golf green soils and 3% of bowling green soils, amongst those samples, there is even a theoretical deficiency of this nutrient. The chances are that a level of deficiency of phosphate for fine turfgrasses in a heavy wear situation is far lower than the 60 ppm extractable phosphate quoted, but there is no general agreement on a particular figure, and in very acid soils where availability of phosphate is very low, there is the possibility that the soil could be deficient in available phosphate even though the extractable phosphate level is above 60 ppm. Even so, widespread routine use of phosphatic fertiliser on fine turf in the United Kingdom and Ireland appears to be a questionable procedure in terms of actual plant needs. A similar survey of golf greens in West Germany also concludes that phosphate fertiliser has been over supplied during the period 1973-1982 (Büring 1984).

The results for extractable potash show levels which are more depressed at the lower end of the range in comparison with available phosphate. This may reflect lower application rates, the effects of more rapid leaching, the effects of luxury uptake, or, most likely, a combination of these factors. However, in the absence of more information, one possible interpretation on the practical use of these figures is that potash should continue to be a relatively important part of the sphere of fertilization of fine turfgrasses (dependent, of course, upon individual soil analysis and an assessment of site conditions in each case, particularly soil type and drainage) given the important interrelationship between potash availability and nitrogen uptake, along with its effects on disease and drought susceptibilities in turfgrasses.

REFERENCES

Büring, W. (1984). Nutrient status of sports turf soil in the German Federal Republic, 1973-1982. *Zeitschrift für Vegetationstechnik* **7**, 45-55.

Appendix B

Reprinted from *The Journal of the Sports Turf Research Institute,*
Vol. 62, 1986

THE PLAYING QUALITY OF LEVEL BOWLING GREENS
By G. HOLMES & M.J. BELL
The Sports Turf Research Institute, Bingley, West Yorkshire, BD16 1AU

INTRODUCTION
Four criteria are often cited in popular bowling literature as being indicative of the ideal level bowling green: a level surface, fast green speed, an even draw on both backhand and forehand and a good cover of fine turfgrasses, yet rarely are all these criteria met in an objective sense. Robinson (1977) suggested that although bowling can be enjoyed at a recreational level on a "less than perfect" green, as the standard of play increases, so the requirements of the players become more stringent and greater emphasis is placed on the above criteria. Indeed, Robinson ventured to suggest that a green should be of such quality that the result of a competitive game is solely dependent on the relative skills of the players and is not a matter left to chance.

The purpose of this work was to: (i) identify the playing characteristics of level bowling greens that are most important to bowlers; (ii) measure the playing quality of a sample of bowling greens and (iii) propose test methods and standards for playing quality.

In order to develop standards for bowling greens, data on surface levels and green speed were collected over a three year period between 1985 and 1987. Seventy-four bowling clubs from most regions of Great Britain agreed to take part in the survey. The bowling clubs included members of the English, Scottish and Welsh Bowling Associations and the English Bowling Federation. Of this sample, 54 (73%) were members of the Sports Turf Research Institute. Although the clubs were selected randomly from County Handbooks with an equal split of members and non-members, it appears that members of the Institute were most willing to co-operate with the research. Ten of the greens were maintained by Local Authorities, the remainder by the clubs themselves.

MATERIALS AND METHODS
Measurement of surface levels
An automatic surveyor's level was used to survey the 74 bowling greens and surface height was measured to an accuracy of 1 mm. Thirty-four greens were surveyed with spot heights at 2 m centres, 29 at 3 m centres, two at 4 m centres and nine at 5 m centres. Measurements of surface height were made around the edges of the greens as well as on the main playing area of each green. The statistical analyses of the data were restricted to the measurements taken on the main playing area of the green although the measurements around green edges proved to be useful in the proposal of standards.

Four statistics were used to assess the variation of surface levels within a green: (i) the range or difference between the highest and lowest points on the green; (ii) the maximum gradient between contiguous spot heights, which allows for the different sampling grids used; (iii) the standard deviation of the spot heights and (iv) the kurtosis of the spot heights (see below). The surface levels of a bowling green are best described using a group of statistics as, individually, none of the above measures adequately describes the variations in surface levels.

Although it was intended to keep the tests of playing quality simple, with the objective that they could be easily understood and employed by the 'lay-person', it soon became obvious that simple measures were poor descriptors of surface evenness. Hence, statistical measures such as standard deviation and kurtosis have been employed with the justification that they summarise sets of data but retain descriptive power.

Kurtosis is a measure of the 'peakedness' of a frequency distribution. A positive kurtosis value indicates that the distribution of spot heights is narrower and more peaked than a normal distribution while a negative kurtosis value indicates that the distribution of spot heights is wider and flatter than the normal distribution. A normal distribution of spot heights would give a kurtosis of zero (see Equation 1). The ideal situation for a bowling green surface is a high and positive kurtosis value which would indicate that most of the spot heights are very similar.

The kurtosis is calculated from:

Equation 1

$$k = \frac{\sum_{i=1}^{N}[(X_i - \overline{X})/s]^4}{N} - 3$$

where: k = kurtosis; N = number of spot heights; X_i = value of the ith spot height; X = mean value of the spot heights; s = standard deviation of the spot heights.

Tests were also made of the surface evenness of greens over 2 m lengths using a profile gauge (Holmes & Bell 1986b). Four sets of ten measurements were taken on each rink, the evenness of a rink being expressed as the average of the sample standard deviation for the four sets of ten measurements.

Measurement of green speed

Green speeds were measured in two ways: (a) the average distance rolled by ten non-biased bowls (five observations from each end of a rink) when released from 1 m height down a ramp and (b) recording by stopwatch the time taken for a biased bowl to travel from the bowler's hand and stop within 0.15 m of a jack sited 27.4 m (30 yards) from the front edge of the bowling mat. The second measure of speed gives a time in seconds and is the definition of green speed given in the Laws of the Game (English Bowling Association 1986). Only bowls that stopped within 0.15 m of the jack were used to measure green speed. Twenty bowling clubs assisted by recording the speed of one or more rinks on their greens during the 1985 season, using the second method described above. The number of green speed measures varied from one per week to two per season.

The correlation between green speed (method b) and the distance rolled test (method a) was studied using 62 pairs of green speed/distance rolled values collected in 1985. All the green speed tests above 13 seconds were measured on synthetic bowling greens. Linear regression was used to predict green speed from the mean distance rolled by ten non-biased bowls.

Bowlers' perceptions of playing quality

Bowlers were asked to complete a questionnaire that asked their opinion of the surface levels, the uniformity of bowl bias on each hand and the speed of the green they had just played on. Seventy-nine questionnaires were collected in 1985, 366 in 1986 and 329 in 1987, a total of 774. The basic data set consisted of coded responses to the questionnaires with the values for green speed (if measured) and the different measures of surface evenness for each record. Each record also contained the playing quality measurements for the rink on which the individual played.

Uneven surface levels can prove disruptive to a game if they occur in the vicinity of the jack, usually between 25 m and 32 m from the mat. Within this area bowls generally roll slowly making them susceptible to uneven levels. Knowing the directions of play and rinks upon which bowlers detected a difference in the reaction to bias on left and right hand draw, the green evenness data were used to test if local gradients at rink ends influenced the reaction to the bias of a bowl (Holmes & Bell 1986a).

If there is an even decline in surface levels from a relatively high left hand edge of a rink towards its right hand edge, then a bowl released down the left hand side of the rink will need to be drawn wider than one sent down the right hand side, in order to stop in the rink centre. Following this supposition, the replies given by bowlers to the question concerning the reaction to bowl bias on each hand were coded according to those responses that would be predicted by analysis of the surface geometry at the rink end and those that would not (Holmes & Bell 1986a). The surface evenness data were analysed by subtracting the spot heights R1 and R2 from the spot heights L1 and L2 respectively (Figure 4.1) and using the criteria shown in Figure 4.2, the expected response to the bias of a bowl was compared with the responses as perceived by players. In figure 4.1, C denotes the centre of the rink.

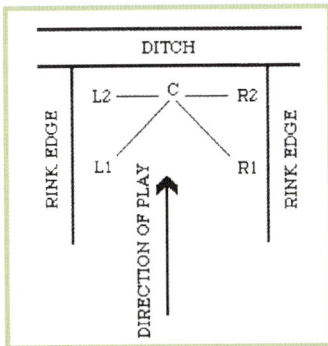

FIGURE 4.1. The position of spot heights used to calculate the gradient of rink ends.

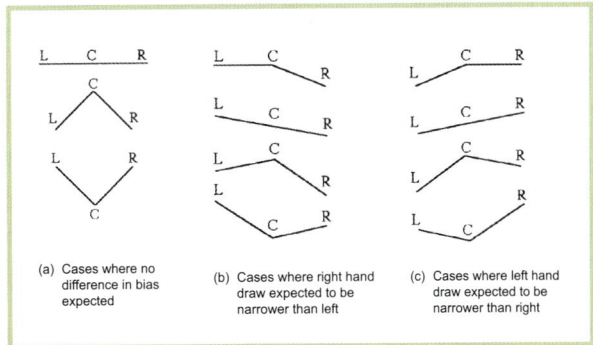

FIGURE 4.2. Schematic view of the criteria used for determining expected variations in the draw of bowls.

Other data

The surface hardness of five greens was measured by a Clegg Impact Soil Tester in 3 x 3 m test plots covering the whole green. A 0.5 kg hammer was dropped from a height of 0.3 m and five observations were made in each test plot. Tests of surface hardness were also combined with green speed measurements at 33 rinks to ascertain if green speed was affected by the hardness of the bowling surface.

The clubs that co-operated with the work in 1985 were asked to record the number of hours use each rink received per day and the time spent on different maintenance jobs each day. The hours of green usage were expressed as the sum of the total number of hours use each rink received. Of the 50 clubs that agreed to keep these records, 19 returned usage data for the full season and 21 recorded the maintenance carried out during the season. In addition, 15 clubs completed a questionnaire that asked for more details of the maintenance procedures carried out and for an estimate of the total expenditure on maintenance.

RESULTS

Variation of heights within the sample of bowling greens

Figure 4.3 shows the frequency of height ranges found on the 74 surveyed bowling greens and for individual rinks where questionnaire responses were obtained.

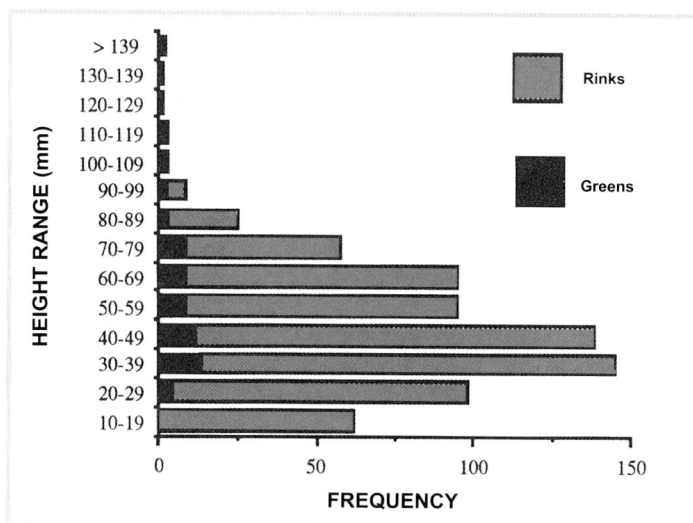

FIGURE 4.3. Height ranges of the surveyed bowling greens and individual rinks.

Both frequency distributions have a modal height range of 30-39 mm. For the main playing areas of greens, the lowest height range of 23 mm was found on a newly-constructed green. The largest height range for the main playing area of a green of 226 mm was for a green thought to be over 200 years old. The average height range for the main playing areas was 65 mm. The maximum height range for individual rinks was 96 mm and the minimum was 12 mm. The standard deviation of the spot heights for the main playing areas of greens varied from 4.4 mm to 60.7 mm. The maximum standard deviation recorded for a rink was 25.7 mm and the minimum was 3.4 mm. Maximum slopes between adjacent spot heights ranged from 0.17° to 1.06° with a mean of 0.50°. The kurtosis values ranged from -1.36 to 2.67, the mean being -0.13.

Figure 4.4 shows the distribution of spot heights on two greens, one with comparatively good surface levels (kurtosis = 2.67), the other with relatively poor levels (kurtosis = -1.03).

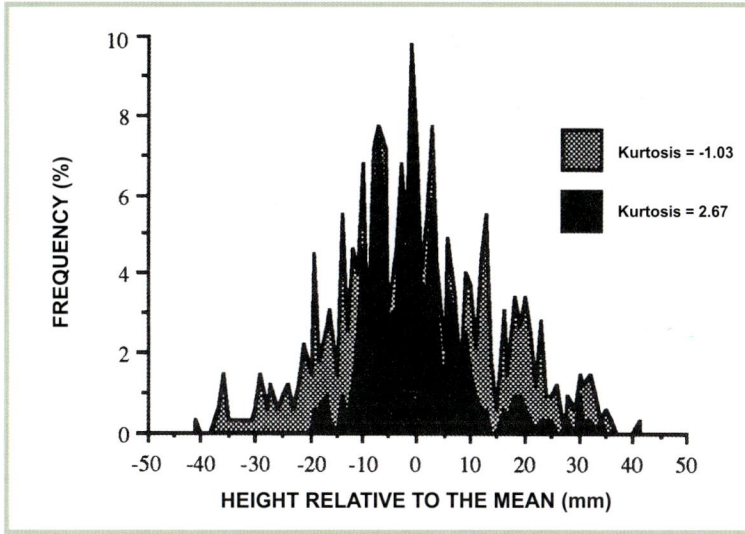

FIGURE 4.4. Surface height variations for two bowling greens.

Figure 4.5 shows the variability in the surface evenness of rinks for which questionnaire data were collected and for the 74 greens surveyed. Thirty-two percent of the rink standard deviations occurred in the range 10-14 mm and 20% in the range 5-9 mm.

The frequency of rink standard deviations as measured using the profile gauge is given in Figure 4.6. The distribution is symmetrical with 52.3% of the rinks occurring in the range 1.5-1.999 mm.

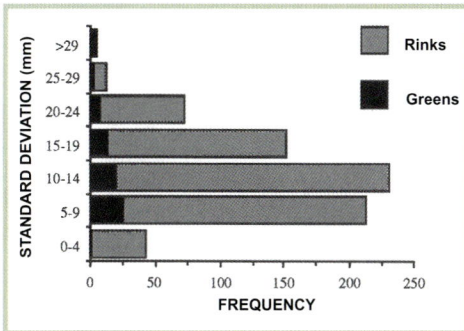

FIGURE 4.5. Rink and green standard deviations in surface evenness.

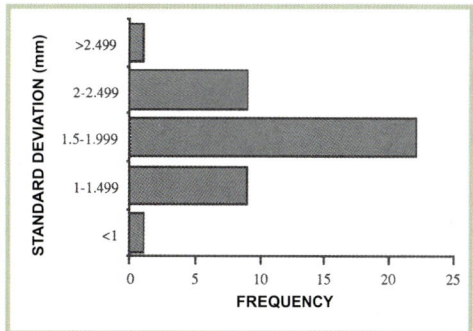

FIGURE 4.6. Rink standard deviations measured using profile gauge. Measured green speeds.

Figure 4.7 shows the relationship between green speed as measured by the 30 yard test and the distance rolled by a non-biased bowl. The distance rolled and green speed are strongly correlated (r = 0.98***) so that green speed can be predicted from the distance rolled using the equation:

Equation 2

$$Gs = 6.01 + 0.36Dr \quad (\pm 0.34)$$

where: Gs = green speed (s); Dr = distance rolled (m) by a non-biased bowl released from 1 m down a ramp.

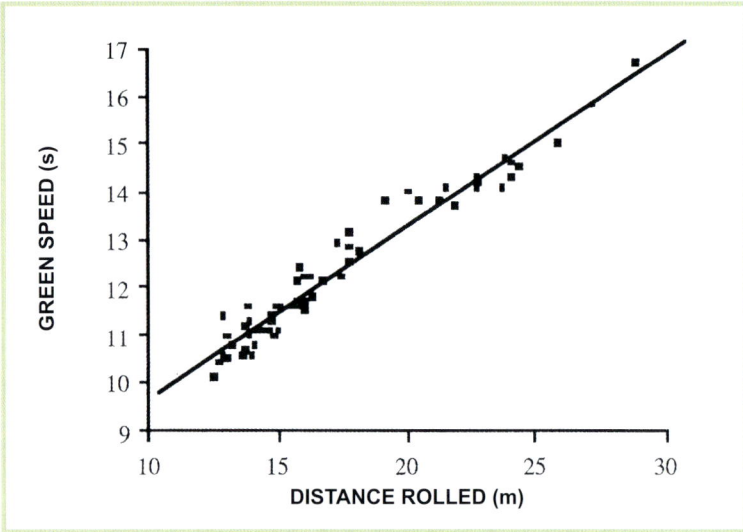

FIGURE 4.7. The relationship between distance rolled and green speed.

Figure 4.8 shows the frequency of green speeds measured during the project. The figure consists of 262 measures made by the authors and co-operating clubs in 1985 using the 30 yard test and 75 measures of distance rolled by non-biased bowls in 1987 that have been converted to a green speed in seconds using Equation 2. These data are not averages for greens but mean values recorded for individual rinks. The majority of green speed measures were between 10s and 12s, with an average speed of 11.0s.

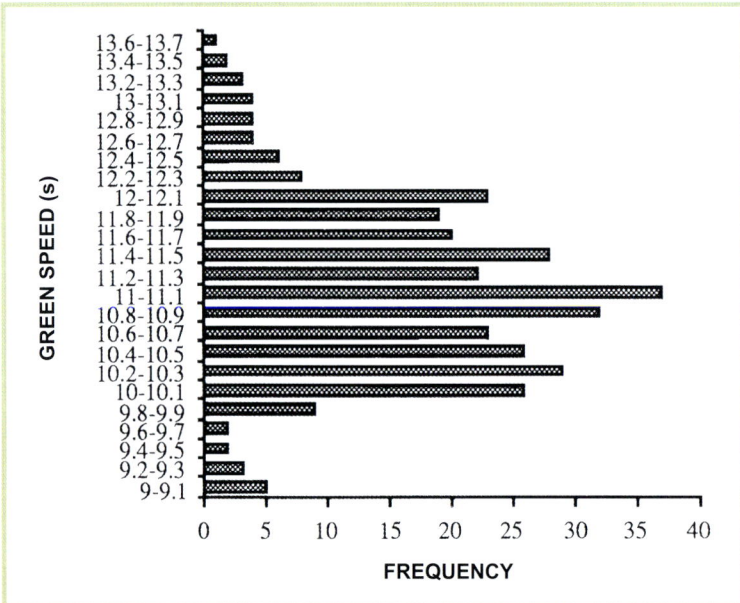

FIGURE 4.8. Green speeds recorded during the survey.

The speeds of different rinks on the same green were found to vary by as much as 3.7s at the same time of day, although the mean variation in green speed between rinks on the same day (67 cases) was 0.67s.

Players often speak of a rink speeding up during a game. To examine the effect of successive bowl roll along the same track, a non-biased bowl was released 16 times along the same line using a ramp with a release height of 1 m (so ensuring that the bowl was released with constant initial velocity) on a green with a measured green speed of 10.9s. Figure 4.9 shows that the distance rolled by the bowl increased by almost 2 m during the test, an estimated increase in green speed of c. 0.5s.

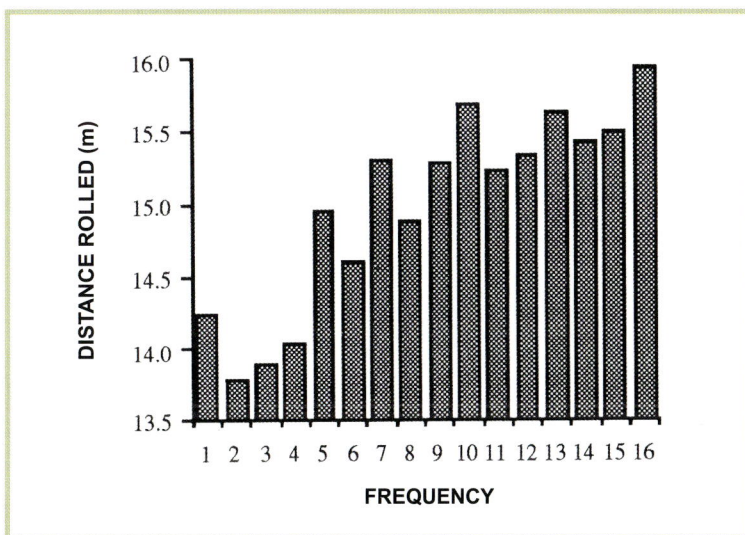

FIGURE 4.9. Progressive increase in the distance rolled by a bowl.

Surface hardness

Figure 4.10 illustrates the variability in surface hardness of one bowling green. As expected, the rink ends were among the hardest areas of the green and softer areas occurred nearer the green centre. Although players continually walk between rink ends and down the centre of rinks, most wear and compaction occur at the rink ends where the players congregate. The relatively lower amount of pedestrian traffic walking over the centre of the green may allow an increased accumulation of dead plant material known as "thatch" in the centre of bowling rinks. Thatch often causes a soft, sponge-like playing surface.

Lush (1985) reasoned that surface hardness should be positively correlated with green speed. She inferred that a bowl would deform the surface less on a hard green than on a soft green and consequently the deceleration of a rolling bowl would be smaller. This hypothesis is confirmed by the positive relationship between green speed and Clegg Impact hardness ($r = 0.47***$) found in this study.

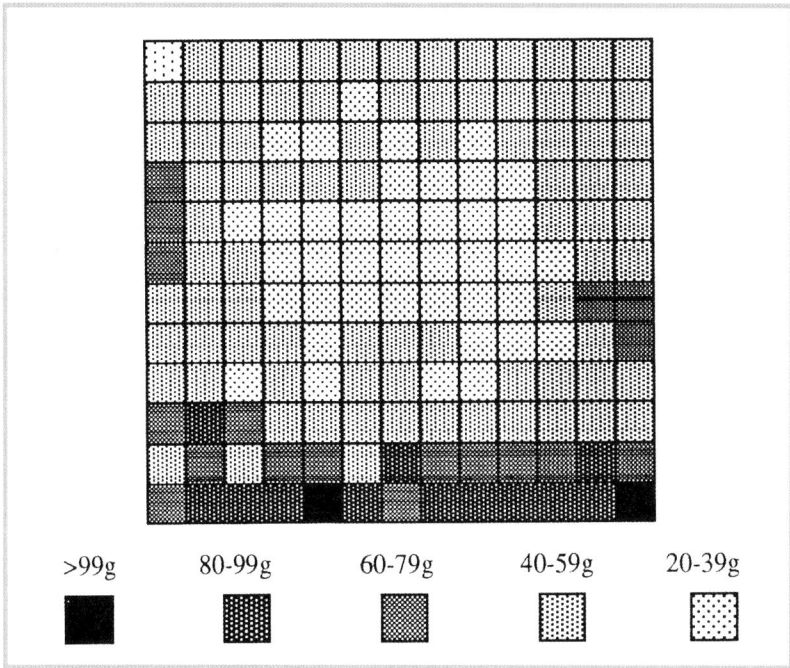

FIGURE 4.10. Surface hardness variations within a level bowling green.

It is clear from Figure 4.10 however that considerable variations in surface hardness can be found within one bowling rink. This suggests that the deceleration of a bowl may vary along its course in response to changes in the hardness of the playing surface. The deceleration of a bowl may also vary because of differences in sward characteristics (see section on green speeds).

DISCUSSION
Surface evenness
The four measurements of surface evenness show that the levels of bowling greens vary greatly. Gooch & Escritt (1975) recommended that the levels of a newly constructed green should be within ±6 mm of the average height of the green. The Sports Turf Research Institute (1985, 1987) suggested that if levels were within ±18 mm from the green average (i.e. a range of 36 mm) then the surface could be improved by selective top dressing and hollow tining. However, if the discrepancy was greater than this figure, more extensive work such as returfing was recommended. None of the 74 greens surveyed during the study would satisfy Gooch & Escritt's recommendation and only 13 (17.6%) would not require the extensive remedial action suggested by the Sports Turf Research Institute (1985, 1987).

The surveys revealed that local gradients between adjacent spot heights were up to 1.06° with an average of 0.50°. For comparison, the British Crown Green Bowling Association (1983) recommends that a new c. 37 m x 37 m green should have a crown height of 0.305 m, giving average gradients of 0.62° from the crown to the corner of the green and 0.95° for the shortest distance between the crown and the ditch. Thus, many level greens have local gradients similar to the overall slopes found on crown greens.

Green speeds

The English Bowling Association (EBA) considers that the ideal speed for a level bowling green is 12-13s, and that speeds of less than 10s "should not occur" (J.F. Elms *pers comm*.). The green speed results show that of the 337 speed tests carried out, only 13.3% fell within the EBA's ideal range and that 6.2% were below 10s.

There was little difference found between the speeds of different rinks on the same green when recorded at the same time of day, with a difference of 3.7s at one green being the largest variation. The latter difference cannot be easily explained as the rinks had received similar amounts of play in the week preceding the test and on other occasions throughout the season the speeds had been similar or their rank order had been reversed. A possible explanation is that popular rinks may be more compacted because of greater pedestrian traffic and, given the relationship found between green speed and surface hardness, the surface of a rink that is less favoured may become relatively softer and slower.

The average club player may not be greatly concerned about the speeds of adjacent rinks being dissimilar, but in competitions, when bowlers may play consecutive games on different rinks, the effect could be important.

Variability of speed within a bowling green has long been thought to be caused by differences in grass species composition. As part of the project, a trial was set up in June 1986 at the Sports Turf Research Institute's trial ground to assess the influence of species composition on the rolling resistance of bowls (Canaway, Baker & Pye unpublished). Five turfgrass species were used: *Festuca rubra* ssp. *commutata* 'Frida', *Festuca rubra* ssp. *litoralis* 'Dawson', *Agrostis castellana* 'Highland', *Agrostis tenuis* 'Bardot' and *Poa annua* 'Commercial'. Each species was replicated four times in randomised blocks. Three non-biased bowls were released down a ramp from a height of 0.5 m in opposing directions on each plot, giving 24 measurements for each species. The tests were made on 27 July 1987 when the turfgrass had been cut at a mowing height of 5 mm.

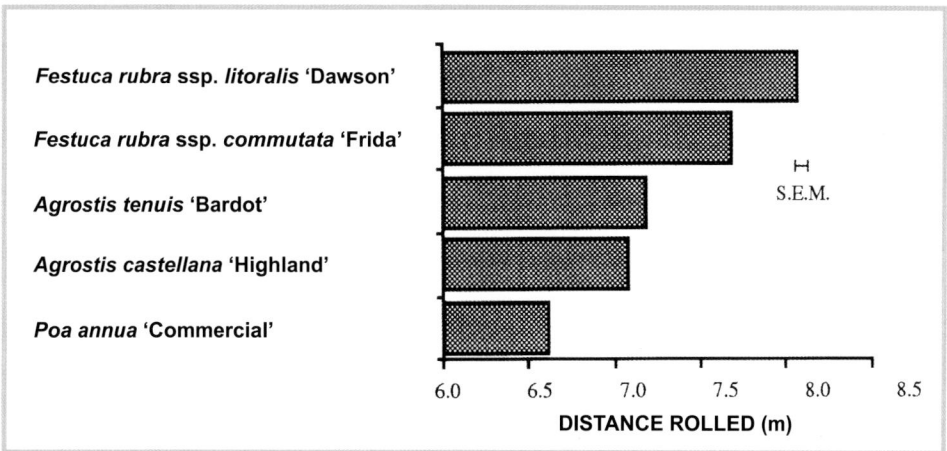

FIGURE 4.11. Distance rolled by a non-biased bowl on five turfgrass species.

The data shown in Figure 4.11 are the distances rolled on each grass species. The average distance rolled on the *Poa annua* was 6.62 m whereas the *Festuca rubra* ssp. *litoralis* produced the longest distance rolled of 8.07 m. All the 'fine' turfgrasses gave longer rolling distances than the annual meadow-grass, with the two fescue species having the longest rolling distances. Canaway *et al.* also examined the influence of cutting height on green speed but surprisingly found smaller differences in speed between cutting heights than between grass species.

Bowlers often speak of a rink becoming faster during the day and on one occasion the speed of one rink was found to increase by 0.6s in three hours. Thus, there are likely to be diurnal variations in green speed as well as longer term changes. The experiment described earlier in which ten bowls were released down the same track highlights the changes in green speed that may occur throughout a day. The successive tracking of bowls is thought to have flattened the grass so reducing its rolling resistance. This point is important as the green speed before a game is likely to be different to that recorded during the game's final stages.

Brearley & Bolt (1958) measured the distance rolled by biased bowls and the duration of rolling on three greens in Australia that were considered to be "fast", "medium" and "slow". The minimum, maximum and mean values of R/T^2 for each green and the corresponding green speeds are shown in Table 4.1.

TABLE 4.1. Minimum and maximum values of R/T2 for "fast", "medium" and "slow" greens (adapted from Brearley & Bolt 1958).

Green	Minimum value of R/T^2	Distance of minimum R/T^2 (ft)	Corresponding green speed (s)	Maximum value of R/T^2	Distance of maximum R/T^2 (ft)	Corresponding green speed (s)
"Fast"	0.41	57.7 64.4 89.4	14.8	0.46	47.7	14.0
"Medium"	0.48	11.5	13.7	0.56	43.9 91.2	12.7
"Slow"	0.57	55.4	12.6	0.67	21.9	11.6

Table 4.1 also gives an indication of the spatial variability of speed within a green. The fact that different length bowls produced different values of the ratio R/T^2 means that the speeds of the greens were not constant over the whole green. Using the method described in section 2 however, the mean value of R/T^2 gives a good estimate of the green speed to within about ±0.5s. It is interesting to note that a "medium" green speed in Australia (12.7-13.7s, Table 4.1) would probably be considered relatively fast in the UK.

THE QUESTIONNAIRE SURVEY

For the purposes of comparing the data from the questionnaires with the playing quality test results, each test has been categorised into arbitrary classes (e.g. for the green speed test: 10-10.4s, 10.5-10.9s, etc.) and the number of responses to each question given in the form of cells. The columns shown in Figures 4.12 and 4.13 are the categories for the test results and the rows record the different responses to each question. The cells are shaded to indicate the proportion of responses within each cell expressed as a percentage of each column, e.g. what proportion of the players that played on a surface with a green speed between 10.0s and 10.4s thought that the speed was "slow" or "satisfactory".

Bowlers' perceptions of surface evenness

Of the 713 bowlers who replied to the question "Does the green undulate?", 258 (36.2%) answered "yes" and 455 (63.8%) answered "no". In response to the question asking if the surface of the green was bumpy, 530 bowlers (82.0%) said that the surfaces were "satisfactory". These responses suggest a general satisfaction with surface levels among bowlers although there appears to be a higher level of dissatisfaction expressed about the larger scale variations in surface evenness (undulations) than smaller scale variations (bumpiness).

The standard deviations of spot heights within rinks show that the majority of bowlers thought that the rinks did not undulate at standard deviations between 0-25 mm (Figure 4.12). At standard deviations between 25 mm and 30 mm the majority of bowlers (53%) thought that the rinks undulated. The highest proportion of bowlers who considered that the rinks did not undulate was 88% in the standard deviations category of <5 mm (Figure 4.12). A standard deviation for a rink of less than 5 mm would appear to be ideal but players still find standard deviations greater than 5 mm acceptable.

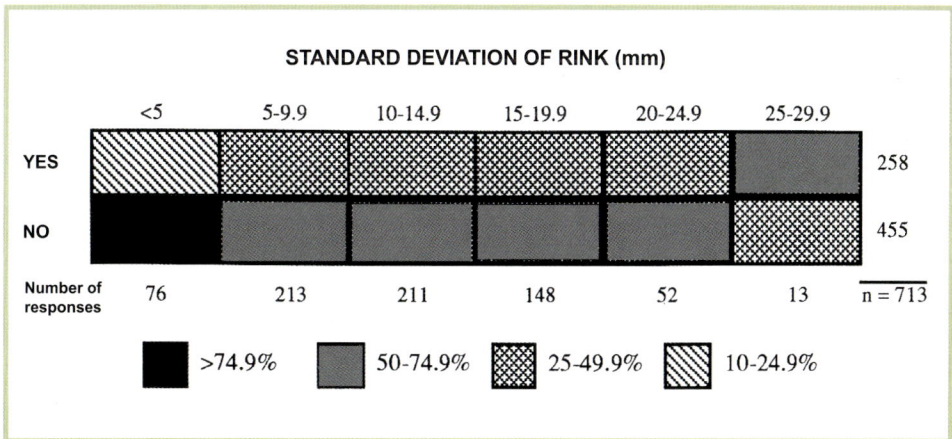

FIGURE 4.12. Bowlers' perceptions to the question "Does the rink undulate?" by standard deviation of rink spot heights.

Of bowlers who had played on rinks with green speeds over 11.5s, 84% thought that the rinks were "fast". Seventy-seven percent of the bowlers who said that the speeds were "unacceptably slow" had played on rinks with speeds below 10.5s. The survey showed that 85% of the bowlers stating that the green speed was "satisfactory" had played on rinks with speeds between 10.5s and 12s and that none thought the speed to be "satisfactory" below 10s. The highest proportion of "satisfactory" responses (77%) occurred for green speeds between 11s and 11.4s. At 12-12.4s, 65% thought that the speed was "fast".

The distribution of responses to the question regarding the smaller-scale variations (bumpiness) of the green showed that the majority of the bowlers stated that the surfaces were "satisfactory" at standard deviations of less than 3 mm, as measured by the profile gauge. At standard deviations between 0.5 mm and 1 mm none of the bowlers thought that the rinks were "bumpy" or "unacceptably bumpy". At standard deviations between 1 mm and 2.5 mm however, the proportion of bowlers that described the green surfaces as "bumpy" was 22%. A standard deviation for this test of ≤1.5 mm may be appropriate for the average bowler.

A sample of 612 bowlers replied to the question asking if the rink they had just played on gave an equal reaction to bias on both hands. Of these, 372 (60.8%) said the reaction to bias was not equal, although only about half of these responses were as predicted for the L1/R1 and L2/R2 slopes using the criteria given in Figure 4.2.

A total of 240 bowlers stated that there was no difference in reaction to bias on the rink they had just played on. The only cases where such responses would be predicted are if the slopes either side of the rink centre are equal or if the rink is perfectly flat (i.e. L1-R1=0 and L2-R2=0) or that any difference in slope is negligible. However, this rarely occurred on the greens surveyed in this study but approximately 50% of the total number of bowlers who detected no difference in bias did so at L-R values of 8 mm or less. This may be an indication of the difference in levels at the rink end below which the majority of bowlers do not detect a difference in the reaction to bias.

Bowlers' perceptions of green speed
Of the 405 players who answered the question concerning the speed of the rink they had just played on, 29 (7.2%) stated that the rinks were "fast", 283 (69.9%) said that the speeds were "satisfactory", 75 (18.5%) said they were "slow" and 18 (4.4%) said they were "unacceptably slow". No bowlers were of the opinion that the rinks were "unacceptably fast".

A total of 326 questionnaires were completed for occasions when a green speed test had been carried out immediately before matches. Figure 4.13 shows the relationship between bowlers' opinions of green speed and the green speed measurements in these cases. There is good agreement between green speeds recorded before matches and players' opinions (Figure 4.13). The chi-square test was used to test for equality in the distribution of responses by cells. Chi-square equalled 187.8***, indicating that the responses were not equally distributed within the cells.

The responses regarding green speed were probably influenced by the playing characteristics of the greens the bowlers had played on most recently. In a hot and dry summer, similar green speeds to those found during the survey would probably result in more "slow" and "unacceptably slow" responses. In the summer of 1985 and during June 1987, when most of the questionnaires were collected, the EBA's "ideal" speed may have been regarded as "fast" by the average club player.

It is suggested that the perception of a "fast" green speed is a positive comment rather than a statement of a green's poor performance. The interpretation of the data presented in Figure 4.13 therefore presumes that "fast" equates with the ideal speed and that "satisfactory" should be the minimum desirable speed. Thus, it is concluded that a green speed in excess of 12s would be considered ideal by the average player.

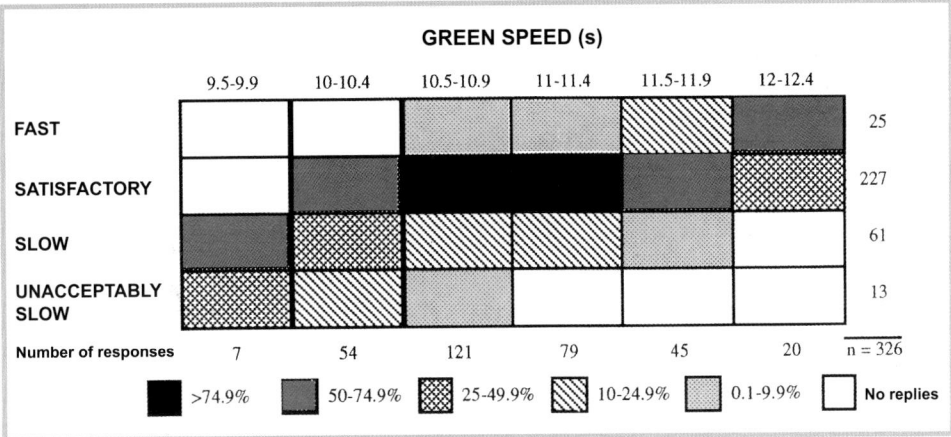

GREEN SPEED (s)							
	9.5-9.9	10-10.4	10.5-10.9	11-11.4	11.5-11.9	12-12.4	
FAST							25
SATISFACTORY							227
SLOW							61
UNACCEPTABLY SLOW							13
Number of responses	7	54	121	79	45	20	n = 326

>74.9%   50-74.9%   25-49.9%   10-24.9%   0.1-9.9%   No replies

FIGURE 4.13. Bowlers' perceptions of green speed by measured green speed.

STANDARDS FOR LEVEL BOWLING GREENS
Existing recommendations
Qualitative standards have been applied by turf specialists to evaluate the playing quality of bowling greens. For instance, by rolling bowls over a green the experienced adviser could get an impression both of the quality of surface evenness and the speed of the green. Judgements on the evenness of bowling greens are often based on the spacing and range of contours shown on survey plans.

Few formal standards exist for surface levels though Gooch & Escritt (1975) recommended that a newly constructed bowling green should have surface levels within ±6 mm from the mean. With regard to green speeds, the English Bowling Association suggested that the ideal speed is between 12s and 13s and that speeds below 10s are unacceptable. Escritt (1978) gave two categories of green speed using the 30 yard test: a "slow" green, he suggested, would have a green speed of 10s and a "good fast" green would have a speed of 15s.

The Sports Turf Research Institute (1983) measured the time taken for a bowl to just reach or just topple into the ditch when delivered from the opposite ditch. Using this test, a time of 18s was considered to be "very fast by average club standards", 14s was considered "satisfactory" and 12s was "excessively slow". The R/T^2 test (Holmes & Bell 1986a) can be used to convert these figures to equivalent speeds using the 30 yard test. Assuming that the figures were based on times for greens of the average dimension of 38 m x 38 m, they equate with speeds of 15.3s, 11.9s and 10.2s, respectively for the 30 yard test.

Proposal of standards
The questionnaire survey was mainly conducted at local club competitions and matches and although some County and International representatives completed questionnaires, the standards proposed are directed at local leagues and competitions and are given as "Preferred" and "Acceptable" values. The preferred values for surface evenness were determined by taking the category of surface evenness where the highest proportion of the players stated that the surface was "satisfactory". For green speed the preferred minimum speed was set by taking the category where the majority of players thought that green speed was "fast".

It is recognised that certain important competitions are played on specific rinks on a green that are known to be of high quality and the proposed standards attempt to account for this. It is recommended that at least three of the rinks on any green should meet the specified requirements.

Recommended test procedures and test conditions

Surface evenness

A survey of surface levels should be made with a surveyor's level to an accuracy of 1 mm. Spot heights should be measured at 2 m centres over the whole of the green and related to a permanent benchmark. All heights should be given in millimetres and the following tests refer to heights in millimetres. Surface heights should also be measured around the edges of the bowling green and a horizontal distance of 6 m has been found suitable for the spacing of these spot heights. Unless otherwise stated, the proposed limits for green evenness refer to the spot heights measured within the main playing area of the green and the heights recorded around the edges of greens should not be included in the analyses.

The profile gauge can be used to determine the maximum variation in surface levels over a 2 m length of the green surface. This instrument may be particularly useful where areas of a green have been returfed or there is an area where poor levels are suspected.

Green speed

(i) *The 30 yard test:* A jack is placed 30 yards (27.4 m) from the front edge of the bowling mat. The time taken (measured to the nearest tenth of a second) for the bowl to roll from the bowler's hand and stop within 0.15 m of the jack is recorded by stopwatch. The average of three tests in each direction is taken as the speed of the rink.

(ii) *The distance rolled test:* A non-biased bowl is released from a vertical height of 1 m down a ramp inclined at 30° to the horizontal. The distance the bowl rolls along the ground is measured to the nearest centimetre from the end of the ramp to the centre of the bowl. Five tests are conducted in each direction on a rink and the average of the ten measures is used in Equation 2 to give the equivalent time for the 30 yard test.

(iii) *The R/T^2 test:* Three bowls are delivered corresponding to "long", "medium" and "short" lengths and the travel time (T) for each bowls is recorded by stopwatch to the nearest tenth of a second. The distance travelled (R) by each wood from the front edge of the bowling mat is also recorded. This procedure is then repeated from the opposite end of the rink. R/T^2 is calculated for each of the six bowls. The average R/T^2 value (X) can then be used in Equation 3 to give the equivalent time for the 30 yard test.

Equation 3

$$\text{Green speed} = \sqrt{\frac{D}{\overline{X}}}$$

where: D = 27.4 m, 30 yards or 90 feet, depending on the units used to measure R.

Climatic variables

There are problems in setting maximum levels of rainfall prior to testing. The problem is particularly relevant to bowls as summer rainfall can be intense and the rainfall total for one day may exceed the total for the remainder of the month. The following conditions are suggested only as guidelines and in most circumstances it will be the duty of the test organisation or club to decide if the weather conditions are typical.

Prior to testing, the rainfall shall not exceed any of the following: 5 mm in the last hour; 10 mm in the last five hours; 15 mm in the last ten hours and 25 m in the last 24 hours.

Playing surface conditions
Before testing is undertaken, the playing surface must be prepared as it would be before play. For instance, if the green is usually mown or brushed before play, the same conditions must apply for testing. The test of green speed should be made in the early afternoon once any dew has evaporated.

PROPOSED STANDARDS FOR SURFACE EVENNESS

TABLE 4.2. Proposed standards of surface evenness for individual rinks			
	Differences between adjacent spot heights (mm)	**Standard deviation of heights (mm)**	**Standard deviation using profile gauge (mm)**
PREFERRED MAXIMUM	6	10	1.5
ACCEPTABLE MAXIMUM	10	15	2

It is recommended that the limits for the difference between adjacent spot heights should apply to the outer 2 m around the edge of the bowling green as well as the main playing area. It is therefore suggested, for instance, that a decline or incline of more than 10 mm over the outer 2 m of a bowling green is unacceptable.

PROPOSED STANDARDS FOR GREEN SPEED

TABLE 4.3. Proposed standards for the speed of individual rinks	
PREFERRED MINIMUM SPEED (s)	12
ACCEPTABLE MINIMUM SPEED (s)	10

It is further recommended that all the rinks on a green that will be played during a competition should meet the above requirements and, in addition, should have green speeds within 0.5s of one another.

No upper limits have been set for green speed. The justification for this is that "quicker" greens are generally thought to demand a greater level of skill from the player. It is therefore thought inappropriate to propose upper limits for green speed. It is also worth noting that synthetic greens are already providing the average player with some experience of fast green conditions (i.e. 13-15s).

REFERENCES

Brearley, M.N. (1961). The motion of a biased bowl with perturbing projection conditions. *Camb. Phil. Soc. Proc.* **57**, 131-151.

Brearley, M.N. & Bolt, B.A. (1958). The dynamics of a bowl. *Q.J. Mech. Appl. Math.* **11**, 351-363.

British Crown Green Bowling Association (1983). *Official Handbook*, Graphic Press, Coventry, 76 pp.

Clegg, B. (1976). An impact testing device for *in situ* base course evaluation. *Australian Road Res. Bur. Proc.* **8**, 1-6.

Dury, P. & Dury, P.L.K. (1983). *A study of natural materials (dynamic/particulate) in the provision of synthetic non-turf sports facilities, particularly for soccer and other winter games*. Nottinghamshire County Council Education Department, Playing Fields Service, 78 pp.

English Bowling Association (1984). *Official Year Book*, Dotesion, Bradford-on-Avon, 296 pp.

Escritt, J.R. (1978). *ABC of Turf Culture*, Kaye & Ward Ltd., London, 239 pp.

Cooch, R.B. & Escritt, J.R. (1975). *Sports Ground Construction – Specifications*, 2nd Ed., National Playing Fields Association, London, 126 pp.

Holmes, G.H. & Bell, M.J. (1986a). The playing quality of level bowling greens: A survey. *J. Sports Turf Res. Inst.* **62**, 50-65.

Holmes, G.H. & Bell, M.J. (1986b). A pilot study of the playing quality of football pitches. *J. Sports Turf Res. Inst.* **62**, 74-91.

Langvad, B. (1968). Sambandet mellan fotbollens studshöjd och klipphöjden på sportsturf. *Weibulls Gräs-tips* **10-11**, 355-357.

Lush, W.M. (1985). Objective assessment of turf cricket pitches using an impact hammer. *J. Sports Turf Res. Inst.* **61**, 71-79

Robinson, G.S. (1977). What the bowler wants in a bowling green. *N.Z.I.T.C. Sports Turf Review* **112**, 171.

Sports Turf Research Institute (1985). Special problems concerned with the maintenance of flat greens. *Sports Turf Bulletin*, No. 149, April-June, 8-11.

Appendix C

Reprinted from *The Journal of the Sports Turf Research Institute,*
Vol. 68, 1992

BALL ROLL CHARACTERISTICS OF FIVE TURFGRASSES USED FOR GOLF AND BOWLING GREENS

By P.M. CANAWAY & S.W. BAKER
The Sports Turf Research Institute, Bingley, West Yorkshire, BD16 1AU

SUMMARY

Ball roll tests were carried out to determine the green speed of five turfgrasses: *Festuca rubra* ssp. *litoralis* 'Dawson', *F. rubra* ssp. *commutata* 'Frida', *Agrostis capillaris* 'Bardot', *A. castellana* 'Highland' and *Poa annua*. Measurements were made on four occasions for bowls and three for golf under variations in mowing height and surface moisture. Averaged over all assessment dates *F. rubra* ssp. *litoralis* provided the fastest surface for both golf and bowls, and *P. annua* was consistently the slowest. *Agrostis* species did not provide the fastest playing surface on any occasion, although 'Highland' ranked second overall for bowls. Surface moisture decreased green speed and a reduction in cutting height generally increased it, although there were some inconsistencies. In view of the differences found it is suggested that further research should be carried out on playing quality of grass species and cultivars.

INTRODUCTION

For sports played on fine turf such as golf and bowls, ball roll characteristics of the surface are of great importance. A ball decelerates as it moves across the playing surface because of the effects of rolling resistance, which can be considered as a force acting at the point of contact between the ball and the surface in a direction opposing that of forward motion (Bell *et al.* 1985). The effects of rolling resistance are referred to by players in terms of green "speed", the "faster" is the surface, the lower is its rolling resistance and *vice versa*. Although bowlers and golfers would both agree on what is a fast green, the means of characterising the surface have developed in different directions in the two sports. In flat green bowls the method which has been developed and generally used has been to record the *time taken in seconds* for a biased bowl to travel from the bowler's hand and come to rest within 0.15 m of a jack (target ball) sited 27.4 m (30 yards) away. Because on a fast surface the bowl decelerates more slowly it can be released at a lower initial velocity and it also travels in a wider arc, this leads to the seemingly paradoxical situation where a fast green has a higher value, e.g. 15 s, than a slow green, e.g. 12 s. Bell & Holmes (1988) studied the speed of 74 bowling greens and obtained questionnaires from 774 bowlers to determine minimum standards for green speed and these, together with earlier standards, are given in Table 1. No upper limits were proposed for green speeds, players generally equating faster greens with a demand for a greater level of skill.

In golf the approach has been to measure the *distance rolled* by a golf ball when released from a standard ramp known as the Stimpmeter (Stimpson 1974). Because of the importance of green speed in tournament conditions, a green speed test comparison table was proposed by the United States Golf Association (USGA) as long ago as 1977 (Radko 1977). This is reproduced in its metric equivalent in Table 2 (note the figures given by Bell *et al.* (1985) were converted inexactly).

TABLE 1. Standards for green speeds on bowling greens		
Source of reference	**Green speed (s)**	**Subjective description**
Escritt (1978)	15	Fast
	10	Slow
Anon. (1983)	15	Very fast
(Converted by Bell &	12	Satisfactory
Holmes 1988)	10	Slow
Bell & Holmes (1988)	12	Preferred minimum speed
	10	Acceptable minimum speed

TABLE 2. USGA green speed test comparison table (Radko (1977) after conversion to SI units)		
	Distance rolled (m)	**Green speed**
Regular membership play	2.59	Fast
	2.29	Medium-fast
	1.98	Medium
	1.68	Medium-slow
	1.37	Slow
Tournament play	3.20	Fast
	2.90	Medium-fast
	2.59	Medium
	2.29	Medium-slow
	1.98	Slow

Because of its ease of operation the Stimpmeter has been widely used in the USA, both in preparation of courses for tournaments (Thomas 1978) and in research studies, for example the effects of mowing (Engel *et al.* 1981), cultivars of ryegrass for overseeded greens (Batten *et al.* 1981, Dudeck & Peacock 1981). In the UK Lodge & Baker (1991) studied the effects of irrigation, construction and fertiliser nutrition on golf green speed. However, there have been no systematic studies of green speed of different grasses used for fine turf. The objective of the work therefore was to study the green speed for both bowls and golf of some grass species commonly used for fine turf in the UK.

MATERIALS AND METHODS
Trial construction and management
The trial was constructed on a loamy sand soil (9% clay, 10% silt, 81% sand) at the Sports Turf Research Institute, Bingley (NGR SE 095 391). The average slope in the direction of roll was <0.01%. The trial was laid out in four randomised blocks with the plots of the different grasses being 7.5 m in length by 1 m width. The five grasses included in the work and their sowing rates were as follows:

Festuca rubra L. ssp. *litoralis* (G.F.W. Meyer) Auquier 'Dawson' (slender creeping red fescue)	35 g m^{-2}
Festuca rubra L. ssp. *commutata* Gaud. 'Frida' (Chewings fescue)	35 g m^{-2}
Agrostis capillaris L. 'Bardot' (browntop bent)	10 g m^{-2}
Agrostis castellana Boiss. & Reuter 'Highland' (Highland browntop bent)	10 g m^{-2}
Poa annua L. "Commercial" (annual meadow-grass)	35 g m^{-2}

The seedbed fertiliser was a 15:9:15 ($N:P_2O_5:K_2O$) material containing IBDU and 2% MgO, which was applied at a rate of 50 g m^{-2}. Both seed and fertiliser were applied on 20 June 1986 and the subsequent maintenance treatments are given in Table 3.

TABLE 1. Standards for green speeds on bowling greens	
Mowing	First cut on 30 July 1986 at 50 mm and the cutting height was gradually reduced through the first year of growth reaching 10 mm on 1 December 1986. The cutting height was further reduced in 1987, down to 8 mm on 3 April, 6 mm on 1 June and 5 mm on 22 June.
Fertiliser	The total fertiliser inputs (kg ha^{-1}) were: N P_2O_5 K_2O 1986 170 45 107 In three applications including seedbed fertiliser 1987 155 0 64 The 1986 fertiliser programme included compound granular fertilisers plus ammonium sulphate. The 1987 programme included ammonium sulphate, potassium sulphate, sulphate of iron and dried blood.
Irrigation	During seedling establishment and until 24 July 1986 the trial was watered on a total of ten occasions to ensure that the seedbed remained moist. Thereafter no irrigation was applied, except for the light applications to wet the surface during monitoring work (see main text).
Top dressing	One light application of a 3:1 mix of sand and sterilised compost in 1986 and two applications of 1.5 kg m^{-2} in 1987.
Mechanical treatments	The trial was verticut on six occasions between 29 July 1987 and 5 October 1987 and spiked on eight occasions between 3 April 1987 and 24 December 1987.

Measurement techniques

For bowls, green speed was obtained by releasing an unbiased bowl from a height of 0.5 m down a standard ramp (Bell & Holmes 1988) inclined at an angle of 30° to the horizontal. Six measurements were made on each plot with three tests in opposite directions. The distance travelled (R, in metres) and the time taken before the ball stopped (T, in seconds) were recorded. Green speed (in seconds) was calculated using an equation given by Bell & Holmes (1988):

$$\text{Green speed} \quad \sqrt{\frac{27.4}{R/T^2}}$$

For golf, the speed of the surface was assessed using a Stimpmeter (Radko 1977) and the distance rolled was measured. A total of six measurements were made per plot, with three readings in opposite directions. The measurement dates, cutting heights and antecedent rainfall conditions are given in Table 4.

The initial measurements were recorded as either dry or moist, depending whether there had been recent rainfall. The surface was subsequently irrigated using a watering can immediately before measurement on each plot, adding a depth of water equivalent to 1.2 mm.

TABLE 4. Measurement dates, cutting height and antecedent rainfall

Date (1987	Bowls	Golf	Cutting height mm	Antecedent rainfall (mm)		
				Previous day	Previous 3 days	Previous week
29 May	✓		8	1.6	1.6	5.2
1 June	✓		6	0.7	1.7	3.3
5 June		✓	6	0.1*	22.0	27.2
27 July	✓		5	10.3	10.3	11.9
30 July		✓	5	12.5	13.6	25.0
31 July		✓	5	0.2	13.8	24.1
23 October	✓	✓	5	<0.1	16.0	33.5

Statistical analysis

Analysis of variance was used to examine differences in ball roll behaviour of the grass species and subspecies (simply referred to as 'species' hereafter). In the tables and diagrams the least significant difference (LSD) at P=0.05 is given to allow comparison of the treatment means. The effect of irrigation was examined using paired t-tests, again using a significance level of P<0.05.

RESULTS
Bowls

Green speed values for the individual measurement dates are given in Table 5 and mean values over all dates in relation to species composition are given in Fig. 1.

TABLE 5. Effect of grass species and moisture conditions on bowls green speed (s) (all dates 1987)

	29 May		1 June		27 July		23 Oct.
	Dry	Wet	Dry	Wet	Dry	Wet	Moist
F. rubra ssp. litoralis	11.3	11.2	11.4	11.3	11.7	11.9	11.2
F. rubra ssp. commutata	10.8	10.5	10.3	10.4	11.6	11.6	10.9
Agrostis capillaris	10.7	10.2	10.8	10.4	11.2	11.4	10.7

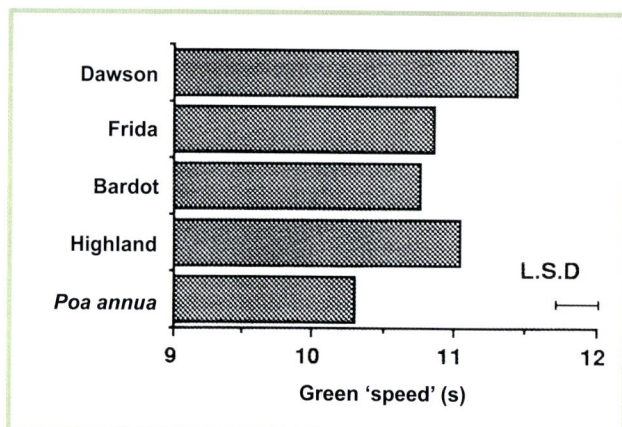

FIGURE 1. Green speed for bowls for the different grass species averaged over all sampling dates. (In both figures Dawson = F. rubra ssp. litoralis, Frida = F. rubra ssp. commutata, Bardot = A. capillaries and Highland = A. castellana.)

Grass species caused a significant difference in green speed on all sampling occasions, except on 27 July following irrigation. Green speed was greatest on *F. rubra* ssp. *litoralis*, averaging 11.45 over all sampling dates, whilst *P. annua* gave the slowest surface with an average green speed of 10.45.

Green speed appeared to increase as the cutting height was lowered and was greatest on 27 July 1987 at a cutting height of 5 mm. The effect was, however, not entirely consistent and, for example, there was no difference in ball roll values at the 8 mm and 6 mm cutting heights.

The effect of irrigation was also inconsistent. On 29 May and 1 June 1987 green speed decreased after irrigation but on 27 June 1987 there was a significant increase in green speed (P<0.05) after irrigation.

Golf
The pattern for ball roll for golf was similar to that for bowls (Fig. 2, Table 6). Averaged over all dates the rolling distance was greatest for *F. rubra* ssp. *litoralis*, i.e. 1.96 m and least for *P. annua*, averaging only 1.57 m.

TABLE 5. Effect of grass species and moisture conditions on distance rolled (m) for golf (all dates 1987)					
	5 June		30/31 July		23 Oct.
	Moist	Wet	Dry	Wet	Moist
F. rubra ssp. *litoralis*	1.87	1.78	2.21	2.01	1.93
F. rubra ssp. *commutata*	1.72	1.69	2.10	1.95	2.05
Agrostis capillaris	1.69	1.67	2.10	1.92	1.91
Agrostis castellana	1.73	1.66	2.09	1.93	1.71
Poa annua	1.49	1.37	1.72	1.64	1.62
LSD (5%)	0.182	0.140	0.232	0.185	0.131

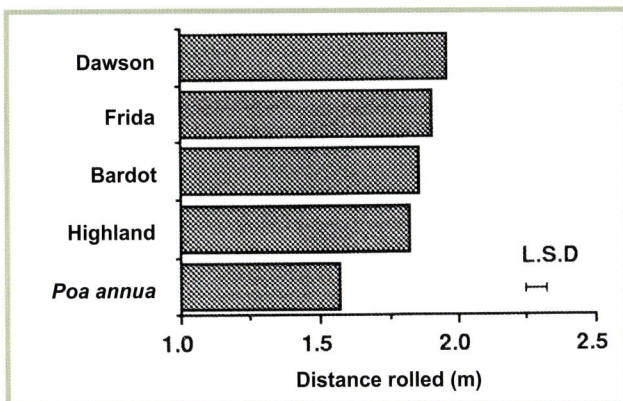

FIGURE 2. Distance rolled by a golf ball for the different grass species averaged over all sampling dates.

There was a significant difference in ball roll (P<0.001) following irrigation, averaging 1.87 m when dry and 1.76 m when wet. Ball roll values were greatest under dry conditions at a cutting height of 5 mm on 30 July 1987 when ball roll for all the grasses except *P. annua* was greater than 2 m.

Over all dates, ball roll ranged from 1.37 m for *P. annua* on 5 June 1987 at a cutting height of 6 mm and after irrigation to 2.21 m for *F. rubra* ssp. *litoralis* under dry conditions on 30 July 1987 (5 mm cutting height).

DISCUSSION

Considering first the results for bowls, none of the measurements reached the preferred minimum speed of 12 s given by Bell & Holmes (1988). However, only one species (*P. annua*) failed to reach the acceptable minimum speed of 10 s on one occasion of measurement. Overall, *F. rubra* ssp. *litoralis* 'Dawson' always gave the fastest surface and *P. annua* always gave the slowest surface. The two *Agrostis* spp. and *F. rubra* spp. *commutata* were intermediate in performance and not statistically different from one another except on 1 June when *A. castellana* was significantly faster than *F. rubra* ssp. *commutata*. Overall, it would be fair to state that these three species were comparable in performance. Evans (1988) stated "long experience indicates that the most common causes of excessive slowness are the dominance of annual meadow-grass in the sward and the presence of a sub-surface thatch or fibre layer". The trial certainly confirmed this long held view of *P. annua*. Evans (1988) also stated "fescue produces a tough wiry type of turf and a fast bowling surface". The trial also bore out this comment although clearly the type of fescue which is chosen could have a large bearing on the speed of the green. Newell & Gooding (1990) demonstrated a considerable range of values for: shoot density, leaf width, leaf numbers, shoot phytomass and thatch depth for a number of species and sub-species of *Festuca* and hence there could be a large, undiscovered source of variation in green speed among different fescues.

For golf, during the trial no attempt had been made to emulate tournament preparation and hence the trial would equate with regular club greens. The figures given in Table 2 for golf green speeds should not necessarily be equated with those given for "minimum standards" for green speed of bowling greens in Table 1. The purpose of the USGA green speed comparison table was not to propose minimum standards for different categories of green speed, but rather to provide an objective test of green speed to enable superintendents to work towards more uniform putting conditions over 18 greens (Engel *et al.* 1980). Indeed, it is not stated whether the figures given refer to the minimum value for each category or its mid-point. Furthermore, the inference is that such precision was not intended. However, some general comparisons can be made. The *P. annua* gave consistently the slowest surface and would have corresponded with slow to medium-slow in the USGA table. Only the *F. rubra* ssp. *litoralis* would have been rated medium-fast on 30 July (dry). All of the remaining data fell into the medium or medium-slow categories.

The effect of moisture was generally to decrease green speed for both bowls and golf as would be expected, although it apparently increase for bowls on one occasion of measurement. Results of t-tests carried out on the pooled data for wet versus dry showed significant differences for both bowls (t = 2.23, p = 0.04) and for golf (t = 5.61, p = 0.0003). The effect of moisture was greater for the smaller golf ball than for the relatively massive bowl. Only 1.5% reduction in green speed due to wetness was observed for bowls, whereas the reduction was 6% for golf (calculated as (dry – wet/dry) x 100).

Overall, the trial showed interesting species differences in ball roll characteristics, which suggests that a wider screening of species and cultivars, for use on UK golf greens, for green speed could yield fruitful results, especially for seed companies marketing cultivars for the golf course market. It was originally intended to continue the trial for a further year, however significant amounts of *P. annua* invaded the plots of the other species (12% overall on the worst affected species, with some plots having individual amounts up to 35%). It was felt that this *P. annua* contamination would undoubtedly mask species differences and therefore the trial was ended.

ACKNOWLEDGEMENTS
The authors wish to thank the Sports Council (London) for support for work on bowls, Messrs. Pye, Smithies and Birtle for technical assistance and Mrs. D.S. Hill for preparation of the manuscript.

REFERENCES
Anon. (1983). The speed of golf and bowling greens. *Sports Turf Bulletin* **143**, Oct.-Dec., pp. 11-12.

Batten, S.M., Beard, J.B., Johns, D., Almodares, A. & Eckhardt, J. (1981). Characterisations of cool season turfgrasses for winter overseeding of dormant bermudagrass. In: *Proc. 4th Int. Turfgrass Res. Conf.* (Ed. R.W. Sheard), University of Guelph, Canada, pp. 83-94.

Bell, M.J., Baker, S.W. & Canaway, P.M. (1985). Playing quality of sports surfaces: a review. *J. Sports Turf Res. Inst.* **61**, 26-45.

Bell, M.J. & Holmes, G. (1988). Playing quality standards for level bowling greens. *J. Sports Turf Res. Inst.* **64**, 48-62.

Dudeck, A.E. & Peacock, C.H. (1981). Effects of several overseeded ryegrasses on turf quality, traffic tolerance and ball roll. In: *Proc. 4th Int. Turfgrass Res. Conf.* (Ed. R.W. Sheard), University of Guelph, Canada, pp. 75-81.

Engel, R.E., Radko, A.M. & Trout, J.R. (1980). Influence of mowing procedures on roll speed of putting greens. *USGA Green Section Record* **18**, 1, 7-9.

Escritt, J.R. (1978). *ABC of Turf Culture*. Kaye & Ward Ltd., London, 239 pp.

Evans, R.D.C. (1988). *Bowling Greens: Their History, Construction and Maintenance*. The Sports Turf Research Institute, Bingley, 196 pp.

Lodge, T.A. & Baker, S.W. (1991). The construction, irrigation and fertiliser nutrition of golf greens. II. Playing quality assessments after establishment and during the first year of differential irrigation and nutrition treatments. *J. Sports Turf Res. Inst.* **67**, 44-52.

Newell, A.J. & Gooding, M.J. (1990). The performance of fine-leaved *Festuca* spp. in close-mown turf. *J. Sports Turf Res. Inst.* **66**, 120-132.

Radko, A.M. (1977). How fast are your greens? *USGA Green Section Record* **15**, 5, 10-11.

Thomas, F. (1978). The stimpmeter and the Open. *USGA Green Section Record* **16**, 6, 7-9.

Stimpson, E.S. (1974). Putting greens—how fast? *USGA Golf J.* **27**, 2, 28-29.

The following Trade Companies kindly supplied photographs for this new edition:–

SISIS Equipment (Macclesfield) Ltd.
Hurdsfield, Macclesfield, Cheshire SK10 2LZ
T. 01625 503030   E. info@sisis.com   W. www.sisis.com

Better Methods (BMS Europe) Ltd.
Unit 22 Cosgrove Way, Luton LU1 1XL
T. 01582 758444   E. info@BMStools.com   W. www.bms-europe.co.uk

Dennis Mowers
Ashbourne Road, Kirk Langley, Derbyshire DE6 4NJ
T. 01332 824 777   E. info@dennisuk.com   W. www.dennisuk.com

Par 4 Irrigation Ltd.
Unit 1 Ebor Business Park, Ure Bank Top, Ripon, Yorkshire HG4 1JE
T. 01765 602175   E. admin@par4.co.uk   W. www.par4.co.uk

Sportsmark Group Ltd.
Sportsmark House, 4 Clearwater Place, Lower Way, Newbury, Berkshire RG19 3RF
T. 01635 867537   W. www.sportsmark.net

Techneat Engineering Ltd.
2 Henry Crabb Road, Littleport, Ely, Cambridgeshire CB6 1SE
T. 01353 862044   E. info@techneat.co.uk   W. www.techneatengineering.co.uk

Tillers Turf Company Ltd.
Grange Court , Grange Lane, North Kelsey, Market Rasen, Lincolnshire LN7 6EZ
T. 01652 678 000   E. sales@tillersturf.co.uk   W. www.tillersturf.co.uk

223

STRI

STRI (The Sports Turf Research Institute) is an independent, non-profit organisation whose objectives are to provide advice and education and to carry out research in the sphere of sports turf. The Institute has its origins in 1929 when the 'Board of Greenkeeping Research' was founded by The Royal and Ancient Golf club of St. Andrews and the four Home Golf Unions to carry out research and to provide advice and education on matters relating to golf turf. In time, it was found that owners and managers of other sports areas also required advice on their turf problems. In recognition of this wider need, in 1951 the STRI was incorporated as a much more broadly based organisation with most of the sports governing bodies being in membership and able to influence policy through their representation on the Board of Management.

As an independent body, the STRI is free to offer an unbiased and unrestrained service to its clients for both construction and maintenance work. This advice will reflect the practical experience of 75 years of service to sports clubs and the findings of the extensive programme of research which is carried out at the Institute. Furthermore, the consultancy services are supported by specialist soil physics, biology and soil chemistry laboratories.